The Brother–Sister Culture in Nineteenth-Century Literature

Also by Valerie Sanders

RECORDS OF GIRLHOOD: An Anthology of Nineteenth-Century Women's Childhoods (*editor*)

EVE'S RENEGADES: Victorian Anti-Feminist Women Novelists

HARRIET MARTINEAU: Selected Letters (*editor*)

THE PRIVATE LIVES OF VICTORIAN WOMEN: Autobiography in Nineteenth-Century England

REASON OVER PASSION: Harriet Martineau and the Victorian Novel

The Brother–Sister Culture in Nineteenth-Century Literature

From Austen to Woolf

Valerie Sanders
Professor of English Literature
University of Hull

palgrave

© Valerie Sanders 2002

All rights reserved. No reproduction, copy or transmission of this publication may be made without written permission.

No paragraph of this publication may be reproduced, copied or transmitted save with written permission or in accordance with the provisions of the Copyright, Designs and Patents Act 1988, or under the terms of any licence permitting limited copying issued by the Copyright Licensing Agency, 90 Tottenham Court Road, London W1T 4LP.

Any person who does any unauthorised act in relation to this publication may be liable to criminal prosecution and civil claims for damages.

The author has asserted her right to be identified as the author of this work in accordance with the Copyright, Designs and Patents Act 1988.

First published 2002 by
PALGRAVE
Houndmills, Basingstoke, Hampshire RG21 6XS and
175 Fifth Avenue, New York, N. Y. 10010
Companies and representatives throughout the world

PALGRAVE is the new global academic imprint of
St. Martin's Press LLC Scholarly and Reference Division and
Palgrave Publishers Ltd (formerly Macmillan Press Ltd).

ISBN 0–333–74930–8

This book is printed on paper suitable for recycling and made from fully managed and sustained forest sources.

A catalogue record for this book is available from the British Library.

Library of Congress Cataloging-in-Publication Data
Sanders, Valerie
The brother–sister culture in nineteenth-century literature : from Austen to Woolf/Valerie Sanders.
    p. cm.
  Includes bibliographical references (p.)and index.
  ISBN 0–333–74930–8
    1. English fiction—19th century—History and criticism.
2. Brothers and sisters in literature. 3. English fiction—20th century—History and criticism. 4. Domestic fiction, English–
–History and criticism. 5. Brothers and sisters—Great Britain–
–History. I. Title.
PR868.B77 S26 2001
823'.809352045—dc21
                                                    2001034805

10 9 8 7 6 5 4 3 2 1
11 10 09 08 07 06 05 04 03 02

Printed and bound in Great Britain by
Antony Rowe Ltd, Chippenham, Wiltshire

For Jennifer and David
Niece and Nephew
Sister and Brother

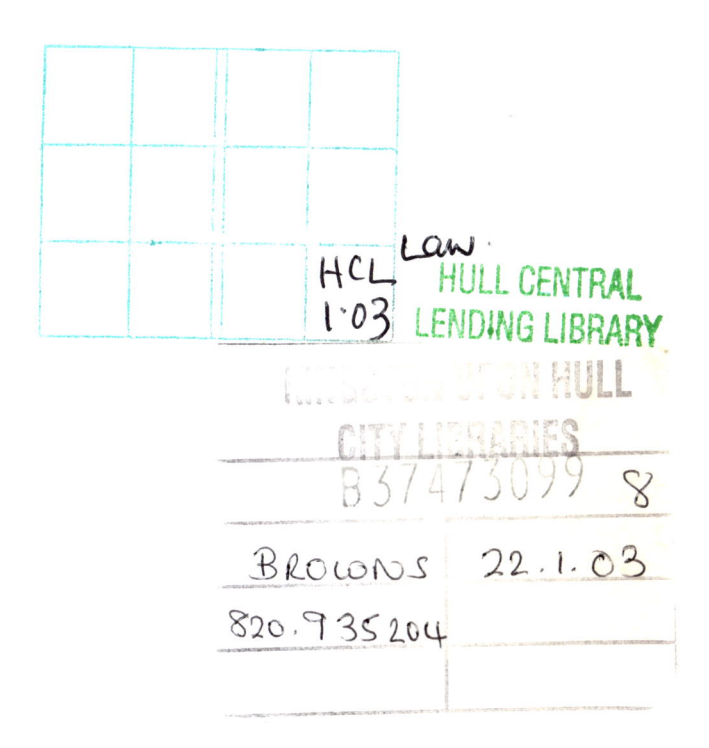

Contents

Acknowledgements	ix
Introduction	1
1 The Brother and Sister Culture	11
2 Brother–Sister Collaborative Relationships	32
Romantic partnerships: the Lambs and the Wordsworths	34
Victorian partnerships: the Brontës and the Rossettis	43
The Sitwell phenomenon	52
3 'One of the Highest Forms of Friendship': Brother–Sister relationships in women's autobiography	57
Margaret Oliphant and Elizabeth Sewell	65
Harriet and James Martineau	69
Conclusion	78
4 The Brother as Lover	80
Jane Austen and Mary Shelley	83
The Brontë novels	88
Family sagas of the 1860s	96
Dickens and George Eliot	99
Conclusion	104
5 The Family Revenge Novel	
Early nineteenth-century Gothic representations	110
Dickens and L. P. Hartley: sisters in wheelchairs	113
Bertha Rochester: the mad sister in the attic	115
Bad Brothers: an introduction	116
Trollope and Oliphant	118
Protective Rivalry: Mary Cholmondeley and William Hamilton	123
6 Changing Places: Siblings and Cross-Gendering	130
The Brontës	139
Walter Pater	142

Sarah Grand's *Heavenly Twins*	145
Eliza Lynn Linton's *Christopher Kirkland*	147
7 'Most Unwillingly Alive': Brothers and Sisters in the First World War	155
Virginia Woolf	164
Vera Brittain and Rebecca West	168
Katherine Mansfield	170
Conclusion	176
Conclusion	180
Notes	186
Bibliography	205
Index	218

Acknowledgements

Many people have contributed to the evolution of this book. In particular, I should like to thank all those who attended seminars where earlier versions of the following chapters were rehearsed: members of the Charlotte Yonge Fellowship and the Martineau Society; staff and students at the Universities of Durham and Newcastle, and Chester College of Higher Education, and those who attended the inaugural conference of the newly formed British Association for Victorian Studies at the University of Hertfordshire in September 2000. Noel O'Sullivan helped with Hegel and introduced me to Jay McInerney's *Model Behaviour*, Pat Brook recommended *This Real Night* and Rebecca West, and Fiona Bagchi told me about F. D. Maurice's brother–sister novel, *Eustace Conway*. Other ideas came from informal and stimulating conversations with people met at conferences or on my travels, especially in Australia. Virginia Blain recounted the fascinating story of Sir William Rowan Hamilton and his sister Eliza, and Ellen Jordan and Joanne Wilkes introduced me to the convolutions of the Newman and Mozley families. Lucy Qureshi of Palgrave provided prompt answers to questions, and a constructive external reader made helpful suggestions about the introduction and conclusion.

I am also grateful to my own brother and sister, Paul and Rosemary, who gave me the direct personal experience of being a sibling. In our case it was an entirely happy one: we rarely quarrelled, and we never wrote each other love-letters. With Paul I invented shared stories called across the landing from our bedrooms after lights out. I am glad to say he still hates mayonnaise and loves coffee cake as much as I do. This book is dedicated to his children in the hope that they too will always value the sibling bond.

For permission to quote from the Martineau papers in their possession, thanks are due to the University of Birmingham, the British Library, and Harris Manchester College, Oxford; for the papers of Norman Austin Taylor, Sarah Vernon on behalf of the Taylor family and the Imperial War Museum, and for the Benson papers in the New Bodleian Library, A. P. Watt Ltd on behalf of the Executors of the Estate of K. S. P. McDowall. Records in the Cheshire Record Office are reproduced with the permission of Cheshire County Council and the depositor to whom copyright is reserved. The cover illustration is by kind permission of Christie's Images Ltd.

Books, lectures, conversation, dancing, could not banish that craving for her brother.

Charlotte M. Yonge, *Heartsease* (1854)

Introduction

> I do not know how love in a cottage may be with a wife. But I am sure it would suit me with a sister.[1]

The relationship between brother and sister is generally one of the longest we experience. Unlike the marital relationship, it spans both childhood and adulthood; it survives long periods of separation; and it cannot be broken by legal intervention. The connection persists, whether or not it is actively sought: in fact for most children it is the first relationship with someone of their own generation, fraught from the start with emotional contradictions. For the first child, the second may be a welcome companion or a hated rival; for the second, the first may be a feared tormenter or a reassuring parent-substitute. Through the course of a lifetime, the sibling relationship will normally undergo extensive changes of mood and intensity; yet as Juliet Mitchell has recently noted, it remains 'the great omission in psychoanalytic observation and theory', overshadowed by the far greater attention paid to the parent–child relationship.[2] For psychologists, too, the subject is neglected. 'At present,' wrote Victor Cicirelli in 1995, 'no theory exists that can account for changes in sibling relationships across the life span, sibling closeness, sibling caregiving and helping, sibling violence and abuse, and so on.'[3] As his list of sibling functions shows, the emotional range within the relationship is enormous, matched only by the variety of roles brothers and sisters adopt towards each other in the course of a lifetime. The rules for conducting a sibling relationship have never been established: ambivalence is its keynote, and instability its underlying condition.[4]

Within literary criticism and history, too, this is an oddly neglected area. Critics have noted, in passing, the prevalence of sibling marriages in Jane Austen or idealized sister-wives in Dickens;[5] many have wondered about Wordsworth's precise relationship with his sister Dorothy,[6] and Juliet Barker has recently stressed the importance of studying the Brontës as a family group, rather than as isolated individuals;[7] but the full significance of sibling relationships to English writers, male and female, from the Romantics to Virginia Woolf, has never been properly addressed and understood. Perhaps this is inevitable in an age that still concentrates its investigative energies on all sexual relationships and the parent–child dyad. Sibling relationships are just 'there' – apparently asexual and neutral – rarely the central relationship in anyone's life.[8] This book argues that for a variety of reasons, the brother–sister relationship assumed an intense emotional significance in English literary and cultural history between the end of the eighteenth century (corresponding with the rise of Romanticism and the popularity of Gothic fiction) and the first third of the twentieth, declining at the end of the First World War – though there is substantial evidence that it continued in a reduced form at least until the Second World War.[9] It was at its height in the nineteenth century, when brother–sister collaborative relationships were particularly active, as with the Rossettis and the Brontës; but whether or not brothers and sisters actually worked together to produce literary works, there are few major poets and novelists who fail to acknowledge a close bond with a favourite sibling. George Eliot's *The Mill on the Floss* is the best-known exploration of this bond, but her male contemporaries, including Matthew Arnold, A. H. Clough, Benjamin Disraeli, T. B. Macaulay, J. H. Newman, Robert Browning, and the Irish astronomer Sir William Rowan Hamilton, depended deeply on their sisters for moral and practical support. The aim of this book is to explore the many ramifications of brother–sister relationships during the period of their greatest intensity, and to suggest that they are an undeservedly neglected guide to understanding the complexity of gender relations at that time.

The period covered by this book is roughly that between 1790 and 1918, during which the English middle-class family evolved into its recognizable 'nuclear' form: a configuration many social historians see as being accelerated by changes brought about by the Industrial Revolution, and the development of the modern state, though not entirely explained by them. These changes were many and complex, involving an increasing separation of paid work from home, as mechanized production took activities such as weaving and spinning out of the family environment and into the factories, and the male wage-earner became distinct from the wife and mother looking after the children. Even if this idealized image was less than universally true, its symbolic appeal was widely acknowledged. Diana Gittins argues that

> the objective of a single male breadwinner per family was one of the most radical changes in family ideology in the modern era, and one that had dramatic effects on notions of fatherhood, masculinity, motherhood, femininity, family life and family policy, and still has.[10]

This shift of emphasis in family ideology allowed middle-class women and children – newly advantaged by the rise of the professions and the wealth made by manufacturers – to develop a new kind of family life within the safety and separation of a domestic space designed for leisure and relaxation. The children, required to do less around the house as their parents became wealthy enough to employ domestic servants, in turn developed a culture of their own, which involved them in elaborately structured games and fantasies in parts of the house rarely visited by their parents. As Michel Foucault has suggested, the fragmenting of the Victorian family into a structure of separate but related networks fostered the growth of secret sexual alliances, and an active commitment to suppressing them where they could be identified.[11]

Leonore Davidoff sees the 1830s as marking the beginnings of modernity in family culture, though she warns against accepting too simple an historical narrative of the nuclear family and industrial society advancing side by side in an unproblematic progress through the decades. Instead, the middle-class family and the industrial process influenced one another; variations throughout both structures further complicating the unfolding of the story.[12] Nor did the family, once formed in its recognizably modern state, remain that way throughout the century. As more children survived infancy, and parents felt less need to replace those lost, family sizes peaked and declined. Awareness of contraception spread, together with the practice of abstinence. By the end of the nineteenth century, the enormous sprawling families which are such a regular feature of Charlotte Yonge's novels of the 1860s and 70s, had given way to more modest groupings of four to six. By the time of the First World War, though some well-known families such as the Asquiths and the Tennants were still sizeable, many of the sisters writing about lost brothers were from sets of only two or three siblings, where such losses were more acutely felt.

With the coming of literary modernism, writers and thinkers became preoccupied with issues of ordering and fragmentation, and returned to the family for exploration of their place in the domestic culture (*Sons*

4 *Introduction*

and Lovers, Howards End, Portrait of the Artist as a Young Man, and *To the Lighthouse* would be good examples). Zygmunt Bauman, a leading theorist of modernity and postmodernity, further sees intellectuals' experience of the postmodern world as being 'one of anxiety, out-of-placeness, [and] loss of direction'. The implications of this for the continuing importance of sibling ties are evident from texts of the 1960s and 70s – briefly mentioned at the end of this book – which continue the inward concentration on brother–sister attraction, openly sexualized, in a culture now conscious of the possibility of child abuse within the family.[13]

The weight newly thrown on brother–sister relationships in the nineteenth century derives from many influences, both historical and literary. For a start, siblings spent more time together in a protected environment. With the middle-classes able to afford lengthier periods of education for their children and keep their daughters at home to await a respectable marriage, closer bonds within the family were inevitable. Brothers who went away to school and college could expect to find their sisters at home when they returned, ready to resume the companionship that might not be available from other sources. Class and location were other key factors. Most of the families discussed in this book were from literary, educational or clerical backgrounds, rather than business or industrial, with a longer history of refinement, and greater reluctance to mix socially with the lower classes. With a full set of playmates at home, there was no real need to go looking for friends beyond the garden gate, especially if the family base was in an isolated rural setting with few other middle-class neighbours.

Siblings, moreover, provided the most readily available and congenial companionship. 'The middle classes,' argues Leonore Davidoff, 'were characterized by strong bonds between siblings, brothers and sisters who grew up together and stayed close all their lives' (p. 126). Given the increasing sexual pressures on the family, this is hardly surprising. The relationship between husband and wife came under urgent scrutiny from at least the time of Mary Wollstonecraft (if not before) and especially following the public debates surrounding the Caroline Norton case from the late 1830s onwards. While social reformers and politicians debated the rights of mothers to custody of their own children, and wives to possession of their own earnings, the brother–sister relationship was increasingly presented as a place of relative safety; an area where men could be trusted to behave, and where women were allowed to show their feelings. There grew up in many Victorian families an aura of romantic loyalty and devotion surrounding siblings, with sisters playing the role of nurturers and carers, and boys that of natural protectors. It was an innocent training in the roles children would ideally adopt as adults. At its least problematic, it was a protected symbiosis that other people respected and understood. Some pairs of siblings found it so congenial that they lived together throughout their adult lives, spared the stresses of childbearing and the inevitable inequality of status that legally divided husbands and wives.

The source of sibling sympathy ultimately derives from Romanticism and its influence on the Victorians – though in a sense it has always been there, starting with Sophocles' Antigone seeing the decent burial of her brother as more important than her own marriage and survival. The notion that a sibling can never be replaced – unlike a spouse or child – has always given the relationship a special resonance exploited by creative writers in most societies.[14] Otto Rank's *The Incest Theme in Literature* (1912)[15] remains the fullest study of sibling relationships in literary and psychoanalytical history, though he regards the parent–child pattern as the more disturbing type of incest. Focusing on German literature, especially the centrality, for Goethe, of his relationship with his sister Cornelia, Rank also turns to Shelley and Byron whose incest themes he correlates with their family fixations in real life. While his is essentially a study of the psychology of literary creation, George Steiner's *Antigones* (1984) tries to explain why eighteenth-century European writers began looking so earnestly for heterosexual mirror-images of themselves. The search for perfect oneness, he argues, arises in Western philosophy, after Kant's emphasis on the separation of subject and object, and the new sense of aloneness in the universe. Whereas Hegel argued that the roots of self-division and thus exile were internal, the Romantic answer was 'an erotic consummation so complete that it annuls the autism of personal identity'.[16] In other words, the lonely ego finds a sense of homecoming after exile in intimacy with another human being, but this must always be unsatisfactory provided the ego has to look beyond its own boundaries. It therefore seeks its ideal mirror-image in the figure of its sister, a self-reflection of the opposite sex, as the perfect sympathizing counterpart, like Narcissus looking for his idealized other, his sister Echo.[17]

In response to the late eighteenth-century cults of idealism and individualism, the Romantics earnestly sought relationships, both in life and literature, that would preserve their own authenticity and intactness as individuals, while saving them from the terrifying isolation of social and intellectual solitude. The philosopher most useful to them here was G. W. F. Hegel, whose *Phenomenology of Mind* (1807) included a section on the perfect nature of brother–sister relationships. 'They are the same blood,' Hegel argued, 'which, however, in them has entered into a condition of stable equilibrium.' What he meant by this was the absence of sexual desire: 'They therefore stand in no such natural relation as husband and wife, they do not desire one another; nor have they given to one another, nor received from one another, this independence of individual being; they are free individualities with respect to each other.'[18] Untainted by the urge to mastery, brother and sister find themselves in one another: to Hegel, the sister even foreshadowed the nature of ethical life, while the brother became the family member 'in whom its spirit becomes individualized, and enabled thereby to turn towards another sphere, towards what is other than and external to itself, and pass over into consciousness of universality' (Hegel, p. 477). Either way the relationship was supposed to have only the most elevating and purifying effects on both siblings. It was also essentially democratic, unlike the rule of the father, which in an age of revolution demanded a philosophical alternative.

For the Romantics, preoccupied with the search for an ideal, complementary 'other,' the emphasis was on the complete, uncritical understanding a sister could offer a brother while unobtrusively refining his very being. Christina Battersby suggests that eighteenth-century culture expressed an increasing respect for 'feminine' qualities found in male creative artists, peaking with the image of the Romantic genius: 'the driving force of genius was described in terms of *male* sexual energies. On the other hand, the genius was supposed to be *like* a *woman*: in tune with his emotions, sensitive, inspired, guided by intellectual forces that welled up from beyond the limits of rational consciousness.'[19] If the source of this irrational inspiration happened to be not merely a muse but also a sister, the creative spirit would be all the purer and less likely to sap the poet's sense of his intact individuality. The parallel image of the double, which also became highly popular at this time, was often more sinister, and concerned with moral conflict, especially issues of free will and evil. According to John Herdman, while brothers are recurring motifs in literature of the double, sisters appear more rarely: presumably because their connection with evil was less appropriate.[20]

The effects of this way of thinking were seen most in the works of Shelley and Byron, where sibling marriages are a favourite plot-device. Cain marries his sister Adah in Byron's poem of that name and Selim and Zuleika, in *The Bride of Abydos* (1813), were brother and sister in the first draft, before they were discreetly turned into cousins. In Shelley's 'Rosalind and Helen' (1818), Rosalind falls in love with a man who turns out to be her father's son; yet 'Day and night, day and night,/ He was my breath and life and light,/ For three short years, which soon were past' (lines 284–6). More commonly, however, Shelley views the sister's perfections from the brother's point of view, as in *Laon and Cythna* (1817), the earlier version of *The Revolt of Islam* (1818), where Laon tells of his 'little sister, whose fair eyes/Were loadstars of delight' (Canto Second: XXI). Spurned by his family and friends, Laon turns gratefully to Cythna: 'As mine own shadow was this child to me,/ As a second self, far dearer and more fair' (XXIV). Only twelve at this stage of the poem, and poised on the edge of puberty, Cythna sleeps in his arms, inspires his songs, and makes him wise: 'What genius wild/Yet mighty, was inclosed within one simple child!' – a view many Victorians, especially Dickens, in his lifelong recreation of his dead young sister-in-law, Mary Hogarth, would propagate in their images of beautiful, pure, prepubescent little sister figures. The point about the pure young sister to a male genius was that she had to be unconscious of her wonderful powers: and, as Shelley puts it, 'Untainted by the poison clouds which rest/On the dark world' (XXV). A wife-figure was already tainted: hence his attraction to unmarried girls like Emilia Viviani in 'Epipyschidion.' Mary Shelley, by contrast, made her hero Frankenstein perpetually uneasy about marrying Elizabeth Lavenza, his sister by upbringing, if not by blood: her image blending with his mother's in a nightmare after he has created the monster.[21]

In Gothic novels of the period, as several critics have noted, the sibling-incest theme was a popular device.[22] To what extent this was to provide cheap thrills, rather than to make a serious social or philosophical comment, is unclear. The more important point being made in women's domestic novels as well as the Gothics is probably that the characters who narrowly escape incest are instinctively attracted to men and women in whom they recognize their own features and characteristics. They feel at home with them in a way that seems unique and uncanny, as happens to the eponymous Evelina in Fanny Burney's novel when she meets Mr Macartney and feels drawn to him. 'The rashness and misery of this ill-fated young man, engross all my thoughts,' Evelina reports, after saving him from shooting himself.[23] In fact Mr Macartney's despair stems partly from his hopeless love for another girl whom he believes to be his half-sister. Encumbered with two possible tabooed relationships, he finds his new friend (Evelina) is his sister, leaving the other to be his wife. In this and most other eighteenth-century novels, the sibling pairs are saved from actually marrying; but there are exceptions. Defoe's Moll Flanders marries her own brother, and M. G. Lewis's Ambrosio (of *The Monk*) has a sexual relationship with his sister Antonia and then murders her (murder of siblings is surprisingly rare in fiction of this – or any – time). The legacy of this tradition lingers in many nineteenth-century novels, where powerful emotions for a brother or brother-substitute (someone with whom the sister has been brought up) complicate relations with a would-be suitor. A triangle of this kind appears in *Mansfield Park* (Fanny, Edmund, Henry Crawford), *Wuthering Heights* (Catherine, Heathcliff, Edgar Linton) and *The Mill on the Floss* (Maggie, Tom, and Philip Wakem/Stephen Guest). In some of these novels, the brotherly relationship is even duplicated, by the presence of an actual brother as well as a brother-like relative (for example Fanny Price loves both William, her real brother, and Edmund, her brother-like cousin, but not Henry Crawford; while Maggie loves Tom, her real brother, and Philip Wakem, her brotherly friend, but not finally Stephen Guest). In each case, the brother-figure embodies an ideal to which the suitor must aspire; the sister in the meantime rehearsing and developing her romantic passions within the privacy and safety of her own family circle.

In the nineteenth century, the brother–sister relationship remained paramount, gaining in complexity as it lost the more obvious erotic overtones associated with its Gothic/Romantic phase. As Steven Mintz has observed, 'few subjects engaged the imagination of the great nineteenth-century novelists more strongly than sibling relations.' The bond with brothers and sisters, he argues, embodies an ideal of loyalty which was 'a way to counteract the problems of generational discontinuity and the anarchy of individualism'.[24] While this is undoubtedly true, a point made by the following book is that the sibling bond is portrayed by the Victorians rather more ambiguously. Although many Victorian writers cleansed the brother–sister relationship of the titillating associations it had for their Gothic predecessors, they also popularized the notion of being *like* a brother or sister to someone who was not a blood relative, thereby exposing the relationship to fresh destabilizing influences. A classic example occurs in a text that is symbolically suggestive about a range of sexual relationships, Bram Stoker's *Dracula* (1897). When Mina Harker offers, after Lucy's death, to be a 'sister' to Lucy's fiancé, Arthur Holmwood, she releases his pent-up grief into an outburst of 'hysterical' sobbing: 'I felt an infinite pity for him,' Mina confesses, 'and opened my arms unthinkingly.' Hastily changing the analogy from sister–brother to mother–child ('I stroked his hair as though he were my own child'), Mina later acknowledges in her journal the strangeness of this emotional freedom, but argues that only a woman 'can help a man when he is in trouble of the heart'. With no real mother or sister to help him, Mina presents herself as a mixture of the two: essentially the appeal of the sister figure in much Victorian fiction. As for Arthur, he freely offers his services as a 'brother', should she ever need 'a man's help'.[25] The fact that Mina is already married to Jonathan Harker seems to be forgotten by both of them, in the enthusiasm of the moment.

Not that brothers and sisters, were, for the Victorians, automatically allies. Though many women autobiographers described their brothers as gods, second selves, ideal companions and intellectual partners, the brother, as an individual in his own right, often disappeared from their adult lives, eclipsed or estranged from his more successful sister, and sisters could become oppressive mother-figures, emasculating their brothers. The politics of envy was an underlying influence on the behaviour of many family groups, and continued to bother succeeding generations of novelists who wrote in other ideological contexts. Initially I had expected the intensity of the brother–sister dyad to reduce after the carnage of the First World War: surprisingly, however, it remained strong in certain families, especially the upper middle classes, as the Sitwells and Lehmanns prove; while the diaries of J. R. Ackerley chronicle the violent mutations of the symbiosis between two siblings whose relationship, according to their editor, 'was a ghastly caricature of the kind of marriage, devoid of sex, that is held together merely by feelings of obligation, pity and guilt.'[26] In fiction, L. P. Hartley's *Eustace and Hilda* (1944) and Evelyn Waugh's *Brideshead Revisited* (1945) explore the unhealthy inwardness of sibling units who turn in on each other, rejecting external influences, and taking the theme to new extremes of emotional exploitation. At a time when social opportunities were wider than they had been in the previous century and class restrictions loosening, it seems surprising that the brother–sister relationship was still seen by many writers in terms of such engrossing urgency.

As Michael Roper and John Tosh have argued in *Manful Assertions* (1991), their study of masculinities since 1800, there is now a strong case for modifying the distinct and separate studies of male and female culture, 'for seeing masculine and feminine identities not as distinct and separate constructs, but as parts of a political field whose relations are characterized by domination, subordination, collusion and resistance'.[27] As their book suggests, the family is the ideal place in which to site such an investigation, and the brother–sister relationship is as central to the debate as the relations between parents and children. After all, it is within the family that the child first discovers his or her identity, first encounters inequalities of treatment based on gender assumptions, and first learns what is expected of an adult male or an adult female in the culture to which the child is still an apprentice. The patterns of rivalry, envy and jealousy, on the one hand, and sexual fantasy, idealism, and sublimated devotion on the other, allowed novelists and poets to probe a vast range of intimate feelings that would have been taboo in standard heterosexual relations. By a deft sleight of hand, the Victorians displaced them on to sibling relationships, where, under an 'innocent' designation, they could be more extensively explored. My book will investigate the ways in which the fractured unity of brother and sister is treated in nineteenth- and early twentieth-century writing – concentrating on English literary texts, but with occasional reference to American examples; it will examine the influence of this unity on the construction – and subsequently deconstruction of the domestic ideal; and consider why the relationship reached its high point in the nineteenth century, polarizing to more violent extremes of dependency and destruction in the warlike century that followed.

Beginning with the historical context for the formation of close brother–sister ties, the first three chapters concentrate on actual families, while the remaining four examine the ways in which the relationship was presented in literary texts. If the number of texts included is ambitious, it was to prove my point – that the Victorian obsession with brothers and sisters was by no means confined to a few eccentric families, but was endemic in the culture. The assumed neglect of sibling relationships by psychoanalysis provided a provocative starting-point, further stimulated by Juliet Mitchell's study of this omission in relation to hysteria, *Mad Men and Medusas* (2000), which was published after I had started writing the book. I have used psychoanalysis where it has been helpful, as well as much recent writing on the social history of Victorian families. But the core of the discussion is the literary texts themselves and what they have to say about the lifelong fascination of the brother–sister bond.

1
The Brother and Sister Culture

She is all his Comfort – he her's. They dote on each other.[1]

In 1841 the British Royal family became a young symmetrical unit again, with a father, mother, and two children – a brother and sister. Victoria, the Princess Royal, was born in the first year of her parents' marriage, in November 1840, while her brother, Albert Edward, known as 'Bertie', followed almost exactly a year later. Not since the early years of George III's reign, in the 1760s and 70s, had there been a young family in Buckingham Palace; and though Victoria and Albert quickly added to their stock of sons and daughters, until there were nine in all, there remained something significant about the first two as a brother and sister pair.

From the first, the balance between them was, by the standards of the time, distorted. All the brains had apparently gone to the girl instead of the boy, as happens with the Tulliver family in *The Mill on the Floss* (1860). While the infant Princess Royal eagerly responded to her father's teaching, Bertie was slow at lessons and difficult to control. The object of his education, according to the Bishop of Oxford, was to turn the Prince of Wales into 'the most perfect man'.[2] Instead, he looked as if he might end up like his great-uncles, the many dissolute sons of George III. The Queen told his new tutor, Frederick Gibbs, in 1852, that the Prince had been 'injured by being with the Princess Royal who was very clever, and a child far above her age; she put him down by a look – or a word – and their natural affection had been, she feared, impaired by this state of things'.[3]

For many Victorians, the brother–sister relationship was the very cornerstone of middle-class family life. Segregated from their parents in nurseries, separated from mothers who were often pregnant or recovering from childbirth, and fathers who were out at work or their clubs, siblings were thrown together for support and companionship. As Karl Miller has suggested, the family is 'an aggregation of pairs and opposites, replications and resemblances', justifying, like mirrors and pools, 'certain strains of dualistic conjecture'.[4] Brother and sister neatly parallel the other pairs of husband and wife and parent and child. Lawrence Stone has stressed how the emotional life of middle-class Victorian families 'was almost entirely focused within the boundaries of the nuclear family. The psychodynamics of this family type have been well described as "explosive intimacy"'.[5] For Foucault, the nineteenth-century bourgeois family became the 'crystal in the deployment of sexuality', an active site of alliance and feeling. For him it was a clear fact 'that sexuality has its privileged point of development in the family; that for this reason sexuality is "incestuous" from the start' – constantly being solicited and refused, 'an object of obsession and attraction, a dreadful secret and an indispensable pivot'.[6]

While there is no evidence of actual incest in the families to be discussed (the Stephen family is a notable exception), there was emotional intensity of a kind that now seems alien and curiously unselfconscious, as if it were perfectly acceptable at the time. This chapter will concentrate on several Victorian middle-class families which best exemplified the development of a sibling culture. While it may seem conservative to focus on the middle-classes, they were the group whose circumstances particularly favoured the growth of close brother–sister bonds. Unlike working-class children, they were not sent out to work in their early teens, but stayed at home until they married, or until the boys, at least, found work after university. Middle-class siblings therefore spent longer together, and often collaborated in the production of family newspapers, elaborate games of make-believe, or other shared entertainments to which their parents were rarely privy. The families selected for this part of the book are the Newmans, Bensons, Farjeons, and Stephens – though reference will be made, where helpful, to other families who shared their experience of the sibling bond.

Most of the families chosen for discussion were from the professional classes, especially the clergy, or literary, rather than manufacturing backgrounds. John Henry Newman (1801–90), the son of a banker, was close to two of his sisters: Harriett (1803–52), his favourite, who married Thomas Mozley, and broke off relations with her brother before his conversion to Catholicism; and Jemima (1808–79), who married another Mozley brother, John, the same year that Harriett married Thomas (1836), but managed to stay on friendlier terms with her brother. A third sister, Mary (1809–28), died young, before she could enter into these ideological complexities. In her twenties, Harriett still liked to be assured of John Henry's feelings for her: 'I hoped you loved me, dear John, whenever I thought of it – but I could never persuade myself that there was any thing in me that could inspire the same feeling towards me that I feel for others, much more you.'[7] As in many of the families discussed below, their brother was an intellectual lifeline for the sisters, and much of their early correspondence concerns the work he is doing at school or university, and any vicarious benefit they can gain from it. Subsequently, however, John was unwilling to discuss his beliefs with Harriett, and she turned instead to her younger brother Francis. In happier days, she had kept house for John when he was working as a clergyman at Ulcombe near Maidstone, Kent.

Edward White Benson (1829–96), was Bishop of Truro and subsequently Archbishop of Canterbury (1882–96). His marriage and family have recently attracted considerable attention from social historians because of the peculiar nature of their domestic life, which they recognized themselves. As David Newsome has noted, 'It is possible that no family in history has written so prolifically about itself.'[8] When she was only twelve, Benson selected a 'child bride' in his cousin Mary Sidgwick (1842–1918), and waited for her to grow up and marry him. None of their six children married, and two – Maggie (1865–1916) and Arthur Christopher ('A.C.') (1862–1925) experienced mental breakdowns, Maggie permanently. Martin, the eldest, died at school of meningitis, aged 17, and Eleanor (Nellie) in 1890 of diphtheria; Hugh (1871–1914) converted to Roman Catholicism after being ordained in the Church of England; and Fred (E.F) (1867–1940) became a society novelist, author of the Mapp and Lucia series. They were all intensely literary and inward-looking – besides what Maggie called 'an unmarrying family' – well educated (even the girls went to Oxford), but melancholy and neurasthenic. 'They had so many gifts,' writes Betty Askwith, 'but there is something twisted about them, something lacking, as if the pressures of their diversely endowed parents had been too much for them.'[9]

The Stephens famously also suffered from 'diversely endowed parents' – the indefatigable Julia Duckworth, who died in 1895, casting her widower, Sir Leslie Stephen, into all-engrossing gloom which his four children and three stepchildren had to manage between them. Vanessa (1879–1961) and Virginia (1882–1941) gained much from each other's support, but Virginia also looked to their brother Thoby (1880–1906) for intellectual companionship and access into the masculine world of

Cambridge. Their other brother Adrian (1883–1948) never seems to have figured very closely in their childhood, though their half-brothers George and Gerald Duckworth, have now become notorious among Virginia Woolf's biographers for their clumsy attempts at sexual abuse of their sisters. As with the Bensons, what one senses most about the Stephens is their lack of contact with other children outside the family, and total focus on what went on within the walls of their home. In young adulthood the Stephens holidayed together and set up shared houses, until all the surviving siblings were married. Their closeness as a group helped them to survive the trauma of their parents' and stepsister Stella's early deaths.

The Farjeons – of whom the best known is the poet and children's writer Eleanor (1881–1965) – were born around the same time as the Stephens, and grew up in Hampstead as members of a rather more bohemian and cosmopolitan household. Their father, Ben, was a playwright and novelist, and their mother, Margaret Jefferson, an American, also from a theatrical family background. Nellie, as she was known, was the only girl in a family of boys: Harry (1878–1948), whom she saw as the law-giver of the nursery, Bertie (d.1945), and Joe (1883–1955). When Harry wanted them to snap out of their fantasy identities, into which he often cast them during their games, he would declare: 'We're Harry – Nellie – Joe – and – Bertie,' restoring them to their consciousness of being an unbreakable foursome.[10]

All these families were, of course, more or less eccentric, which perhaps makes them unrepresentative of Victorian family life in general – except that all the famous nineteenth-century families had their peculiarities, and most were equally conscious of having particularly close sibling ties. I could of course have talked about the Brontës and the Rossettis (whose collaborations are discussed in Chapter 2); other families where sibling relations were influential include the Martineaus, with James (1805–1900) and Harriet (1802–76) both pursuing active careers; and the Arnolds and Macaulays, where the sisters provided intelligent companionship to better-known brothers intent on their own careers. But their support always went further than mere understanding of their work. What both brothers and sisters longed for, and usually gained from each other, was warmth of feeling, a sense of being at ease with someone who understood them.

A good place to start is the openly passionate language they used with each other, especially in letters – both in childhood and adulthood – occasionally ornamented with Latin and French phraseology. Eleanor Benson addressed her eldest brother Martin, away at Winchester, as 'dear marmoset', 'Darlingus superbus', and 'My own –', signing herself 'Your pussycat', and sending him 'a loving kiss from my coral-red lips'.[11] Twenty years later, Virginia Stephen was addressing her elder brother Thoby, away at Clifton College, and reluctant to send letters back, as 'your Mightiness', or 'Milord', and signing off as 'your loving Goatus Esq.'[12] While it may be tempting to dismiss these as cases of adolescent enthusiasm appropriate to young girls, adult males, such as Macaulay were writing to and about their sisters in much the same language. 'Dearest, dearest sister', he told Hannah Macaulay, when his other favourite, Margaret, had married, 'you alone are now left to me. Whom have I on earth but thee?': a view close to Disraeli's at a crisis point in his life, when he wrote to his father, 'I wish to live only for my sister.'[13] When Sarah Disraeli wrote the preface to their jointly written novel, *A Year at Hartlebury* (1834), she, in turn, pretended they were a married couple: 'Our honeymoon being over, we have amused ourselves during the autumn by writing a novel. All we hope is that the Public will deem our literary union as felicitous as we find our personal one.'[14] Dorothy Wordsworth's lifelong adult devotion to her brother William is too familiar to need extensive quotation here, but he also wrote of her in language that we would now find extravagant: 'Oh my dear, dear sister with what transport shall I again wear out the day in your sight. I assure you so eager is my desire to see you that all obstacles vanish. I see you in a moment running or rather flying to my arms.'[15] For the Sitwells, little had changed over a hundred years later, when Edith Sitwell wrote to her youngest brother as 'My own darling Sachie,' declaring, 'I miss you most dreadfully.'[16] Alice James's biographer, Jean Strouse, notes that William James addressed his sister as 'You lovely babe', and on one occasion sent a 'thousand thanks to the cherry lipped apricot nosed double chinned little Bal for her strongly dashed off letter, which inflamed the hearts of her lonely brothers with an intense longing to kiss and slap her celestial cheeks'.[17] Among the successful middle classes whose letters have survived, this language is used alike by children and adults, men and women, with more or less equal frequency. The historical 'moment' – post-Romanticism, but largely pre-Freud – fostered the development of this kind of emotionally uninhibited writing, while family letters even during the crisis of the First World War tended to be more restrained.[18] Nor did the Victorians 'characterize normal family behavior' – whatever they had to say about its etiquette and good conduct.[19] Park Honan, in his study of Matthew Arnold, suggests that the Victorian family was simply less embarrassed by sentiment than we are, 'and since people did not blindly exalt sexual love, or fear that every kiss implies sexual desire, they permitted more physical contact between brothers and sisters and between heterosexual friends than we do.'[20]

What may surprise us most is the dependency of adult males on their sisters. While this was more common with younger brothers and older sisters (such as the Lambs, or Edward Lear with his eldest sister Ann), where the sister might become a mother-substitute, Macaulay, for example, leant on two sisters who were ten and twelve years his juniors. The astronomer Sir William Rowan Hamilton, wanted his four sisters to live with him at Dunsink Observatory in Dublin, and share his interest in astronomy, as Caroline Herschel had done with her brother William; while Matthew Arnold relied on his sister Jane for critical and personal advice, though she was only a year older than himself. 'My poems are fragments,' he told her in 1849, '...I am fragments, while you are a whole.'[21] Sisters were expected to offer a calming influence and stabilizing advice, while brothers provided practical assistance and access to intellectual stimulus which might otherwise be difficult for sisters to find on their own or through their governesses.

Repeatedly, in Victorian culture, sisters are assigned the passive stay-at-home role of the spiritual mentor, while brothers are permitted degrees of freedom and inconsiderateness which their sisters simply have to bear. As Carol Dyhouse has suggested, 'Girls were taught that deference towards brothers was part of the natural order of things.'[22] E. W. Farrar, writing in 1836, insists that 'sisters should be always willing to walk, ride, visit with their brothers, and esteem it a privilege to be their companions'; at the same time, they should use the occasion to promote their brothers' moral well being and domestic tastes.[23] Charlotte Yonge, in *The Girl's Little Book* (1893), agrees: 'No one can do more for a brother than his sister,' Yonge argues, 'above all by her prayers, but also by her influence.' She recommended a sister to 'give up her own pursuits for [her brother's] holiday time to aid in his, and if she does so cheerfully she will have a hold on him.'[24] Working-class women autobiographers sometimes note that while they were expected to undertake domestic chores as soon as they were old enough, their brothers were free to help or not, as they pleased. Hannah Mitchell recalls 'the fact that the boys could read if they wanted filled my cup of bitterness to the brim'[25]; while Molly Hughes, who was from a more affluent family, remembers being served last at meals. 'I was expected to wait on the boys, run messages, fetch things left upstairs, and never grumble, let alone refuse.' This she actually enjoyed because she liked running about, and her brothers 'never failed to smile their thanks', and bring home treats for her.[26] Girls were frequently flattered into feeling superior to their brothers in order that they would accept an inferior position in the family. It was also widely accepted by commentators that the sister risked eventual loneliness and abandonment as her brother progressed to other relationships. Harriet Martineau felt that 'of all natural relations, the least satisfactory is the fraternal. Brothers are to sisters what sisters can never be to brothers as objects of engrossing and devoted affection.'[27] Her view is contradicted by the emotional dependency of many successful Victorian men on their sisters, but one object of this study is to explore the consequences of the widely accepted view that sisters were to put their own needs behind their brothers', specifically on the politics of envy this was likely to establish within the Victorian family.

Any study of the Victorian brother–sister relationship has to focus on the schoolroom, the place where the differences between them first became manifest. While a middle-class girl might expect to be mainly educated at home, by her mother initially, but subsequently by a governess and possibly masters, with perhaps a couple of years in her teens at a boarding school, a boy would normally be removed to school at the age of eight or nine, at a point where brother and sister were becoming conscious of each other as intellectual companions as well as playmates. Advice books written in the first third of the century carefully instructed mothers on the different approaches they should adopt towards the upbringing of their sons and daughters. Sarah Ellis, for example, has separate chapters in her *Mothers of England* (1843) on the training of boys and girls. Believing that boys had a natural energy which they needed for their future careers and responsibilities, she felt they must be humoured, and their mother must charm them into wanting to be useful around the house; but whereas she felt it was right to send boys away to school, there was no reason to do the same for girls. This did not necessarily mean their education was inferior, nor that they could not share certain studies with their brothers. 'In the study of botany, geology, and many other pursuits of more lasting interest than those which afford amusement only,' Ellis argued, 'girls may very properly be associated with their brothers.'[28] In this section of her book, Ellis quotes approvingly from the work of an earlier theorist, Isaac Taylor (1787–1865), author of *Home Education* (1838), who, while recommending that girls be kept at home, believed that they were benefiting from a superior education to their brothers':

> Girls, well taught at home, may tacitly compel their brothers to feel, if not to confess, when they return from school, that, although they may have gone some way beyond their sisters in mere scholarship, or

in mathematical proficiency, they are actually inferior to them in variety of information, in correctness of taste, and in general maturity of understanding; as well as in propriety of conduct, in self-government, in steadiness and elevation of principle, and in force and depth of feeling.[29]

Taylor's belief, like that of many contemporaries, was that a sister would profit intellectually from contact with her brother, while the brother would be morally elevated by his sister's influence. Nevertheless, it clearly occurs to him that in some cases the sister might well overtake the brother intellectually: a situation he tries to reassure his readers should be only temporary: 'It may happen that the girls of a family surpass their brothers in intelligence, and in assiduity, and might with ease be made to advance step by step with them, even in the severer studies,' he admits. 'Nevertheless the former must be made to buckle on an armour, and to gird themselves for a conflict with which it would be not merely useless, but a positive disadvantage to the latter to have any thing to do' (Taylor, p. 196). Though Taylor was happy to see siblings being educated at home together in early childhood, and enjoying what he quaintly called the 'gentle and sparkling friendships of brothers and sisters' (Taylor, p. 26), he had no doubt that they must ultimately be separated, and the male standard be taken as the norm. While boys were to buckle on their intellectual armour, girls were to retain 'the pleasurable associations of intellectual pursuits' (p. 197) and concentrate on practical experience, as opposed to the abstractions pursued by their brothers.

A popular educational book used by many children in the nineteenth century was the *Early Lessons*, or Harry and Lucy series begun by Richard Edgeworth in 1780 and continued by his daughter Maria in 1813. *Harry And Lucy Concluded* (1825), which had run to a fourth edition by 1846, demonstrates the complementary skills girls and boys were assumed to have. While both children are eager to learn, their parents fully expect Harry to be more interested in the mechanical details of how things work, while Lucy is more imaginative and literate. The book opens with Lucy's lament to her mother that she and her brother seem to be going in opposing intellectual directions: ' "Harry has grown so excessively fond of mechanics, and of all those scientific things which he is always learning from my uncle and papa...".' As much as anything, Lucy is concerned that she has lost her own former interest in them, which her mother assures her is exactly right: ' "Yes, mamma, I remember your saying, just after that happy barometer time, that I thought of nothing but experiments"' Lucy replies; '"papa said, that must not be. Then I was not allowed to go into his room with Harry in the mornings. However, I learned more of arithmetic, and drawing, and dancing, and music, and work."'[30] Lucy's mother warns her that though she may now resume her studies with Harry, she must 'submit to be inferior' to her brother for some time.

The theme of sisters prevented from studying with their brothers reverberates through nineteenth-century literature, with Latin the favourite symbol of male intellectual exclusiveness. In 'The Sister's Expostulation on the Brother's Learning Latin', which appears in Mary and Charles Lamb's collection of poems for children (1809), the sister feels the classical language has come between them:

> Once you lik'd to play with me –
> Now you leave me all alone,
> And are so conceited grown
> With your Latin, you'll scarce look
> Upon any English book.

Unlike Tom Tulliver, the brother recognizes that

> Many words in English are
> From the Latin tongue deriv'd,
> Of whose sense girls are depriv'd
> 'Cause they do not Latin know. –[31]

Latin appears most famously as a male preserve in *The Mill on the Floss*, when Maggie shows off her pleasure in Latin sentences on her visit to Mr Stelling's school, but is told that girls are 'quick and shallow'[32]; and in Charlotte Yonge's *The Daisy Chain* (1856), where Ethel May is ordered to stop competing with her brother Norman in Latin and Greek. '"From *hic haec hoc* up to Alcaics and *beta* Thukididou we have gone on together, and I can't bear to give it up,"' Ethel complains to her elder sister Margaret, who nevertheless insists that she must: '"we all know that men have more power than women, and I suppose the time has come for Norman to pass beyond you. He would not be cleverer than any one, if he could not do more than a girl at home."'[33] ... She reluctantly yields, only when her duty to her father is mentioned, and when Norman himself says, with a degree of bluff tactlessness, that '"it really is time for you to stop, or you would get into a regular learned lady, and be good for nothing"' (p. 164). In a sense, however, Ethel has the last word, in that studying never makes her ill, whereas it gives Norman a nervous breakdown. Neither George Eliot nor Charlotte Yonge indicates that her heroine has been intellectually defeated by her brother.

Similarly, in *Harry and Lucy*, the younger sister soon begins to assert herself intellectually, and proves to be brighter at arithmetic and literature than her brother, even if she has a shorter attention span. Harry calls her 'Mrs Quick-Quick' (much as Tom Tulliver, similarly discomfited, will call Maggie 'Miss Wisdom') though her father says she is '"what is vulgarly called birdwitted"' (II, 213). Edgeworth tries to preserve an intellectual balance between them, suggesting that in exchange for her poetic tastes, he imparts his love of science: the text meanwhile shuttles uneasily between scenes where Lucy is humbled, to others where she refuses to be put down. The book ends with Harry keen to invent something, and Lucy grateful for her parents' permission to '*go on* with Harry': when he was temporarily disabled by rescuing a child from a house fire, Lucy realized it was her '"greatest happiness to feel that he liked to have me with him always, reading and talking to him, and being interested in the sorts of things which he liked best"' (III, 311–12). For all her fiery quickness, the main lesson Lucy has to learn is acceptance of her underlying mental inferiority to Harry.

That fiction seems to have been a reflection of at least some families' practices in real life is suggested by a stream of references in nineteenth-century women's autobiography to the sharing of Latin lessons with brothers, and the awkwardness this sometimes caused if the sister outpaced the brother. Mary Martha Sherwood, author of the infamous children's book, *The History of the Fairchild Family* (1818–47), in which the recalcitrant children are taken to see a corpse on a gibbet, recalls that although she and her brother Marten were educated at home until he was nine or ten years old, they were 'by no means under the same management'. While she was taught by her mother, he received lessons from his father; but, 'no authority being used, he made such small progress in his Latin, that it was at last suggested that I should be made to learn Latin with him.' Though their mother took over as tutor to both children, Mary stayed in the lead. She admits that 'it is generally observed that, all things being equal, girls learn more rapidly than boys during the years of childhood.'[34] Although it has been traditionally accepted for many years that Victorian boys studied the classics, and their sisters on the whole learned modern languages, there is plenty of evidence to suggest that girls were taught Latin at home by their parents, shared their brothers' tutors, or found some other way of acquiring Latin and occasionally Greek that was not necessarily disapproved by their parents. Elizabeth Barrett recalls reading Homer 'in the original with delight inexpressible, together with Virgil'.[35] She studied Latin and Greek with Mr McSwiney, her brother Edward's tutor. Mary Somerville, the mathematician, taught herself enough Latin to read Caesar's *Commentaries*, but told her uncle Dr Somerville that she feared it was in vain: 'for my brother and other boys, superior to me in talent, and with every assistance, spent years in learning it' – the argument used against Ethel May by her sister. Though Dr Somerville himself gave her temporary help with Virgil, she later borrowed her brother Henry's tutor Mr Craw to hear her demonstrate some problems from Euclid, a book he had imported, at her request, from Edinburgh.[36] Her chances of obtaining this sort of access to the classics and mathematics would have been slim without the intermediary role of her male relatives, especially her brothers, who brought both books and tutors into the house. Later in the century, girls with brothers still seem to have had an intellectual advantage over all-girl families. The childhood diary of Naomi Mitchison (b. 1897) mentions 'Doing Latin with Boy' (her elder brother, J. B. S. Haldane)[37]; later she was the only girl at a boys' school. Ivy Compton-Burnett went on learning Greek and Latin with Mr Salt, her brothers' tutor, after they had gone to school.[38] As recently as 1987, Penelope Lively's Booker Prize-winning novel, *Moon Tiger*, which is partly about an incestuous brother–sister relationship, notes its heroine's jealousy of her brother's relationship with his Latin tutor, and her insistence on being allowed to join the lessons. In this case, the fictitious narrator, Claudia Hampton, recalls, it was not just the subject itself that appealed, but also the intimacy of adult male companionship: '"I noticed two things: that Gordon was enjoying what he was doing and that there was an affinity between them...I went to find Mother, among her roses, and announced that I wanted to learn Latin."'[39]

Normally, however, what went on at boys' schools remained something of a mystery to girls kept at home with their governesses. Whereas boys, according to John Honey, were sent to school to develop their manliness, and in the second half of the century, at least, 'home – and particularly mothers and sisters – were taboo subjects,' girls were trained specifically *for* the home, to grace it and make it a pleasant place for their fathers and brothers, later their husbands and sons, to return to.[40] Boys were under pressure to conceal any longings for their families, while girls could only sit at home and wait for news. 'O! what I suffered for Jas. when he went to the grammar school at Norwich!' Harriet Martineau told her friend Fanny Wedgwood when her eldest son was about to start school. Martineau's sympathies were all with the anxious elder sister, Frances, known as 'Snow', who might not only have to face her own sense of bereavement, but also the stigma of her brother's embarrassment. 'I trust (but it is a case in which I could never be sure) that she will not have to endure what most sisters have to go through from the school boy shame at sisters. Few boys are strong enough to eschew that weakness.' Martineau's opinion was that this was a fairly common experience.[41] Though the cult of manliness at public schools is usually seen as a later development, taking place in the second half of the century, Martineau's testimony suggests that it had already started to take root. In *Tom Brown's Schooldays*, published in 1857, but set back to the period of Dr Arnold's headmastership of Rugby in the late 1830s, little Arthur is warned on his arrival never to '"talk about home, or your mother and sisters."' Tom duly avoids mentioning his family, 'as his blundering school-boy reasoning made him think that Arthur would be softened and less manly for thinking of home'.[42]

Separation at nine or ten was clearly the most serious threat to the symbiotic relationship of brother and sister, and one that was likely to have long-term effects on the maturation process of both sexes: boys regarding domestic life as inimical to the tough stand they were developing in their other relationships, while girls often had no other significant contacts to replace their lost companionship with their brothers. The faithful correspondence of sisters such as Nellie Benson, Harriett and Jemima Newman, and Virginia Stephen, full of reminders of family birthdays and accounts of dull visits, reveals not only the unexciting pace of life at home, but also pain at how little news came back from their brothers' far more expansive worlds. John Henry Newman, who sent his sisters 'a list of the quantities of the terminations of as many Greek words as I could collect without much trouble', also sent verses in Latin written on the back of a letter ('I do not wish to tear a fresh sheet of paper'), and warned his sister Mary that the only way to make him remember her birthday was to send him a letter the day before. From Oxford, he tried to convince Jemima of how little time he had for answering letters, promising to write at greater length when he had finished his degree.[43] Charles Dodgson, before he became Lewis Carroll, ends one of his letters home from Oxford to his sister Elizabeth with a barrage of questions about domestic issues, as if making up for neglected duties, or else trying to give home life its due: 'Has Fanny found any new flowers? Have you got any new babies to nurse? Many new pictures to paint? Has Mr Stamper given up the ball room yet? Will you tell me whose and when the birthdays in next month are?'[44] Underlying Dodgson's mock-seriousness is perhaps a sense that these were the only matters his sisters had to think about while he was enjoying life at Oxford. Molly Hughes was rarely even allowed out of the house, 'and never taken to anything more exciting than a picture gallery', whereas the boys roamed freely round the tourist sights of London.[45]

The periodic return of boys from public schools for the holidays was a major event in most middle-class families, as their letters and diaries testify. The Benson family correspondence is particularly illuminating in this respect. Eleanor (Nellie) Benson writes to her brother Martin at Winchester more frequently than he writes to her, planning his holidays well in advance of his return. 'When you come home (Ah rapturous moment) we will (Oh what bliss) study if you have (Dear! impossible idea) got as far as me,' she wrote on one occasion; on another, in 1874, she talks of his setting her sister and herself a Latin exam: 'I hope you will for your exams are so easy at least they (or rather it) was last time.' Her flirtatious tone plays with a sense of the different worlds they inhabited, and tries to cover up her disappointment at not receiving enough letters. She constantly counts up the days till the next holiday, draws cats with balloons coming out of their mouths saying 'Hurray Hurray, Martin comes home on Wednesday', worries that he might be 'too grand now (Winchester man that you are) to be called marmoset', and begs him to write to her: 'Write *oh* write *Oh* write to me. *please* do, *please* do, *please* do' – with increasingly urgent underlining under each 'please'. Though Martin died at school in 1878, and both Nellie and her sister Maggie went to Truro High School, followed by Lady Margaret Hall, Oxford, their letters suggest that the girls needed their brothers to give full validation to their intellectual experiences. Nellie even fantasized about being her brother's fag: 'I shouldn't much mind being your fag for I don't imagine you are *very* severe Mr Perfect.'[46]

Imagining herself into the life of a boys' school was also tried by Molly Hughes, who had four brothers, one at Shrewsbury, the rest at Merchant Taylors'. 'So much did I hear about the school and the masters that I feel almost an old Taylorian myself'. On Speech Day each year, she 'seemed to get right inside the life of the boys', and could even join in the school song.[47] A similar experience is recounted by Vera Brittain in *Testament of Youth*, Uppingham Speech Day being one of the pre-war landmarks in her young life. Its significance as marking the end of peace time is clearly its main claim on her memory, but she also recalls being keenly interested in meeting her brother Edward's friends about whom she had heard so much.[48] As long as brothers and sisters mainly attended single-sex schools, and as long as boys' public schools remained the academic elite, sisters went on feeling excluded from a strongly masculine preserve. Rarely did they feel their academic achievements were to be compared with their brothers'. Virginia Woolf was still resentful of the amount of money spent on educating the males of middle-class families, while their sisters made do with whatever was left, when she claimed that 'Arthur's Education Fund' changed the face of the landscape for a woman visiting Harrow or Eton, Oxford or Cambridge. 'To you it is your old school... the source of memories and traditions innumerable. But to us, who see it through the shadow of Arthur's Education Fund, it is a schoolroom table; an omnibus going to a class.'[49] Perhaps she was recalling a visit to Thoby's school, Clifton College, in 1898, when she attended a luncheon and garden party during his last year there. 'I have never really seen your residence,' she wrote, treating it jokingly as a country house, '– and this time next year you will be flitting.'[50] Newman described his Trinity College room to his sister Jemima in mock-heroic terms ('On turning to the right a massy chimney-piece of marble discovers itself surmounted by a handsome pair of bronze figures...') which play on her ignorance and his own position of privilege (*Letters* I, 70).

The effect of their sisters' influence on brothers sent away to public school also needs to be considered. Kept in a masculine stronghold, and sent home only after many weeks away, boys were bound to have difficulty adjusting back to the presence of sisters in a domestic context. As Peter M. Lewis has argued, male institutions like boarding schools 'construct a system in which masculinity is defined by absence of the feminine. Boys are removed from home because home is the site above all of a compassionate love (but also of other "feminine" qualities and emotions) which weakens resolve and impedes progress to manhood.'[51] Although some school reformers were concerned about the rough atmosphere in which public school boys traditionally had to live, their attempts to remedy it continued to omit the feminine. William Sewell, the first Warden of Radley, based his idea of the school on the model of the family, 'with the Warden as father, the Fellows as elder brothers, all living under one roof...' Sewell did, in fact, acknowledge the absence of any women in this idealized family, and admitted that 'Of that family the Warden himself must be the father and the mother too.' He also proposed 'the introduction of ladies,' but trembled 'at the audacity of the idea'. Where the ladies came from or what they were meant to do when introduced was left somewhat obscure, though Sewell clearly felt they served a beneficent purpose.[52] In fiction, *The Mill on the Floss* shows Tom's awkwardness on returning home from school and finding Maggie passionate to be with him again and share his activities. It takes him some days to adjust to her emotional demands, and characteristically, she wins his approval only for success in catching a fish – a masculine sport he can respect. In the real-life reminiscences of several Victorian families, elaborate make-believe games instigated by older brothers or sisters kept the family together in between absences at school, much as the Brontës' Glasstown, Angria and Gondal sagas survived their frequent departures for school or work, and enabled elder brothers to maintain a reputation for active leadership.

The games of the Benson children have been particularly well documented, as have their troubled dynamics as a family. Martin became one of the legendary dead siblings characteristic of nineteenth-century family culture, whose early disappearance marked the others for the rest of their lives. (Other examples are Maria Brontë, dead at eleven from tuberculosis neglected at Cowan Bridge Clergy Daughters' School, and also remembered as an intellectual prodigy; Thomas De Quincey's sister Elizabeth, who died in 1792, and gave his mind 'a permanent tinge of melancholy'[53]; and Thoby Stephen, handsome, intelligent and athletic, dead of typhoid at the age of 26). When the Benson brothers and sisters were all at home together, they each had their special companion; they also contributed to the shared imaginative games that needed the presence of elder brothers to be properly organized. E. F. Benson (Fred) recalls having a 'special alliance' with Maggie, 'which continued till the end of her life...'; though when their elder brother Arthur (A. C.) Benson wrote his memoir of his sister, he claimed her as his own 'special ally'.[54] Within large Victorian families, various combinations of two were possible; indeed were probably essential to provide some sense of belonging to a smaller, more intimate unit than the whole tribe. According to John Tosh, 'a passionate attachment between brother and sister was not uncommon, nor was it frowned upon'.[55] With children encouraged to make friends within their own social group, especially as other brother–sister combinations might provide future spouses, the choice was often limited. What is most striking about the Benson family letters and other biographical materials is the infrequent mention of any friends' names in childhood, though they subsequently formed one or two close same-sex relationships in young adulthood, and all, like their mother, showed some leaning towards homosexuality. A. C. Benson admits in his memoir of his sister that they mixed with few families in Truro when his father was Bishop; a practice repeated by the young Stephen children holidaying in St Ives. 'We never had any friends to stay with us,' Virginia Woolf recalled. 'Nor did we want them. "Us four" were completely self-sufficient.'[56] Fred Benson describes the

Saturday Magazine they wrote as a family group (something that was also done in Lewis Carroll's family, Eglantyne Jebb's, and Virginia Woolf's), and notes that they were all keen hobbyists – 'draughtsmen, ornithologists, conchologists, geologists, poets and literary folk' (*Our Family Affairs*, p. 54). In addition, they played a game called 'Pirates' – 'evolved by the family generally' (p. 94) – and convened a 'mystical "Chapter," of which Arthur was warden, Nellie, Maggie, and myself sub-warden, secretary and treasurer, and Hugh was Henchman' (p. 97). By 1884, they were writing plays together in the holidays; another year they dramatized *The Rose and the Ring* in operatic form with original lyrics set to popular tunes (p. 179). Later he and Maggie tried to write a story together, which rehearsed some ideas for his later *Dodo* (p. 180).

Other extensive memories of sibling games and fantasies are reported of the Hamiltons and Farjeons. Sir William Rowan Hamilton, as the only boy in a family of five siblings, organized his sisters into games re-enacting the Trojan War. In his early teens, he arranged them 'into a government entitled the Honourable Society of Four', omitting the remaining sister who was too young for office: 'He himself was peer, Eliza and Sydney were commoners, Grace was lady lieutenant, and their father was king, with veto power over all legislative acts (crimes were punishable by slaps on the back).'[57] Eleanor Farjeon, the only girl in a family of four, tells a similar story of male domination of the playroom. Again, she was close to one brother, Harry, and recalled that 'if ever sister longed for identity with her brother, Nellie did.' Harry led complex games of 'TAR' (named after Tessy and Ralph, from *The Babes in the Wood*, which they had seen in the theatre), by announcing ' "We are This Person and That," and we instantly *were* those two, till some movement in the drama necessitated an exit or another entrance.'[58] Like Tom Tulliver, Harry was a stern lawgiver, who recognized no gradation between honesty and dishonesty: 'he invented rules and codes with Spartan strictness' (pp. 250–1). Looking back on her total commitment to Harry's games, Farjeon wonders whether their effect on her psychological development was altogether healthy. Her descriptions credit Harry with dictating the very nature of her being: 'I could not "be" anybody till Harry said so,' Farjeon recalls (p. 321); 'Harry was Prometheus and I his figure of clay, till he breathed into me the stolen fire' (p. 324). More than a game, TAR took over her life, and halted her progress towards adulthood. Farjeon claims not to have been aware of her own sex until she was 'nearly thirty years old, and it took at least ten years more for emotional crudeness to get abreast of mental ripeness' (p. 324).

Evidence gathered from several autobiographies recalling childhoods spent towards the end of the previous century or the beginning of the next evokes a fantasy-life that was largely separate from the downstairs world of the children's parents – as E. Nesbit's novels at the beginning of the twentieth century so often suggest.[59] As they grew up, the relationship between brothers and sisters was placed under increasing strain. While the boys moved on to university, the girls were kept at home in a state of prolonged childhood, which officially ended only when they married, or their parents died and they had to take responsibility for themselves. Even then, married brothers with a home to offer were expected to house their sisters, and it was not unusual throughout the nineteenth century for adult and orphaned sets of siblings to keep house together. This was Dorothy Wordsworth's ambition from the moment she was reunited with William after they had spent their childhoods apart; Macaulay hoped to live with one or both of his younger sisters; Walter Pater did live with his, and Charles Lamb with his older sister Mary; and Virginia Stephen, before her marriage to Leonard Woolf, lived first with all three siblings, and then with her younger brother Adrian. Even after she had gone to West Africa, Mary Kingsley returned to keep house for her brother – until he next chose to travel: 'I must do it,' she explained, 'it is duty: the religion I was brought up in. When he does not want me, I go back to West Africa for the third time, perfectly content to stay there if it chooses.'[60] In fiction, too, adult brothers and sisters are often found keeping house. Mr Bingley, in *Pride and Prejudice*, is accompanied to Netherfield by both his sisters, including one who is married; Mary and Henry Crawford leave the house of their reprobate uncle in London to live with their married sister, Mrs Grant, near Mansfield Park; as soon as they are released from their jobs, Tom and Ruth Pinch, in *Martin Chuzzlewit*, set up house together; Thurstan and Faith Benson in Elizabeth Gaskell's *Ruth* become the orphaned and pregnant heroine's substitute parents and spiritual and worldly advisers; Harriet Gresley goes to live with her clergyman brother James in Mary Cholmondeley's *Red Pottage* (1899), even though they have entirely different values; and adult pairs of siblings living together in Henry James's novels include Paul and Rose Muniment in *The Princess Casamassima*, and Dr Sloper and Lavinia Penniman in *Washington Square*, whose hero, Morris Townsend, also lives with his widowed sister, Mrs Montgomery. It was partly just a matter of economic necessity or convenience that adult siblings should live together; partly a need for respectability and protection at a time when it was practically unheard of for young middle-class single women to live alone. Sisters-in-law with an active and respectable social circle were also a means of introducing younger sisters to potential marriage-partners. In fiction, the adult sibling relationship is usually treated positively, but there are exceptions, as will be seen later. Dickens often has maladjusted younger brothers cajoling their saintly elder sisters to marry men of the brother's choice, so as to improve his own prospects. Normally, though, living with a brother or sister seems to have offered a more democratic lifestyle than was the case where ageing adult children lived at home with even older parents – quite apart from the other personal advantages sibling living arrangements might offer in the way of career advancement and marriage opportunities through introductions to brothers' friends.

For some women in their twenties and thirties, the older brother who was 'out in the world' provided a continuing source of intellectual support and advice which proved invaluable later on. Jane Austen, who was fond of all her brothers, relied most perhaps on Henry, four years her senior, for opinions of her novels as she was writing them; particularly with her later works keeping careful note of what he thought. Henry also negotiated with publishers for her, even dictating a letter to John Murray about the copyright of *Emma, Mansfield Park* and *Sense and Sensibility* when he was too ill to write. The fact that Austen herself took over a few days later and urged Murray to call on her and sort things out, shows that she was fully capable of dealing directly with publishers: only a pretence continued that a woman should have a man to mediate with businessmen.[61] For Emily Davies, however, founder of Girton College, Cambridge, her older brother Llewelyn was invaluable in helping her make the transition from a limited home life in Gateshead to essential networking in London. Though Llewelyn, a former Fellow of Trinity, had been embarrassed at the prospect of her meeting his college friends, he apparently had no such inhibitions by the time Emily was in her late twenties. Her biographer, Daphne Bennett, comments on a visit she paid him in 1859: 'At last she was discovering an atmosphere in which she could breathe and expand mentally, in which she could discuss anything without giving offence.' He also helped by 'introducing her to his friends, some of whom were among the most influential men in England.'[62]

On other occasions, a brother was still needed for intellectual dialogue. Close though she was to their elder sister Vanessa, and willing though her father was to help with advice on reading, Virginia Stephen turned to Thoby when she wanted to discuss Greek literature, Shakespeare, or current affairs. He was less forbidding than their father, and during his short lifetime, she treated him as someone more learned than herself, whose opinions were worth seeking. In 1901 she was writing for advice on which Sophocles play she should read, and wondering why the characters in *Cymbeline* appeared so inhuman: 'I shall want a lecture when I see you; to clear up some points about the Plays.' By 1903, when she was 21 and nursing their dying father, she was lamenting: 'I don't get anybody to argue with me now, and feel the want. I have to delve from books, painfully and all alone, what you get every evening sitting over your fire and smoking your pipe with Strachey etc. No wonder my knowledge is but scant. Theres [sic] nothing like talk as an educator I'm sure.'[63] Back in 1724 Elizabeth Tollet felt much the same way as she studied alone, imagining her brother at St John's College, Cambridge, relaxing after his work with congenial friends: 'In books good subjects for discourse are found;/Such be thy talk when friendly tea goes round.'[64]

One of the best examples of the brother's continuing advisory role is in the relationship of Arthur Hugh Clough with his sister, Anne Jemima, who subsequently became the first Principal of Newnham College, Cambridge. Left at home in Charleston, South Carolina, while her brothers went to school in England, Anne Jemima had to wait till adulthood to be on close terms with Arthur. Her niece, Blanche Athena Clough, comments: 'They wrote to one another while he was at school, and he discussed large questions with her, such as the advantages and disadvantages of an Established Church, and planned that they should spend their future lives together in some quiet vicarage.'[65] Like many other brothers, real and fictional, he provided her with books and intellectual guidance. She was afraid she might have 'become fanatical and foolish' if she had stayed in America, 'and not come to England and been taught better by Arthur' (*Memoir*, p. 25). Anne Jemima seems honestly to have believed her brother to be wiser and better than she was, as her private journals indicate. He took her on her first journey abroad after America, to Germany and Switzerland, and engaged her in stimulating intellectual conversations. Reading between the lines, the conflict between sisterly and other kinds of love becomes evident: 'Some talk with Arthur about marriage,' she notes on one occasion, 'also about the duties that single women owe to their families' (*Memoir*, p. 60). Although Deborah Gorham feels that 'she thought much more about him than he ever did about her',[66] Anne Jemima was devastated when Arthur died in 1861, and called his loss 'the closing in of my most cherished hopes' (p. 100). Women bereft like this in midlife often channelled their energies into active public service of a kind their brothers would have approved.

The Cloughs were both achievers, and in different fields; more often, an adult spinster sister is found in the background of her successful brother's life, attending to his manuscripts, fair-copying, listening, and supporting: a role famously performed by Dorothy Wordsworth, but also by Sarianna Browning and Sarah Disraeli. Browning's sister moved back in with him after the death of his wife, Elizabeth, and according to a chronicler of Browning's youth, was a major intellectual companion: 'with the exception of about twenty years in the middle of their lives, "Dearest Sis" was his closest confidante throughout his life.'[67] Sarah Disraeli's interest in her brother's career, meanwhile, became 'a method of vicariously satisfying her own frustrated hopes and ambitions';[68] even after his marriage in 1839 to Mary Anne Wyndham, and in return for campaigning for him in Parliamentary elections, she was idealized in his fiction.[69]

In the nineteenth century, it was usually the brother who helped the sister enter the world of publishers' deals and contracts; by the twentieth century, the balance of power had shifted, and sisters were just as likely to help brothers if they were older and more successful. As the baby and only brother in a family of older sisters, John Lehmann was often the victim of tricks, practical jokes, and elaborate games; subsequently, however, his sister Rosamond advised him on his writing, and shared with him the development of her own writing career.[70] The Sitwells took it in turns to take the initiative: Edith introducing her younger brothers to the world of the imagination when they were children; Osbert retaining her as his mentor and 'chief adviser on what to read'; later Osbert and Sacheverell suggesting she set her *Façade* poems to music by William Walton, whom they had met at Oxford, proving that the masculine world could still produce connections not so readily available to sisters who were not yet university-educated.[71]

As Chapter 3 will show, when brother–sister relationships declined in adult life, they tended to go seriously wrong, exacerbated by the positive childhood associations which had subsequently been betrayed. Support of incurably helpless siblings, however, seems to have been a good deed silently taken for granted in the lives of many Victorians: rarely spoken about, but consistently performed. Even Gladstone, who had been spiritually guided by his older sister Anne (another of the legendary sibling 'saints' who died young), was repeatedly baffled by what to do with his other sister Helen, who alienated her staunchly Church of England brother by deciding in 1842 to become a Roman Catholic; she was also an opium addict. The journalist J. R. Ackerley's sister Nancy (1899–1979) was, according to their friend E. M. Forster, in love with her brother;

while his diaries suggest that apart from his homosexual relationships, he was more in love with his dog, Queenie. Suicidal and lonely after the breakdown of her marriage, Nancy expected Joe to look after her; Joe in turn reminded himself: 'She was my sister only, my only sister, but my sister only, and her assault upon me was more than the assault of a lover, a wife.' To the novelist Clifford Kitchin, seeing them coming home after a morning's drinking, they looked like Charles and Mary Lamb.[72]

The brother–sister relationship has emotional nuances missing from the sister–sister relationship, intense and full of jealousies as that often is. While sisters may be rivals for the love of the same man, they essentially exist as equals: educated in the same way, and subject to the same constraints imposed on them as women in a male-dominated society. For many Victorians, a sibling of the opposite sex acted as a platonic marriage-partner. While living with a brother, an unmarried sister could claim a roof over her head and all the affection and protection afforded to a wife, without the sexual obligations. Provided her brother was no disciplinarian, she could combine the best of childhood with the best of adulthood: emotional security with freedom and independence. Adult siblings gave each other an extension of the family home and a continuation of the natural affinity they had felt as children, whereas marriage involved the strains of constructing intimacy with a stranger. Nevertheless, as Theodore Zeldin has argued, the search for an ideal soul-mate has often been frustrated by rivalries too closely embedded in the sibling relationship: 'All over the world, the disappointment individuals have had with their own brothers and sisters has led them to seek artificial siblings outside the family, to invent relationships from which envy would be excluded.'[73] Brothers marry wives and exclude their sisters; sisters prefer other men to their brothers; both fight over the distribution of family property. Sisters remember how little was spent on their education, brothers remember how they had to work all their lives while their sisters were looked after at home. Other friends come between them, as do children, so that one may need intimacy when the other has it from a relationship outside the family. The brother–sister relationship is simultaneously the longest and the most stable, yet also the most unpredictable that many of us experience. Its uneasy representation in the works of nineteenth- and early twentieth-century writers is the subject of the rest of this book.

2
Brother–Sister Collaborative Relationships

> Now reader, how were those two connected? they were not lovers – they were not man & wife – they must have been, a marked resemblance in their features attested it, brother & sister – [1]

From the Lambs to the Sitwells, the late eighteenth to the twentieth century produced a succession of literary families whose collaborative relationships generated poems, novels, journals, letters, legends, mysteries, and speculative psychoanalytical responses. The most common configuration of these family groups was the brother–sister pair or trio: hence Henry and Sarah Fielding, Charles and Mary Lamb, William and Dorothy Wordsworth, Benjamin and Sarah Disraeli, Branwell, Charlotte, Emily and Anne Brontë, Dante Gabriel, Christina and William Rossetti, Edith, Osbert and Sacheverell Sitwell, and in the United States, Gertrude and Leo Stein, and William, Henry and Alice James. Sister–sister pairs, by contrast, are rare – unless one breaks down the Brontë group, or looks at minor writers such as Maria and Geraldine Jewsbury; brother–brother equally so, unless one separates the Rossettis, or looks to Germany for the Brothers Grimm. In most cases, there was something about the interaction of the sexes that was more fruitful of literary achievement than the same-sex partnership.

To some extent, this meant sheer practical assistance, such as Dorothy Wordsworth was able to provide in acting as her brother's amanuensis, or Dante Gabriel Rossetti offered in approaching publishers on his sister's behalf; but there was a good deal more than this, which it is the object of this chapter to uncover. The brother–sister collaborative partnership of the Romantic or Victorian period cannot avoid to some extent being a model of gender-relations of the time, though it may also be atypical and transgressive. Society may also query its internal dynamics and public image, so that whereas there was a general acceptance of the Lambs' and Wordsworths' living and working relationships (occasionally spiked by suspicious gossip), the Sitwells were to a considerable extent damaged by their image as an eccentric threesome. Moreover, it may be all too easy to assume that the sisters took a lesser role and were patronized by the brothers, when in all probability they created each other in roles of their own designing. It is with this construction of each other – in poetry and prose, in biographical memoranda as well as in art, for private and public consumption – that this chapter is most concerned.

The function of these collaborative relationships in literary history is complex and variable from family to family: nevertheless, certain general conditions prevail, beginning with the fact that most of these brothers and sisters never married, or, like Charlotte Brontë, did so late in life and briefly. Neither of the Lambs married (though Charles proposed, and was rejected)[2] but in each of the other families, one member successfully found a partner: William Wordsworth, Benjamin Disraeli, William Rossetti, Sacheverell Sitwell, Leo Stein, and William James. It seems significant that except for Charlotte Brontë, the married sibling was never the sister. Though most of them had other friends, the family grouping remained tight throughout their lifetime: Dorothy Wordsworth, for instance, ending her life peacefully in her brother's house; all the Brontës returning home from their forays into the outside world; Christina and William Rossetti living with their mother well into adulthood; and the Sitwells working together on projects such as *Façade*, and contributions to literary journals like *Wheels*. Close brother-and-sister bonds provided a supportive alternative to marriage in a way that we tend to have difficulty comprehending: hence the prurient speculation as to whether the Wordsworth relationship was incestuous.[3] Commentators on the Wordsworths are either aghast at the very idea, or feel, with Molly Lefebure, that they must *at least* 'have endured an agonising frustration of full physical expression of their love.'[4] One senses that many people would like the Wordsworth pair to have been incestuous because that would have made them more understandable. The reality is that we will probably never know, and reading biographical data into texts may well mislead. What we may discover from the work of collaborative brother–sister groups, however, is imaginative projections of male/female roles which are commentaries on the experience of writing from a family basis. This chapter will not be concerned with the mechanics of collaborative writing; it will instead selectively examine the work of siblings to discover to what extent their sense of writing from within a mixed sex group affected their ability to transcend gender barriers, or whether they simply reinforced conventional codes.

Romantic partnerships: the Lambs and the Wordsworths

The Lambs and the Wordsworths separately reached a point in their lives when they set up house together and for a while adopted a 'child'. For the Wordsworths, this happened at Racedown, Dorset, in 1795, when they looked after Basil Montagu; the Lambs were rather older when in 1823 they took on a 'daughter', Emma Isola, who eventually married the publisher Edward Moxon. For both couples, a mock family for a time seemed necessary or desirable, implying a wish to imitate the standard pattern for 'normal' married couples. Were brother–sister pairs consoling themselves for missing out on marriage? Were they imitating the wedded household because their own model was insufficiently established or emotionally unsatisfactory? Charles Lamb, who said his sister 'cleaved to him for better, for worse' (echoing the language of the wedding service),[5] tries to pinpoint, in 'A Bachelor's Complaint of the Behaviour of Married People', what it is exactly that he finds irritating about couples; while Mary Lamb's letters struggle to describe her relationship with her brother in terms that entirely satisfied her: 'you would like to see us as we often sit writing on one table (but not on one cushion sitting) like Hermia & Helena in the Midsummer Night's Dream, or rather like an old literary Darby and Joan,' she told her friend Sarah Stoddart in 1806. They were either two girls together or an elderly couple; the gender boundaries further confused by Mary's admission that she was 'taking snuff & he groaning all the while & saying he can make nothing of it'.[6] If anything, Mary, who was eleven years his senior, was Charles's mother-figure: an age-gap he retains when in his *Elia* essays, he recreates his sister as Bridget Elia, his cousin – 'my sweet cousin', as he calls her in 'Mrs Battle's Opinions on Whist', where he envisages a timeless tableau of card-playing:

> That last game I had with my sweet cousin (I capotted her) – (dare I tell thee, how foolish I am?) – I wished it might have lasted for ever, though we gained nothing, and lost nothing, though it was a mere shade of play: I would be content to go on in that idle folly for ever. The pipkin should be ever boiling, that was to prepare the gentle lenitive to my foot, which Bridget was doomed to apply after the game was over: and, as I do not much relish appliances, there it should ever bubble. Bridget and I should be ever playing.[7]

The passage fixes them for ever in a strange state of suspended animation, perfectly balanced: though he has won all the suits ('capotted her'), he imagines a situation in which they play for ever, gaining nothing, and losing nothing, with the pipkin for ever boiling, the soothing foot treatment for ever anticipated: the whole an affectionate piece of comic whimsy that ironizes Keats's frozen lovers on the Grecian Urn, permanently about to kiss. Similarly, Dorothy Wordsworth struggles to find a convincing way of telling *her* best friend, Jane Pollard, exactly how she feels about *her* brother, William. 'I am willing to allow that half the virtues with which I fancy him endowed are the creation of my Love,' she admits, 'but surely I may be excused!' Kindly incorporating Jane into the fantasy, she too envisages a static picture of domestic bliss: 'think of our moonlight walks attended by my own dear William; ... Think of our mornings, we will work, William shall read to us.'[8] In later years, their relationship would be difficult both for her to describe and other people to understand. Coleridge thought Wordsworth had made a mistake in taking her to Goslar in 1798–9: 'His taking his Sister with him was a wrong Step... Sister is considered as only a name for Mistress,' he worried.[9] While their immediate friends and relatives in England seemed to accept their closeness, De Quincey noticed that his 'coarse-minded neighbours' were suspicious: 'It is Wordsworth's custom whenever he meets or parts with any of the female part of his own relations to kiss them – this he has frequently done when he has met his sister on her rambles or parted from her and that in roads or on mountains...'[10]

Were the Lambs and the Wordsworths ahead of their times, or behind them? Though most family historians see close brother–sister relations as typical of the age in which the two pairs were living, contemporary evidence suggests that they were also constructing variations of this model which they themselves recognized as a little extreme, and which were specifically designed to suit their emotional and psychological needs. Both the Lambs suffered from bouts of mental disturbance, Charles Lamb drank heavily, and Dorothy Wordsworth eventually succumbed to a form of dementia through which she was nursed in her brother's house. Charles Lamb particularly disliked the way married couples flaunted the fact of having been chosen, so that 'you cannot be in their company a moment without being made to feel, by some indirect hint or open avowal, that *you* are not the object of this preference.'[11] The attraction of the brother–sister household was that choice was not an issue, or at least not the main one, as in marriage: the relationship had existed in some form since infancy, and simply needed maintaining – or in the case of the Wordsworths, rediscovering after their long separation as children. Alan Grob makes the point that Dorothy was 'to be not only his "dear, dear Sister" bound to him by ties of blood, but also his rationally chosen partner and companion, a "dear, dear Friend," whose invaluable intellectual assistance to him he would gladly acknowledge.'[12] She in turn chose William, rather than Richard or John as her lifelong companion. For the Lambs, mental infirmities were part of the package: they both needed looking after by someone who would understand their peculiarities, and avoid passing judgement where there was little to be achieved by so doing; but if Mary Lamb was also his housekeeper and mother-substitute (even before their mother was killed), it is less easy to assign *him* a familial role with a name we recognize (too young to be father, too old to be son). As with the Wordsworths, she described their relationship informally, in letters, while he explored its nature in his published works. In each brother–sister pair it was the brother who formally shaped and reconstructed the relationship for public consumption, while the sister's feelings were divulged only to friends, and sometimes only to herself.

'We house together, old bachelor and maid, in a sort of double singleness,' Lamb reports in another *Elia* essay, 'Mackery End, in Hertfordshire'.[13] When Mary Lamb killed their mother in 1796 in an attack of rage while they were preparing a meal, Charles avoided condemning her, seeing her instead as the 'unconscious Instrument of the Almighty's judgements to our house'[14] As defined by Elia, 'Bridget' is always middle-aged, unglamorous and eccentric; but she also has a wild, ungovernable streak, which bursts through in the essays, however hard her cousin tries to restrain her. In 'Mackery End,' Lamb notes her preference for 'some modern tale, or adventure', while he prefers the quaint or antiquarian; she likes to read in company; she lacks formal education; and she dislikes being told her faults. 'She was tumbled early, by accident or design, into a spacious closet of good old English reading, without much selection or prohibition, and browsed at will upon that fair and wholesome pasturage,' Lamb explains, turning her into a roaming animal – perhaps the 'lamb' of their surname.[15] When they revisit their old family haunts at Mackery End, Bridget (who 'in some things is behind her years', p. 91) shows her joy more effusively than Elia, whose memory of the place is less distinct. He can only watch in silence as 'Bridget's memory, exalted by the occasion, warmed into a thousand half-obliterated recollections of things and persons, to my utter astonishment, and her own–' (p. 92). More instinctual and primitive than her fastidious house-mate, Bridget takes over the occasion, and enacts the disruptive incursion into the social order approved by French feminist theorists such as Hélène Cixous and Julia Kristeva. 'If woman has always functioned "within" the discourse of man,' Cixous argues, '...it is time for her to dislocate this "within", to explode it, turn it around, and seize it; to make it hers, containing it, taking it in her own mouth, biting that tongue with her very own teeth to invent for herself a language to get inside of.'[16] While it remains true that Lamb is ventriloquizing his sister here, her irrepressible vitality, like the Duchess's in Browning's dramatic monologue, 'My Last Duchess', threatens the more staid dominance of the external male speaker.

This is even more the case with Lamb's essay 'Old China', which Bridget hijacks, and diverts entirely from Elia's original direction. While Elia begins by acknowledging his 'almost feminine partiality for old china', Bridget bursts into nostalgia for the 'good old times' when they struggled to make ends meet, instead of indulging themselves with trifles. Most of the blame for this she deflects towards him, lamenting, above all, the loss of adventure in their more prosperous way of living. Instead of walking into the country and taking their food with them, they '*ride* part of the way – and go into a fine inn, and order the best of dinners'; they now take the best seats at the theatre instead of struggling into the galleries; they buy whatever books they want; and they no longer enjoy the sense of having a special treat. Elia lets her speak for most of the essay – 'Bridget is so sparing of her speech on most occasions, that when she gets into a rhetorical vein, I am careful how I interrupt it' – but at the end delivers a rational rebuke, which returns her to the subject of 'Old China': 'And now do just look at that merry little Chinese waiter holding an umbrella, big enough for a bed-tester, over the head of that petty insipid half-Madonnaish chit of a lady in that very blue summer house.'[17] Again, the reader thinks of Browning's poem, which ends with the envoy urged to admire 'Neptune taming a sea-horse' – apt symbol of the Duke's taste for dominance. Alison Hickey thinks we should read the essay as 'an extended act of prolonging his own voice,' 'an act of possession or imposition on his part, no matter how much he would give to her.'[18] The essay's ending certainly supports this, as Elia reinscribes the woman as an insipid 'chit', a pretty image on willow-patterned china needing manly protection.

Jane Aaron has shown that Charles Lamb saw himself as having what we now regard as permeable ego boundaries: 'His personal correspondence indicates that Charles experienced himself as a conglomeration of parts rather than a whole.'[19] This clearly allowed him to ventriloquize further female roles in *Mrs Leicester's School* (1808), a joint-production for which Mary wrote the greater part, while Charles was initially credited with being sole author. One of his three contributions, 'Maria Howe; or the effects of Witch Stories', is spoken by a 'weak and tender-spirited' girl, who recalls her closeness to her father's unmarried elder sister, ten years his senior; but the aunt is recalled ambivalently as a woman whose oddness terrified her, and seemed witch-like. She was 'a source of both love and terror to me'.[20] While both the Lambs write of displacement and broken families, Charles is clearly here exploring ambiguous feelings for his sister, especially a fear of her 'wickedness', her potential to do harm, as Mary had done to their mother. Another of Lamb's contributions, 'Arabella Hardy; or, the Sea Voyage', describes how an orphan girl was cared for by an effeminate-looking sailor, nicknamed 'Betsy', on a voyage from the East Indies to England. To entertain his small charge, 'Betsy' 'would enter into my thoughts, and tell me pretty stories of his mother and his sisters, and a female cousin that he loved better than his sisters, whom he called Jenny'.[21] Jane Aaron suggests the narrative is 'centrally concerned with the arbitrary nature of conventional gender-role differentiation, and the limiting prejudices the system creates'.[22] Lamb certainly was drawn to androgynous images of men which break down such barriers, as we see in 'Old China': 'I love the men with women's faces, and the women, if possible, with still more womanish expressions,' he says of the china tea-cups he admires (p. 287); but while he warms to the effeminate men, he intensifies the femininity of the women, making them more clearly 'womanish'. Exploring the lawless world of witches, dream-children, painted Chinese men and women, bachelors, maids, and poor relations, Charles Lamb voices in his essays and contributions to *Mrs Leicester's School* a fear or distrust of female duality: an explosive combination of gentleness and fury, both of which Mary had shown for their mother, Elizabeth.

Wordsworth noted similar propensities in Dorothy. Though never likely to murder anyone, she is often depicted in his poems as 'wild' – the 'wild ecstasies,' and 'the shooting lights/Of thy wild eyes,' remembered in 'Tintern Abbey' – in a way that has certainly troubled critics, whether or not they troubled him. De Quincey also saw her in these terms, as 'the very wildest (in the sense of the most natural) person I have ever known', and thought she 'humanized' his otherwise austere nature. Her contributions to the partnership were, in his view, distinctly feminine, ingrafting by a 'sexual sense of beauty, upon his masculine austerity' certain delicacies and graces which he would otherwise have lacked.[23] To more recent critics, however, as James Soderholm has shown, the brother is blamed for seeing his sister as intellectually or spiritually inferior to himself: certainly at an earlier stage of mental development, which reflects an outgrown phase of his own.[24] Wordsworth often shows himself to have been disturbed by whatever it was that Dorothy's example taught him. The cancelled opening of 'Nutting', which was originally addressed to 'Lucy', begins with a shudder of horror at the damage done to the hazel grove Wordsworth subsequently depicted himself as devastating:

> Ah! what a crash was that! with gentle hand
> Touch these fair hazels – My beloved Friend!
> Though 'tis a sight invisible to thee
> From such rude intercourse the woods all shrink
> As at the blowing of Astolpho's horn.[25]

As many critics have noticed, the speaker urges Lucy (generally identified with Dorothy), her cheeks flushed 'with a tempestuous bloom', her look 'Half cruel in its eagerness', to rest on a bed of heath and 'sink into a dream/Of gentle thoughts.' Seen in sexual terms, Lucy/Dorothy frightens her brother, who fears what Gregory Jones calls her 'erotic independence':

> He recognizes that she has it in her to live a completely independent life, erotically and otherwise, and he no doubt wants this for her in one sense. But he simply cannot bear the thought of losing their tightly bound relationship – their co-dependency, I suppose we would call it now.[26]

It is hard to know whether Wordsworth was concerned about losing her: after all, he had already formed one relationship with Annette Vallon, and would marry Mary Hutchinson in 1802. Of the two, he must have realized he was the more likely to break up the dyad. On the other hand, he sees her as intrinsically bound up with his own identity. 'Nutting' was originally intended as part of a poem on his own life, and indeed was reclaimed as such when he deleted the lines about Lucy. Whenever he writes most intently about his own development as a poet, especially his changing relationship with nature, he defines himself in relation to her co-development, which he sees as being more spontaneous and uncontrolled than his own. Wordsworth never seems sure whether to envy this or reproach her for it. She is an earlier version of himself, a stage he has passed through – equated with his youth – which paradoxically pointed the way forward for himself. At the end of 'Tintern Abbey' he hears in her voice the 'language of my former heart': 'Oh! yet a little while/ May I behold in thee what I was once,/ My dear, dear Sister!' – and seems to will her emotional stasis, so that she remains a child-replica of himself.

Much of Wordsworth's best-known poetry enacts a battle to control Dorothy's influence on his life and work, even as he pays tribute to it. James Soderholm wonders whether we have simply become too suspicious of their relationship. 'Why do so many recent critics insist,' he asks, 'contrary to all biographical evidence, that William secretly has it in for Dorothy when he writes a poem including and even celebrating her?' (Soderholm, p. 315). Yet she herself knew that he sometimes found the language of her journal entries too strong an influence: 'After tea I read to William that account of the little boy belonging to the tall woman, and an unlucky thing it was, for he could not escape from those very words, and so he could not write the poem.'[27] Wordsworth's need for 'escape' from his sister's influence took several forms: moments originally shared, as in 'I wandered lonely as a cloud', become solitary ones; and poems apparently written to commemorate Dorothy's gifts can be read as diminishing her, even if this was not the original intention. Douglass H. Thomson, for example, notes that 'one of the chief difficulties involved in a reading of the Lucy poems is the persistent and progressive diminution of the cycle's main character'.[28] Thomson argues that because of the close identification between Lucy and himself, she becomes an emblem of his own 'unquiet heart', which needs to be chastened and re-educated; while Kenneth R. Johnson suggests that Wordsworth, who used the Lucy poems to explore the possibility of his sister's death and what this would mean to him, was also trying to grapple with his incestuous feelings for her. The Lucy poems finally 'show the pain of his renouncing her'.[29] Like Mary Lamb for Charles, Dorothy Wordsworth appears to have been for her brother a 'source of both love and terror'; though it seems not so much fear of what she might do that troubled him, as fear of himself. Hence Dorothy's merging with his self-analysis in 'Nutting', 'Tintern Abbey', parts of *The Prelude*, and the Lucy poems.

If Wordsworth and Lamb feared the unruly feminine, while also acknowledging its nurturing qualities, how did the two sisters respond to their brothers in their writing? To a large extent, they avoided writing in the same genre. Dorothy Wordsworth is best known for her *Journals* rather than her poetry, and Mary Lamb for her contributions to *Mrs Leicester's School* (which was more her work than Charles's) rather than her essays, though both produced the *Tales from Shakespeare* (she dealing with the 'lighter' side, however, the Comedies). Mary Lamb's stories from *Mrs Leicester's School* are curiously unpreoccupied with brothers. The key relationship for her, in so many of these stories that are concerned with parents abandoning their children, is that of mother–daughter. In tale after tale, the young female speaker describes being taken to stay in someone else's house, and left there; to make it worse, the parents often trick their daughter and sneak away without telling her when they will be back. Mary Lamb's stories are all of dysfunctional, broken families: of widowed fathers, orphans, substituted children, and motherless daughters; of godparents, grandparents, and stepmothers. No comfort is offered from brothers or brother-substitutes, and the daughter herself often feels inadequate to comfort her widowed father.

Dorothy Wordsworth was also fascinated by broken and abandoned families, as her *Grasmere Journals* show in her constant mention of beggars wandering the Lake District and recounting their family histories. Although Wordsworth was inspired by beggars too, he tended to be less interested in the details of how they came to lose their wives and children. Dorothy, by contrast, noted everything she could remember about the Leech Gatherer, whereas William idealized him into a philosopher-poet who somehow held the secret to peace of mind in adversity.[30] Dorothy, conspicuously, lacks this peace of mind. By implication, she worries about the precarious state of her own future wellbeing, dependent as it is both on William's survival, and his continued good will towards herself. Far from writing him out of her life, as he often does with her, she tries to install him immovably at the centre. There is no fear of him as a 'fell destroyer', only of the circumstances (such as his marriage) which might separate them again, as they had been separated by their mother's death in childhood. She also worries constantly about his health, especially in relation to his 'composing', which she generally depicts as exhausting, rather than invigorating: 'Wm. worked at *The Cuckow and the Nightingale* till he was tired' (8 December 1801); 'William worked at *The Ruined Cottage* and made himself very ill' (23 December 1801); 'Wm. very ill, employed with *The Pedlar*' (28 February 1802). *The Pedlar* was particularly troublesome, sending them both to bed ill on several occasions. Although she records many happy and companionable evenings at Dove Cottage, the most noticeable thing about her journal entries is the number of brief, short-lived physical collapses she mentions. Their day was frequently disrupted by the need to lie down in the afternoons, or to stay in bed late in the mornings. A typical entry reads: 'I was not well in the morning – we baked bread – after dinner I went to bed – Wm walked into Easedale' (3 December 1801).

It may be that she was worried about the incestuous implications of their feelings for one another, but she remains remarkably unselfconscious about them in her Journals, recalling occasions when, for example, she and William sat together in harmonious silence, he making a pillow of her shoulder (17 March 1802). This is very much the state of mind to which William urges his 'beloved Friend' in the cancelled version of 'Nutting': a 'dream of gentle thoughts' enjoyed while they rest on a 'light bed of purple heath' (lines 15–16). Either Dorothy's conscience was clear on the subject of incest, or she was unconcerned about the comments of other people. She expected William to read her Journal, and seems to have been unembarrassed about the effects of his reading passages such as these. At its most harmonious, their relationship allowed them to work side by side, enjoying each other's silent company:

> William worked at *The Cuckow* poem. I sewed beside him. After dinner he slept, I read German, and, at the closing-in of the day, went to sit in the orchard – he came to me, and walked backwards and forwards. We talked about C[oleridge]. Wm. repeated the poem to me. I left him there, and in 20 minutes he came in, rather tired with attempting to write. He is now reading Ben Jonson. I am going to read German. It is about 10 o'clock, a quiet night. The fire flutters, and the watch ticks. I hear nothing else save the breathing of my Beloved, and he now and then pushes his book forward, and turns over a leaf.
> (23 March, 1802)

The passage moves from stillness, to restlessness and back to stillness again, besides quietly slipping from the past tense into the present, as if Dorothy is recording their every movement as it happens, like the Brontë children in their diary papers: brief samples of frozen time, with every member of the family fixed momentarily in a domestic occupation. Dorothy Wordsworth's journals describe a household that was restless, turbulent, emotionally labile; full of people coming and going, with nobody written out. Moments of complete harmony, such as this, were bought at a price.

The Lambs and the Wordsworths lived together and collaborated with an intensity unparalleled by the later examples this chapter will discuss, other than perhaps the Brontës. To a considerable extent they turned their backs on the outside world and lived according to their own emotional needs; but in both these examples, the brothers seem to have been more troubled by the invasive presence of their sisters than the sisters were by their brothers. While Lamb finds Bridget Elia an unpredictable companion, she (as Mary Lamb) can delete his role altogether from her imagined households. While Wordsworth needed to erase or control Dorothy, who doubled as an undisciplined version of his now austere self, she appears to have felt no anxiety as to his influence over her, and wanted only more of it.[31] While both brothers urge their sisters to be kindly and 'gentle', they register femininity as something self-contained, explosive, and threatening to their own equilibrium. The sisters, meanwhile, concentrate on turbulent households whose male head is frequently absent, moody, selfish or unwell. For all their mutual dependency (or perhaps because of it), the brothers and sisters of the Romantic period are under no illusions about what it means to live together.

Victorian partnerships: the Brontës and the Rossettis

For much of their adult lives, the Brontës and the Rossettis lived together with their surviving parent much as they had done when children. Some left home – all the Brontë children to work for brief spells, Dante Gabriel Rossetti to live a bohemian artist's life, his elder sister Maria to join an Anglican Sisterhood – but both families remained largely loyal to a childhood configuration of parents and children forming a household. Moreover, most were published authors or well-known artists. They understood each other's professions, and were able to give each other moral support. Marrying out of the family circle proved difficult for most of them, only William Michael Rossetti achieving any long-term success as a husband and father. In fact, what gives both these families something in common is the increasingly dissolute lifestyle of one brother (Branwell and Gabriel), and the parallel self-discipline of the sisters. Their writing about men became steadily more disillusioned.

As children, Charlotte and Branwell Brontë were close collaborators. It was their father's gift of a box of 12 wooden soldiers to Branwell in 1826 that inspired the long series of tales about imaginary kingdoms written by all four Brontë children well into their adulthood; but Charlotte was the only sister to collaborate at length with Branwell, and to debate with him, through their shared fictions, their conflicting ideas about masculinity, poetry, politics and romance. As children, they had a healthy scepticism about each other, as well as a deep bond of affection: Branwell, as the only boy, mocking his sisters' odd appearance and behaviour. As the stories about the Islanders, Glass Town and Angria developed, Charlotte and Branwell shared a cast of characters, but as Christine Alexander has noted, in her extensive research on the Brontës' juvenilia, 'while Branwell directed a background of wars, parliamentary debates and business deals, Charlotte became a purveyor of bedroom dramas.'[32] Her heroes were the Duke of Wellington and his two sons, the Marquis of Douro and Lord Charles Wellesley, while Branwell inclined more towards Napoleon Bonaparte and a succession of male misfit figures – either failed poets, such as Henry Rhymer, also known as Young Soult – or unsuccessful soldiers, such as Henry Hastings. Branwell was inventing these characters even before he was old enough to have tried drink and drugs, and Charlotte was satirizing them for their incompetence before she could have any idea that Branwell would repeatedly fail in whatever career he attempted. Her contributions to the 'Tales of the Islanders', written when she was 14 and Branwell 13, depict the four Brontë children as 'Little King and Queens', with Branwell already somewhat apart from his sisters. 'I forgot to mention that Branwell has a large black club, with which he thumps the children upon occasion and that most unmercifully,' she wrote in describing their imaginary school containing a thousand pupils.[33] In Volume 4 of 'Tales of the Islanders', Little King is found lounging on a bank with three old washerwomen (self-caricatures of the Brontë sisters, like Macbeth's witches): when the Duke of Wellington approaches, 'They courtesied and he bowed, much after the fashion of a dip-tail on a stone.'[34] From the start, Charlotte seems to have seen her brother in foppish, self-conscious terms, as a figure out of touch with normal standards of behaviour. Her evident pleasure in making fun of him can be seen from her character sketches of his alter-egos in her 'Characters of the Celebrated Men of the Present Time' (1829). In particular, she satirizes his inflated opinion of himself and his pretentious language: 'Some of his apostrophes are high and almost sublime, but others are ridiculous and bombastic,' she says of Captain Bud; while of Young Soult (the fictitious son of Napoleon's military commander during the Peninsular War), she says prophetically that 'He appears constantly labouring under a state of strong excitement occasioned by excessive drinking and gambling, to which he is unfortunately much addicted.'[35] This attitude intensifies in her drama, 'The Poetaster' (1830), which purports to be written by Lord Charles Wellesley, and features Henry Rhymer/Young Soult as a self-consciously desperate Romantic poet pining in a garret. In what sounds like one of Thomas Love Peacock's parodies of Coleridge from *Nightmare Abbey* (1818), Charlotte gives Rhymer several bombastic speeches as he sucks up to Wellington's two sons in hope of preferment: 'The wings of poesy are ever expanded, and they often bear this unbending spirit by a sudden involuntary flight afar into the wild realms of imagination,' Rhymer apologizes when he has failed to give them a straight answer. The Marquis of Douro advises him to 'sit quietly down to some honest employment and think no more of writing poetry' – much as Southey was to do in 1837 when Charlotte wrote to him with a sample of her verse. Rhymer, on this occasion, nearly hangs for murdering Captain Tree (Charlotte's character), but when his victim recovers at the last moment, Rhymer skulks away promising to write no more, 'for this poetizing has brought me nothing except misery and mortification.'[36]

In 'My Angria and the Angrians' (1834), Charlotte recreates her brother as Patrick Benjamin Wiggins, dissatisfied with 'being a signpainter at Howard [Haworth]', and determined on a brilliant career which would be commemorated on his tombstone: 'As a Musician he was greater than Bach, as a Poet he surpassed Byron, as a Painter, Claude Lorraine yielded to him –'.[37] Five years later, Charlotte was still satirizing Branwell, though with a more serious undercurrent reflecting his repeated career-failures and his by then established habit of drinking to excess. Branwell's latest Angrian alter-ego Henry Hastings had admitted in an 1837 narrative that he liked a drink at night, 'the same as another'[38]; when Charlotte wrote a tale about him in 1839, she gave him a forgiving sister, Elizabeth, who assures him: ' "Your faults & yourself are separate existences in my mind, Henry." ' Henry has failed as a soldier, and is now on the run after shooting a man and deserting; undaunted, he plans a successful come-back as a politician, while his sister knows him as a 'murderer, an outlaw – a deserter & a traitor'. Passionate, proud, and hot-tempered, Henry Hastings is caught, tried in a court of law, and demoted from Captain to Private, but his sister never gives up on him: 'It was very odd but his sister did not think a pin the worse of him for all his Dishonour – It is private mean-ness – not public infamy that degrade a man in the opinion of his relatives –'.[39] By contrast, Elizabeth quietly makes her own living, as a lady's companion and as a teacher: the gender-divide is strongly marked, with all the common sense and economic independence accruing to the sensible woman, as it will in *Jane Eyre*. Nevertheless, though fully aware of Henry's enormities, she accepts that natural affection 'is a thing never rooted out where it has once really existed' (*Captain Henry Hastings*, p. 242).

Given Charlotte Brontë's evident fascination with her brother's unrealistic ambitions and irrepressible personality, it seems surprising that she avoids giving the heroines of her major novels actual blood-brothers:

Jane Eyre, Shirley Keeldar, Caroline Helstone and Lucy Snowe are all only children. Tom Winnifrith states categorically that 'Emily and Charlotte do not create a character out of Branwell'.[40] On the other hand, as Jane Miller has suggested, the Brontë heroes could be seen more generally as brother *types*: 'bad, spoiled ones and twins, warily watched as second selves and other halves.' She argues that to some extent, the 'difficulties and the contradictions of the relationships between women and men which [Anne and Charlotte] write about start from the difficulties and the contradictions there are in a sister's love for a brother'.[41] Brontë heroines search for an 'affinity' with a man – the ease that one feels with a favourite family member – but this may be achieved only after many bouts of sibling-like squabbling, misunderstanding, or sulking, and there may be a serious obstacle to the relationship the equivalent of consanguinity (Rochester's wife, Paul Emanuel's Catholicism). Actual brothers, such as John Reed and St John Rivers, or Gilbert Markham, in *The Tenant of Wildfell Hall*, tend to be the spoiled centre of their sisters' lives; pairs of brothers, such as the Crimsworths in *The Professor*, and Robert and Louis Moore, are often temperamentally antagonistic, a plot possibly borrowed from Branwell's Angrian stories.[42] In marrying her heroines to men such as Rochester and Paul Emanuel, who share their acerbic view of society, their 'ugly' features, and their difficulty in fitting in, Charlotte Brontë was creating anti-social brother-figures whose 'foreignness' (quite literally, in M. Paul's case, and partly in the Moore brothers') rescued them from any suggestion of incest. In the process of sharing her Angrian stories with Branwell, Charlotte had learnt to express herself as a sardonic and worldly-wise bachelor-narrator – as Charles Wellesley, a brother's brother. Her male characters are never blandly polite carpet-knights. Though surrounded by women in their households, they still belong to the Angrian world where mockery of other men's foibles is the prevailing mode.

As for Branwell himself, we have no mature writings by which to measure the final outcome of his close collaboration with Charlotte; but at various points in his life, all his sisters were crucially important to his psychological development. Winifred Gérin suggests that his closest relationship was originally with his sister Maria, the eldest Brontë child who died when she was eleven: 'In the case of Branwell it may not be too much to say that the death of Maria was the chief cause of his mental instability and of the consequent disasters that dogged his days.'[43] Branwell certainly addressed her by name in his two poems 'Misery' I and II (1835–6), though he disguises her as the dying wife of a fictitious Lord Albert, galloping to her bedside. Branwell habitually associated

Maria with angelic imagery: she was 'Angel bright and angel fair', the one who was going to protect him on his journey through life ('Oh, once we thought to pass together/Through stormiest change of wind and weather'). She reappears as Caroline, the dead sister mourned by Harriet in 'Caroline' (1837), and her brother in 'Sir Henry Tunstall' (1840), a narrative poem about a soldier-son returning home after sixteen years in India, irrevocably changed, but still dreaming of his 'sainted Caroline'. Again, he recalls 'the red fireside of a winter-night,/ With two fair beings seated side by side/ The one arrayed in all a soldier's pride,/ The other sadly pale, with angel eyes'. U.C. Knoepflmacher suggests that Emily Brontë then transmuted Branwell's doomed search for Maria as ghost-child 'into the myth of Catherine/ Heathcliff and their dispersed selves'.[44]

With Maria dead, Branwell turned to Charlotte for close collaboration on the Glass Town saga, but he never idealized her – or, apparently his other sisters, if Charlotte's 'My Angria and the Angrians' is anything to go by. Ventriloquizing her brother as Patrick Benjamin Wiggins, Charlotte has him introduce his three sisters to Lord Charles Wellesley as 'miserable silly creatures not worth talking about. CHARLOTTE'S eighteen years old, a broad dumpy thing, whose head does not come higher than my elbow. Emily's sixteen, lean and scant, with a face about the size of a penny, and Anne is nothing, absolutely nothing'.[45] If this was how Branwell thought of his sisters, Charlotte was under no illusions. At times, though, he found each of them useful or congenial. If Charlotte was his writing partner, Emily was his partner in failure – at least as far as engagement with the outside world was concerned: she was the only sister at home when Branwell returned from his ignominious trip to London when he failed to register as a student at the Royal Academy. Anne subsequently became his working partner when both were employed by the Robinsons of Thorpe Green to teach their children. But all three sisters found a way of surviving long enough to achieve the success their brother seems to have craved more than any of them; and all were sufficiently disturbed by their brother's physical and mental deterioration to incorporate portraits of men hardened by drink and irascible temper into their novels (Charlotte deals with this in her first novel, *The Professor*, and largely abandons it subsequently, though she has many irritable, brutal men in her later novels; Emily in Hindley Earnshaw, and Anne in Arthur Huntingdon). Branwell, in turn, faded from their lives: the fawn smudge of the famous 'pillar portrait' of the three sisters testifying to his once central position in the family, now no more than a columnar blur.

Dante Gabriel Rossetti also painted portraits of his sister Christina, both in her own person, and as the Virgin Mary. He also drew a caricature of her in a 'rampageous' mood, smashing up the household furniture, her feet and arms flying.[46] Though this was a friendly joke, it perhaps registers the groundswell of frustration that most commentators have identified in Christina Rossetti's poetry. Gabriel told their mother that he thought Christina had 'more natural talent' than himself;[47] nevertheless, he took it upon himself to criticize her work, suggest changes to poems, offer alternative titles, approach publishers on her behalf, and generally construct her image in a mode congenial to himself, while declining any reciprocal advice from her. He dedicated his first two volumes of poetry to his brother William, and none to her. Indeed, both the Rossetti brothers tried to shape Christina according to their own tastes: Gabriel by painting her self-absorbed, scared, despondent chastity in the two Virgin Mary pictures, and by rejecting the more 'unwomanly' emotions and themes (such as illegitimacy and anger) expressed in her lyrics; William by presenting her posthumously to the public as reticent, modest, devout, and over-scrupulous. His characterization of her in his 'Memoir' differs strikingly from the one he wrote of their brother, Gabriel. Where he is 'always and essentially of a dominant turn' and 'self-centred always', she is 'replete with the spirit of self-postponement, which passed into self-sacrifice whenever that quality was in demand'.[48] Though William's portrait of her is longer than the parallel one he did for Gabriel, one has the sense that his sister remained opaque to him. He sounds baffled as to why she refused two marriage proposals when she evidently loved the men who had made them; and although she was a devout Anglican, he is uncertain why she always felt spiritually deficient. As he struggles to describe her appearance – again something that was easier with Gabriel – he applies and dismisses all the current clichés of female beauty: 'She was certainly not what one understands by "a beauty"; the term handsome did not apply to her, nor yet the term pretty. Neither was she "a fine woman". She has sometimes been called "lovely" in youth – ('Memoir,' p. lx).

To both her brothers, Christina was a pure and retiring woman of surprising talent, but – unlike them – crucially without sexual experience. Like Branwell Brontë and William Wordsworth Gabriel wondered how he would feel if his sister died young. In 'My Sister's Sleep', he imagines a dying sister ('Margaret') tended by their devoted mother on Christmas Eve, while he himself is present in the death chamber, but at a distance, and emotionally confused:

> Our mother bowed herself and wept:
> And both my arms fell, and I said,
> 'God knows I knew that she was dead.'
> And there, all white, my sister slept.

Her snowy virginity is apparently what most impresses him – with the consciousness that she dies just as Jesus Christ is being symbolically born. As Angela Leighton has argued, 'Without any acrimony between them, the women and men in the Rossetti household seem to have reproduced the main ideological division between the sexes in society at large': in other words, faith for women and doubt for men.[49]

Overtly, at least, Christina seemed respectful of her brotherly mentors. William notes that she had a natural deference for the head of the household, whoever that might be: a deference echoed in a letter of 1880 where she insists that she is unoffended by greater praise of Gabriel than herself: 'Don't think me such a goose as to feel keenly mortified at being put below you, the head of our house in so many ways.'[50] She undoubtedly found Gabriel's encouragement stimulating – pencilling on the fly-leaf of one of her books, 'And here I would like to acknowledge the general indebtedness of my first and second volumes to my brother's suggestive wit and revising hand'[51] – but she was fully capable of asserting herself when he gave her inappropriate advice: for instance, she came out firmly against including a tournament in 'The Prince's Progress'. In her dealings with Gabriel, Christina seems to have put on a good act: of politely listening, obeying whenever she could, but reserving her right to have the last word on her own poems.

Moreover, Gabriel was, on some occasions, right. It was he who suggested *Goblin Market* for the title of Christina's best-known poem, in place of her proposed *A Peep at the Goblins*, and he enthusiastically pushed her first volume of poems with Macmillan. Only two years older than her, he assumed the senior role by virtue of his masculinity – even though she was the first to publish a book of poems. Her sex also disqualified her for membership of the Pre-Raphaelite Brotherhood, which meant that however successful she was in her literary career, she was never going to be part of the club. Instead, she satirized it, feigning humility: 'In these six men I awestruck see/Embodied the great P.R.B.' A second poem, written in the same kind of ironic doggerel, recorded its break-up – largely the result of its members' self-conscious posturings . Her own brother's unwillingness to exhibit any more pictures for a while is summarized in one line: 'D. G. Rossetti shuns the vulgar optic.'[52] Charlotte Brontë's caricatures of Branwell were in a similar vein, aimed at his artistic pretentiousness.

While Christina rarely wrote directly about her brother in her poems – any more than he wrote directly about her in his – his personality and life style seem to have affected the way she thought about men in their relations with women. As he delayed his marriage to Elizabeth Siddall, Christina, according to Jan Marsh, painted the Prince (of 'The Prince's Progress') 'in Gabriel's image'.[53] The mocking style is similar to that of the 'P.R.B.' poem: it pretends to take his position seriously, while neatly undermining it by means of its simple rhymes and exaggerations. Many of the lines describe a mood of vacillation as the Prince meanders on his way over difficult country to meet his waiting bride. At every opportunity, the Prince is distracted from his goal – whether by a milkmaid with fresh milk ('The Prince, who had journeyed at least a mile,/Grew athirst at the sight'), or quite simply by boredom and lack of company. What he chiefly lacks is self-will: 'He half turned away, then he quite turned back.' In the end, he delays so long that when he arrives at the Princess's palace, she is being carried out in her coffin. 'Her heart was starving all the while/You made it wait,' he is told by one of her attendants.

Ironically, this was a poem on which brother and sister collaborated particularly closely – and she spent four years perfecting it. Germaine Greer has suggested that the man against whom Christina directed all her animus in her poems was neither of the two men she loved (James Collinson and Charles Cayley), but her brother Gabriel, who was the first and strongest influence in her life: 'This is not to say that she had an affair with her brother, but simply that she knew that she wanted to be the most important person in his life,' Greer argues.[54] Gabriel was certainly her nearest rival, the only other member of the family working in a similar field. Although their subjects seem to be widely different, both are ultimately concerned with intense emotion; both explored their spiritual and sensual sides, even if, as Dolores Rosenblum has suggested, 'their sexual roles extend to their poetry, as Dante Gabriel enacts risk and excess, Christina conformity and restraint.'[55] While it may not be necessary to agree with Rosenblum that the numerous sister figures in Christina's poetry are really versions of her brother, there seems to me little doubt that she was defining her idea of genuine passion, not only against what she had already experienced in her own life with Collinson, but also against Gabriel's somewhat shoddy emotions for Lizzie Siddall. Christina's poem, 'In an Artist's Studio' (1856), while not referring directly to her brother's obsession with Lizzie's ethereal looks, is nevertheless easily identified with this always troubled relationship:

> He feeds upon her face by day and night,
> And she with true kind eyes looks back on him,
> Fair as the moon and joyful as the light:
> Not wan with waiting, not with sorrow dim;
> Not as she is, but was when hope shone bright;
> Not as she is, but as she fills his dream.

Christina merges her own sorrow with Lizzie's: the yearning, waiting woman who subsequently appeared as the title illustration, drawn by Gabriel, for *The Prince's Progress* (1866), with the line: 'The long hours come and go.' The poem implies that Gabriel's obsession blinds him to her real state of sorrowful decline. It was no wonder that Christina was also drawn to Tennysonian themes of waiting, abandoned women, such as Mariana, The Lady of Shalott, and Ulysses's Penelope. In many of her poems, she urges her male addressees to be decisive, to act on their feelings: 'You talk, you smile, you nothing do,' she rages in 'The Heart Knoweth Its Own Bitterness,' which William saw as one of her most personal poems.[56] At this stage she was not to know that Gabriel would take another three years to marry Lizzie: he had already delayed five before introducing her to his family. Impatience with male indecision remained a theme even after Gabriel had finally married and buried his wife, as in 'Last Night', where the speaker urges her lover to deal fairly with her rival, Kate: 'If you love her best, speak up like a man;/ It's not I will stand in the light of your plan.' More eerily, her early prose story *Maude* (1850) ended with the burial of the poet-heroine's lock-up manuscript book in her coffin, prefiguring Gabriel's decision in 1862 to bury the manuscript of all his unpublished poems with Lizzie (it became necessary to exhume the poems in 1869). In 'The Heart Knoweth Its Own Bitterness', the speaker longs for a serious exchange of feelings, as she does in 'The Lowest Room' (1856), a poem which laments the passing of strong, physical men, as in Homer's day, and longs for the 'Archangelic trumpet-burst,/ When all deep secrets shall be shown,/And many last be first.'

Christina Rossetti's opinion of men is rarely flattering, despite her gratitude to her 'two very brotherly brothers'.[57] Moreover, her poems contain a recurrent sense of defeat – as if she is always going to be beaten by someone stronger or more successful than herself – whose right to dictate she nevertheless challenges. Like Charlotte Brontë, she acknowledges the man's greater freedom to live away from his family and do as he pleases, while higher standards are expected of the stay-at-home woman. Ultimately, in both families, the sister was the survivor. Both Branwell and Gabriel succumbed to addiction and mental chaos; they also became obsessed with unavailable women (Lydia Robinson and Jane Morris). From their brothers, the sisters learned that men were arrogant, ambitious, emotionally dilatory, and self-destructive. In many ways, the gender split inverts the distrust of the feminine, which was more a characteristic of the Romantic sibling partnerships. For these two Victorian families, it was the brother whose ability to live a controlled and balanced adult life was being questioned; while William Rossetti, as the 'surplus' brother, and the final Rossetti to die, developed a new role for himself as the constructor of his siblings' shared and independent histories.

The Sitwell phenomenon

By the beginning of the twentieth century it was less necessary for brothers and sisters to share households and look after each other. With higher education and the professions gradually opening to women, and a dawning acceptance that marriage was not the only purpose of a woman's life, sisters had more options, and brothers less right to detain them. Nevertheless, close familial bonds persisted in literary families of siblings born at the end of the nineteenth century, and launching their careers after the First World War. The four Stephen children in some ways parallel the Rossettis: two boys and two girls, all gifted in different ways. Initially close to Thoby, Virginia's shock at his early death was scarcely assuaged when she set up house with her younger brother Adrian. Notwithstanding, the whole concept of Bloomsbury revolved around the sibling household of the remaining Stephen children. In the United States, Gertrude and Leo Stein lived together whenever they could, sharing their aesthetic interests; and in England in the 1920s the three Sitwells hit the literary and cultural scene with an impact that baffled and amused their contemporaries.

The Sitwells are the first set of artistic siblings in literary history to be treated as a joke. Aldous Huxley (who later took them more seriously) called them the Shufflebottoms – 'each of them larger and whiter than the other'.[58] Noel Coward satirized them as 'the Swiss Family Whittlebot' – Hernia, and her brothers Gob and Sago – in his 1923 show *London Calling*. Wyndham Lewis caricatured them in *The Apes of God* (1931) as Lord Osmund Finnian Shaw, his brother Phoebus, and his sister Harriet, introduced as a 'flying harpy, in her embroidered gold, with a sinister tiara'.[59] Virginia Woolf told Jacques Raverat: 'They take themselves very seriously. They descend from George the IVth. They look like Regency bucks. They have a mother who was in prison. They probably need careful reading, which I have never given them, and thus incline to think them vigorous, but unimportant, acrobats.'[60] Though Edith's poetry enjoyed a revival during the Second World War, and she was welcomed ecstatically on her American tours in 1948 and 1949–50, literary history has always had difficulty knowing what to do with the Sitwells. As Virginia Woolf noted, and F. R. Leavis confirmed – 'the Sitwells belong to the history of publicity, rather than that of poetry'[61] – they were seen as a troupe of performers, rather than as genuine poets: an impression reinforced by their aristocratic background, eccentric names, and in Edith's case, Gothic dress, barbaric jewellery, and dramatic headdresses. The fact that there were three of them only intensified the joke.

In objecting, Edith added more grotesque images to the legend. 'We do not like to be treated as if we were an aggregate Indian god, with three sets of legs and arms, but otherwise indivisible,' she insisted'; nor did they like being seen as a 'hive'.[62] Virginia Woolf was right in thinking that they took themselves very seriously. The eldest by five years, Edith encouraged her brothers Osbert and Sacheverell in their early attempts at writing poetry. She devoted a chapter to Sacheverell in her *Aspects of Modern Poetry* (1934), claiming that he was unjustly neglected and abused. 'I do wish I really thought I could be of any use to the greatest poet of our time,' she told him privately (he was actually rather upset at not being called a poet of genius).[63] In return, they supported her ventures when they were older, the brothers suggesting she put her *Façade* poems to music, and Osbert, despite encroaching Parkinson's Disease, accompanying her on her American trips.[64] There were minor skirmishes: Osbert was upset when Sacheverell married (the only one to do so), and Sacheverell was upset when the other two went to America without him – but on the whole, the Sitwells clung together as a 'closed corporation'.[65] Edith attributed this to their having shared an unhappy childhood, but in reality, it was mainly her childhood that was miserable: her parents had been disappointed that their first child was a girl, whereas Osbert was welcomed as heir to the Renishaw estate. Moreover, like Queen Victoria's eldest two children, and in fiction, like Maggie and Tom Tulliver of *The Mill on the Floss*, the sexes of the two siblings were ill-matched with their abilities. 'As a child,' Osbert recalls in the first volume of his autobiography, 'I was slow as my sister was quick of apprehension. And in each of us this was wrong. She should have been slow, being a girl – '[66] Edith, however, felt her sex disabled her from writing certain kinds of poetry. 'Being a female,' she told Sacheverell, in the course of advising him on revisions to *Dr Donne and Gargantua*, 'I could not *weight* the *blanks* properly (as you know, I never attempt blanks myself, because I am sure they don't lie in a woman's physique).'[67] Nevertheless, she was the one who held them together, living with Osbert at Renishaw during the Second World War, and encouraging Sacheverell in his poetic career. She was aware of the importance of brother–sister relationships in literary history, noting in *English Women* (1942) the closeness of Sir Philip Sidney and his sister, the Countess of Pembroke, as well as the familiar examples of the Wordsworths and the Rossettis. Edith speaks well of both brothers and sisters in this brief patriotic book published during wartime;[68] all three Sitwells, meanwhile, contributed their share to the collective legend of their family collaboration. All wrote autobiographies, and Edith idealized their relationship in her poem, 'Colonel Fantock' (1924):

> But Dagobert and Peregrine and I
> Were children then; we walked like shy gazelles
> Among the music of the thin flower-bells.
> And life still held some promise, – never ask
> Of what, – but life seemed less a stranger, then,
> Than ever after in this cold existence.

For all the Sitwells, the sibling alliance seems to have been their defence against a world in which they felt ill-at-ease. In 'The Octogenerian', Sacheverell finds himself

> Thinking just now
> What an exciting world it was
> When the three of us were young together: –
> Ever in trouble for being young
> and having talent:

They would never have dreamt of satirizing each other, as Charlotte and Branwell Brontë did: instead they threatened libel cases against people who satirized them. Even as an elderly man, Sacheverell felt bereft when his sister died, and wrote a succession of poems in her memory, trying to understand her mysterious nun-like remoteness, and paying tribute to her early influence on him. In 'Serenade to a Sister', he addresses her as she 'for whom and whom only, I wrote poetry':

> To have known and loved you,
> And been your pupil and your brother
> Is all I want of fame.

Viewing her as a nun, a ghost, a prisoner, a statue from Chartres Cathedral, and an 'abbess of the nightingales,/ Who wound up the clockwork in my mortal frame,' Sacheverell reinforces the intensely private nature of their feelings for each other, but also the sense that she was lonely and misunderstood.

Deploring the encroachments of philistinism, the Sitwells pondered their collective and individual past. According to Cyril Connolly, 'all three had a particular awareness of the sadness and transitoriness of things'.[69] Although Edith wrote about the War, the three siblings became increasingly interested in reconstructing and exploring their childhood: either, in Osbert's case, through the medium of leisurely autobiography, or, in Edith's through reminiscences and fairy tales, which were themselves a means of recalling garden landscapes and the perspectivelessness of childhood. Edith admitted that *The Sleeping Beauty* (1924), which she wrote for Osbert, was largely about her life as a child at Londesborough Lodge, Scarborough, her grandparents' home.[70] Despite her unhappy childhood, this poem evokes a timeless nostalgia for youth:

> When we were young, how beautiful life seemed! –
> The boundless bright horizons that we dreamed...
> But age has dimmed our innocent paradise
> With a faint shadow, shaken dust within our eyes, –

The Sitwells were oddities in their own time, more akin to the world of Pope and the eighteenth century than to the broadening democratization of the twentieth. This may help to explain why the brother–sister relationship remained so central to their lives. Though they all had friends of their own, they were looking to a network of emotional support that hearkened back to a time when family connections were closer than mere friendships. The Sitwells established an alternative society to the outside one that often failed to understand them. As with the other sibling groups discussed in this chapter, they were marked by a kind of revolutionary conservatism, which maintained traditional family structures, while reinventing them for purposes of their own. Like the others, too, they contained recalcitrant qualities. For Edith, the family 'corporation' was a place where her role as a single woman was respected; for Osbert where his homosexuality was accepted; for Sacheverell, where his sensitivity was understood – much as Charles Lamb's and Branwell Brontë's drunkenness, Mary Lamb's insanity, Dorothy Wordsworth's arteriosclerosis, Emily Brontë's antisocial silence, and Christina Rossetti's religious intensity were, if not understood, at least tolerantly incorporated into the family picture. Though brothers and sisters at times felt threatened by each other, and practised compensatory strategies, they had, in fact, devised a private mythology of their own which fostered their freedom to write. If brothers created their sisters as guardian angels, ghosts, nuns, abesses, Virgin Marys, and saintly corpses, they also constructed an outspoken Bridget Elia, a clever sister Edith, three witch-like weird washerwomen, a furniture-smashing Christina, and a wild-eyed, bough-breaking Dorothy. If sisters created their brothers as the adored poet 'Wm,', 'darling Sachie,' and 'dear old boy' Osbert (though without recourse to male stereotypes), they also constructed a Henry Hastings on the run, a bombastic Young Soult, a dilatory Prince, a drunken Hindley Earnshaw, and a sulky Gilbert Markham. The relationship was flexible enough to stretch from idealization to caricature. What is most revealing about brothers' construction of sisters, however, is their recognition, from generation to generation, of a transgressive energy searching for a legitimate outlet. For sisters writing about brothers, the tendency was more towards regret and critical acceptance.

3
'One of the Highest Forms of Friendship': Brother–Sister Relationships in Women's Autobiography

> My doll seemed lifeless and no girlish toy
> Had any reason when my brother came.[1]
>
> Little by little we never met again.[2]

Traditional Victorian autobiography by men is dominated by the difficulties of the parent–child – especially father–son – relationship. None of the great names in the field has much to say about sibling relationships. This was something that largely disappeared with the last of the Romantics, Thomas De Quincey and Leigh Hunt. John Stuart Mill, for example, though the eldest of a large family of brothers and sisters, focuses almost entirely on his intense relationship with his father, while Anthony Trollope mentions his five siblings in passing, but four died of tuberculosis, and he seems not to have been particularly close to any of them. Charles Darwin recalls being taught by his sister Caroline, and being slower in learning than his younger sister Catherine,[3] but Newman says nothing about his family relationships in childhood (indeed very little about his childhood altogether), despite his close relationship with two of his sisters, Harriett and Jemima, and the death of a third, Mary, in her late teens. There is no sense in any of the major male autobiographers of the period that relationships with brothers or sisters were at all significant. With their female contemporaries, however, the picture is markedly different, as Harriet Martineau explains in her *Autobiography*:

> Brothers are to sisters what sisters can never be to brothers as objects of engrossing and devoted affection. The law of their frames is

answerable for this: and that other law – of equity – which sisters are bound to obey, requires that they should not render their account of their disappointments where there can be no fair reply. Under the same law, sisters are bound to remember that they cannot be certain of their own fitness to render an account of their own disappointments, or to form an estimate of the share of blame which may be due to themselves on the score of unreasonable expectations.[4]

After the clear opening statement, Martineau's explanation of the emotional complexities of the relationship becomes increasingly obscure, and her language more convoluted and imprecise. By the 'law of their frames', she implies that because girls are physically weaker they are emotionally more dependent, and less able to cope with the inevitable separation of brother and sister in adult life. The second part of her statement implies that because sisters are guilty of unreasonable emotional expectations of their brothers, they may be no fair judge of their own disappointment. Martineau was referring to her younger brother James, the Unitarian theologian, to whom she was devoted – until their religious and other differences drew them apart. The final separation came in 1851, when James wrote a hostile review of his sister's and Henry Atkinson's *Letters on the Laws of Man's Nature and Development*, but in fact the two had been growing apart since her long illness of 1839–45, allegedly cured by mesmerism.[5] Juliet Barker, writing about Charlotte Brontë's disappointment with her brother Branwell, describes her feelings in similar terms: 'he had committed the unforgivable sin of not living up to her expectations of him.'[6]

Martineau's experience is important because it establishes something of a pattern in Victorian women's autobiography: a record of closeness to brothers in childhood and adolescence, followed by intellectual, cultural, or emotional distancing in adulthood. Whatever it was that brothers were able to offer sisters in the first twenty years of their lives seems to have become irrelevant or unavailable in the later stages. Whatever it was that Martineau was unable to articulate in a straightforward way was evidently widely experienced. The object of this chapter is to investigate what repeatedly happened in Victorian women's reconstructions of their family life in their attempts at a truthful retrospective narrative, and to see whether their changing relationships with their brothers registered a wider difficulty in negotiating personal and professional opportunities for their self-development. Perhaps their greatest challenge was to find a way of recounting their side of the family history without unfairly implicating their brothers (and thereby offending patriarchal sensibilities) or casting blame upon themselves as unsympathetic sisters. While George Eliot and Charlotte Brontë avoided direct autobiography completely, the women writers discussed in this section oscillated between fiction, autobiography, journals and letters in the piecemeal recovery of their sibling relationships: fluctuating awkwardly between public disclosure and private confession, while excluding certain aspects of their family experiences altogether. The result is a series of broken narratives with yawning omissions, their central theme frequently displaced on to the fiction discussed in the next chapter. So far as this chapter is concerned, Branwell Brontë's famous 'pillar portrait' of his three sisters with a fawn columnar smudge marking where he once joined them, serves as a convenient emblem of the brother's cancelled presence in his sisters' lives. The continuing presence of the smudge is a reminder, however, of his permanent inerasable influence.

Few of the well-known Victorian autobiographies were written by only children – Ruskin being the most obvious example. Most nineteenth-century children first encountered gender distinction in their own home, accompanied as it was by marked differences in education and career preparation. Several women autobiographers remember the births of younger brothers as a major disruption of their home lives: sometimes the advent of a much wanted male heir. This is certainly the case in Charlotte Yonge's unfinished 'Autobiography'. Apparently destined to be an only child Yonge was six and a half when her only brother Julian was born. Yonge called it 'the greatest event of my life'; yet it clearly disarranged family routines in a way that left her feeling bewildered and neglected: 'He came with rather short notice, and I remember the being left in the dark in my crib and the puzzled day that ensued.'[7] Moreover, her grandiose ideas for a name – Alexander Xenophon – were quietly rejected, and Julian's arrival did little to reduce her emotional dependency on her large families of cousins. Harriet Martineau's memories of her brother James's birth are likewise bewildered. 'That day was another of the distinct impressions which flashed upon me in after years,' she recalls, describing the best bedroom, which in its unused grandeur begins to sound like Jane Eyre's Red Room. Martineau's strongest memory was of struggling across the slippery floor to reach her first view of the baby: the first of several stories told invoking a terrifying sense of physical insecurity.[8] Mary Howitt, one of three girls, was astounded when her parents suddenly produced a boy: 'In the midst of our amazement and yet undeveloped joy arose the question within us, "Will our parents like it?" for we had the impression that they never approved of boys.'[9] In each case, the brother's arrival is registered as occasioning uncertainty, an uneasy revision of the status quo, as the sister immediately recognizes that her life will be permanently changed. In childhood, sisters generally acknowledged that brothers had a more privileged status, embodied their parents' hopes, and were intended for adult engagement with the outside world. Any resentment of this situation was largely repressed in their autobiographies, or more probably sublimated into an ardently romantic fantasy of lifelong devotion and mutual protection. At its least complicated, a sister's love for a brother offered an apparently unchallenged opportunity to feel and show real emotion for another human being without the barriers imposed between parents and children, and later, husbands and wives. There is rarely any suggestion in nineteenth-century autobiographies or novels that sibling love is wrong, or even that it needs to be outgrown; nor do Victorian women seem in the least embarrassed about admitting to it in the most extravagant of terms. 'And he was a kind of god to me – my Frank, as I always called him,' Margaret Oliphant recalls of one of her inadequate older brothers, whom she later had to house and support;[10] while the Evangelical novelist 'Charlotte Elizabeth' (Mrs Tonna) claimed that constant companionship with her only brother gave her 'a habit of deference to man's judgment, and submission to man's authority, which I am quite sure God intended the woman to yield.'[11] From a more secular point of view, Gertrude Stein simply found it useful to have an older brother (Leo), 'because that makes everything a pleasure to you, you go everywhere and do everything while he does it all for you and with you which is a pleasant way to have everything happen to you.'[12]

George Eliot's 'Brother and Sister' (1869) sonnet sequence, though not strictly autobiography, is one of the best records of what close sibling friendship had to offer the younger sister: though as with most of the other records quoted in this chapter, a subtext of inferiority and neglect is never far below the surface. Recalling her devotion to Isaac Evans, three years her senior, in a succession of scenes that parallel the Maggie and Tom fishing sequence in *The Mill on the Floss*, Eliot remembers holding him 'wise':

> and when he talked to me
> Of snakes and birds, and which God loved the best,
> I thought his knowledge marked the boundary
> Where men grew blind, though angels knew the rest.
> If he said "Hush!" I tried to hold my breath
> Wherever he said "Come!" I stepped in faith. (p. 427)

Belief in a brother's godlike wisdom is typical of much autobiographical Victorian women's writing. Unexplained, it is merely offered as a given of the relationship, instinctual and 'natural'. The sister of George Eliot's sonnets accepts that she is the junior partner, though the fact that she always registers differences in their treatment shows that she is certainly aware of her inferior status. As they set off on a fishing picnic, she thinks with joy 'That I should have my share, though he had more,/ Because he was the elder and a boy' (p. 427). As in *The Mill on the Floss*, the will to believe in happy memories, enhanced by a Wordsworthian evocation of nature and timelessness, 'the primal passionate store', is always crossed by an undertow of unhappiness. Left alone in charge of the fishing rod, the dreamy sister falls into a trance in which her surroundings become a dream-world: 'A fair pavilioned boat for me alone/ Bearing me onward through the vast unknown.' Sonnet VIII begins, however, with the rude incursion of reality: no fairy-tale shallop, but 'the barge's pitch-black prow,' heralded by her brother's angry cry (p. 430). She is saved by the lucky chance of finding a silver perch on the end of her line, which instantly transforms her 'guilt' into 'merit' and rewards her with hugs and praises. But the sonnet sequence, of which this is the climactic moment, emphasizes the precariousness of her standing with her brother. Ever poised for disapproval, he watches and judges everything she does: ' "This thing I like my sister may not do, /For she is little, and I must be kind." ' By the end of the sequence, she has lost her dreaminess and learnt her brother's practical skills:

> My aery-picturing fantasy was taught
> Subjection to the harder, truer skill
>   That seeks with deeds to grave a thought-tracked line,
>   And by "What is," "What will be" to define. (p. 432)

Paradoxically, the judgemental brother inspires her nostalgic childhood fantasy while also teaching her to begin defining her better self by deeds of integrity. Her private mental excursion away from him in the middle section of the sonnet sequence is firmly curtailed, and ends with the merging of their two selves in a series of boys' games led by the brother.

Victorian women writing about childhood relations with their brothers usually accept a second place in their shared lives. This feeling of inferiority was usually intensified when the brother went to school and left his sister at home. George Eliot's closing stanza of the 'Brother and Sister' sonnet sequence begins with the dead finality of 'School parted us', a view shared by Mary Martha Sherwood in the statement that 'from the time in which my brother went to school, he never could be to me what he was before'.[13] Like George Eliot, her brother wrote a poem to commemorate their relationship: 'From a Brother to a Beloved Sister, on a Field called the Bee Meadow, where they used to play together in infancy', which Sherwood proudly quotes in her autobiography. Most of it is a conventional evocation of 'a meadow in a halcyon vale', a childhood 'Paradise', culminating in the lines:

> Sister, 'twas here our morning star arose,
> And may in antitype its evening close.

As Chapter 1 argues, the separation of brother and sister when the brother was sent to school was one of the most divisive moments of nineteenth-century childhood. Its emotional effects reverberate through women's autobiography, often urging them to greater intellectual efforts so as to keep up, and retain their brothers' respect during the holidays. Aged eighteen, Harriet Martineau, up since five in the morning, was meeting her brother James at seven 'to read Lowth's Prelections in the Latin' (*Autobiography*, I, 101); when he left for college, he urged her to take up a new intellectual hobby, or plunge into 'authorship', which he declared himself unable to do as a student answerable to his tutors: 'What James desired, I always did, as of course; and after he had left me to my widowhood soon after six o'clock, one bright September morning, I was at my desk before seven beginning a letter to the Editor of the "Monthly Repository"' (*Autobiography*, I, 118). This may have been a backhanded way of allowing his sister an ideological freedom that he lacked himself, but it certainly launched Martineau into a career as a full-time writer. They exchanged letters while he was away at college, from which she 'derived extraordinary advantage', and during the summer of 1824 went on a long Wordsworthian walking tour of Scotland together, covering over five hundred miles.[14]

In teenage years, older brothers acquired for many women autobiographers a glamorous aura, as happened with Eliza Lynn Linton's brother Arthur, 'the perfect embodiment of manly power and moral greatness...He was, and is, the great ideal of my life.'[15] Elizabeth Sewell remembered having similar feelings for her brother William, like herself a novelist. 'I really idolised my brother William, whose great abilities, fervent piety, and warm affection I was beginning to understand and appreciate; and who captivated me with his sermons and poetry and conversation,' Sewell recalled of herself in 1830, when she was fifteen. 'I never loved any one else in the same intense way...' Like Martineau, however, she recognized the emotional risks in this kind of extreme devotion. 'I was so entirely engrossed in my feeling for my brother that I had no thought to give to any one else.'[16] Passed from clergyman brother to clergyman brother in their various country livings, she seems at last to have realized that she was also embarrassing them with the intensity of her feelings, and becoming emotionally unstable. Yet adoration of older brothers seems to have been a safe outlet for adolescent romanticism that in Sewell's case, along with Christian observance, served as a permanent substitute for an adult heterosexual relationship. Where the brother was a clergyman, as with William Sewell, it could be safely passed off as a form of religious discipleship; it could also be a way of escaping charges of uselessness or a wider kind of family drudgery. Sewell's sister Janetta, for instance, lived with another of their brothers, Edwardes, at New College, Oxford for thirty years, thereby finding herself a purpose in life and an intellectually stimulating home. Sibling 'marriages' of this kind solved many problems for Victorian single women, not least of which was the excessive childbearing of their more conventionally married sisters. Where it worked, this kind of arrangement could give a woman all the dignity and security of a male-headed household without the sexual obligations this usually entailed. It could also leave her relatively free to write or pursue other interests of her own.

Martineau's eldest brother Thomas was another family god – silent, reserved, and destined to die young of tuberculosis. 'We revered and loved him intensely, in the midst of our awe of him' (*Autobiography*, I, 43). While her younger brother James encouraged her to write as a way of dealing with her depression when he returned to college, it was her older brother Thomas who officially gave her permission to do so professionally. The story is often quoted of how he praised an article in the *Monthly Repository*, unaware that his sister had written it. When she admitted her authorship, he called her 'dear' for the first time, and urged her: '"Now, dear, leave it to other women to make shirts and darn stockings; and do you devote yourself to this"' (I, 120). Martineau's retelling of this story in a section of her *Autobiography* headed 'First Appearance in Print' gives her entry into professional authorship the stamp of male approval while keeping it within the private domestic sphere. Carefully managed, writing was a way of winning love and attention from an older brother, who often becomes, in literary recollections, the embodiment of public (patriarchal) opinion.

It was in fact fairly common for older brothers to usher their sisters' first publications into the world: something that the sisters seem proud to recall, though they subsequently eclipsed their brothers in later life. Margaret Oliphant's older brother Willie, whose drinking problems were a worry to his family, took the manuscript of her first novel, *Passages in the Life of Margaret Maitland*, to the publishers Colburn in London: later he was employed in fair-copying her manuscripts, so that he might 'retrieve a sort of fictitious independence by getting 10 per cent upon the price of them'.[17] Her family tried to play down the awkwardness of the baby sister's succeeding where the older brothers had failed, by treating her professional authorship as a kind of delightful joke in which all members of the family were entitled to play a part. Four of her novels actually appeared under Willie's name, though he subsequently wrote some of his own.

Oliphant's narrative indicates the beginnings of strain and pretence in the relative distributions of power and influence within the brother–sister relationship: something that damaged most of the families discussed in this chapter. Several felt that the brother must at least have the appearance of worldly activity on his sister's behalf: something that was most marked in the Sewell family, where the sisters all came in a group at the younger end of the family. Sewell herself eventually became their mainstay through her novel-writing, though the pretence of her feminine powerlessness was kept up for as long as possible. Like Martineau she asked her brother's permission before sending an article for publication in a magazine (the humble *Cottager's Monthly Visitor*): 'I asked William whether there could be any objection, and when he said "No", it was sent' (*Autobiography*, p. 66). William was again brought into the secret when her sister Ellen told him she was writing a novel called *Amy Herbert*: 'He looked at the first chapters, and liked them, and begged me to finish the story' (p. 75). Gratified by its success, William 'one day said to me, that having begun writing tales I could go on and write some more' (p. 80). Throughout this stage of her career, as recounted in her *Autobiography*, Sewell makes a great point of stressing her brother's approval and encouragement, while insisting on her own reluctance to be noticed as an author or praised to her face: something Henry Austen also noted of his sister Jane.[18] It was not until the publication of her novel *The Experience of Life* (1853) that Sewell used her own name on the title page: until then, they were stated to be 'By a Lady' or 'by the author of *Amy Herbert*' and 'Edited by the Rev. W. Sewell', giving them the double endorsement of male and clergy approval. When William came to write a novel himself, he claimed *Hawkstone* (1845) used to 'amuse' his sister.[19] Far from introducing a more democratic regime after their father's death, Sewell's godlike brother seems only to have intensified the dictates of patriarchy, until in this – as in so many parallel families – the sister quietly outpaced the brother and his attempts to attach himself to his sister's success.

The brothers went wrong for a variety of reasons, but most were associated with the pitfalls of nineteenth-century masculinity. Financial problems, sometimes exacerbated by alcoholism, were the commonest source of collapse, as with Margaret Oliphant's brothers Willie and Frank, and a Newman brother Charles; alcoholism was the chief cause of Branwell Brontë's decline, intensified by a sense of personal failure; and financial mismanagement William Sewell's. Ideological disagreement, religious and moral, separated Harriet and James Martineau and Isaac and Mary Ann Evans, while Newman's conversion to Catholicism finished his relationship with his favourite sister, Harriett Mozley, who blamed him for the near-conversion of her husband, Thomas. More often, however, brothers and sisters drifted apart because they wanted different things in life. Whereas brothers such as Charlotte Yonge's, Elizabeth Sewell's and Harriet Martineau's were more likely to marry, settle down and have children, their sisters pursued a solitary and celibate life of literary production. In most cases it was the sister, rather than the brother, who took the more unusual career path, widening the gap between them in middle age.

Margaret Oliphant and Elizabeth Sewell

In the later stages of her autobiography, Margaret Oliphant often had to deal with the return of her shabby, failed brother into her own independent and successful life, aware that to many contemporary readers, the proper order of things had been inverted, and the tale needed to be told with the utmost diplomacy. Oliphant, thinking aloud about her brother Willie, found this difficult:

> Willie, who still lives in Rome, as he has done for the last two-or three-and-twenty years – nearly a quarter of a century – among strangers who are kind to him, wanting nothing, I hope, yet also having outlived everything. I shrank from going to see him when I was in Italy, which was wrong; but how can I return to Rome, and how could he have come to me? – poor Willie! the handsomest, brightest of us all.
>
> (*Autobiography*, p. 19)

As for her other brother, Frank, he had married and had four children, slipping into bad health and financial ruin. Oliphant in her account of his collapse, tries to cover for him: 'He was a man without an expensive taste, the most innocent, the most domestic of men, but what he had had always slipped through his fingers, as I well knew' (p. 129). Between them, she and his wife tried to sort things out, taking two of the children each. The only boy, another Frank, fell to Oliphant, who dreamed of training him 'for something better than they had thought of'. When she came to write up this episode in her *Autobiography*, and the further disasters that followed, she was unsure whether the public would be interested in 'family details'; she also knew that 'all can never be told of any family story, except at the cost of family honour' (p. 130). When his wife died a few years after this arrangement had been put in place, Frank returned to his sister's care: 'He came to me like a child glad to get home, not much disturbed about anything that could happen' (p. 131). Oliphant willingly gave him – and his four children – a home, but admits sadly in her *Autobiography*, 'he and I, who had been so much to each other once, were nothing to each other now...he had drifted one way and I another. He did not even take very much interest in me, and I fear he often irritated me.' (p. 132). In a direct role-reversal of the period's expectations for men and women, Frank sat in his easy-chair in the dining-room, while his sister set about earning enough money for his children as well as her own. This turn of events furnished Oliphant with another weary explanation for everything that was unsatisfactory about her potboiling career as a too-prolific novelist. Undaunted by both her brothers' failures, she stresses repeatedly in her autobiographical account of this episode of Frank's collapse that her one thought was to give her own two sons and Frank's Frank the best education she could afford – as if to prevent, in the next generation, the chapter of failures that had ruined the first. The supreme irony of her continuing sacrifice was that they too let her down – her own two sons by gradual decline and early death, Frank by a less annoying kind of death in India. News of the elder Frank's fatal illness and his wife's death broke – five years apart – on both occasions in the middle of a party, symbolically ruining Oliphant's attempts to relax from the pressures of being her brother's keeper. In the end, she was resigned, vaguely guilty, and defensive about it: 'I did all I could for him, grudging nothing, but we had veered far away from each other, and I do not know that I was always kind' (p. 146). In mourning him, she showed none of the intensity that marked her grief for each of her three surviving children.

By the time Branwell Brontë died, his sister Charlotte had also achieved the requisite emotional distance, though she could not conceal her intense disappointment at his wasted opportunities. 'I do not weep from a sense of bereavement,' she told her publisher, William Smith Williams, '– there is no prop withdrawn, no consolation torn away, no dear companion lost – but for the wreck of talent, the ruin of promise, the untimely dreary extinction of what might have been a burning and shining light.'[20] Though Branwell had long since ceased to be the lively, competitive companion he was in their Angrian days, she could not forget that he had been the object of her aspirations and ambitions; nor could she easily ignore her sense of pity and bitterness on his behalf (Emily, normally sympathetic, dismissed him as a 'hopeless being').[21] George Eliot hardened herself in a similar way against her brother Isaac, who insisted on replying formally through the family solicitor when in 1857 she finally told him of her relationship with George Henry Lewes: 'I dare say I shall never have any further correspondence with my brother, which will be a great relief to me,' she admitted – though twenty-three years later, when Isaac reopened the dialogue, she assured him their long silence had never broken her affection for him, 'which began when we were little ones'.[22] Ties of this intensity were impossible to shrug off entirely, however grossly the finer sensibilities had been offended.

Elizabeth Sewell outlived her glamorous older brother William, but her *Autobiography* crumbles into diary entries and brief updates on her own and her family's situation without going into details of his humiliating failures as a businessman and founder of high class new schools. In her adolescence, William was apt to be patronizing. He caught her reading Butler's *Analogy* one day, and commented: '"You can't understand that."' For years she was unable to tell anyone that 'Butler's *Analogy* had been to [her] as it has been to hundreds, the stay of a troubled intellect and a weak faith' (*Autobiography*, pp. 53–4). Sewell seems to have early learnt a habit of self-repression which prevented her from communicating freely with her brothers or acknowledging her own abilities. This stood her in good stead when she came to write her *Autobiography*, which was also meant to be a family history, written at her mother's request. William had a tendency to run up huge debts whenever he became involved in the founding of a new school: first with St Columba's, near Dublin in 1843; then with Radley, whose first Warden he became in 1853, fleeing to Germany ten years later after debts had reached a sum of £28,000, three thousand more than he had accumulated at St Columba's. 'He was not a man of business habits,' his sister excused him in a tactful understatement; moreover he was devoted to beauty, and believed that the boys in his schools would grow up with purer hearts and minds for being educated in civilized surroundings. According to Elizabeth Sewell, her brother's 'delight in seeing beauty around him often showed itself in a way which caused him to be misjudged and thought careless of expense' (*Autobiography*, p. 165). It was hard to see how outside observers could judge him otherwise.

Little precise information about William's disasters is to be found in the *Autobiography*: Sewell understates the extent of the debts, and is vague about the explanations for them, as befitting a younger sister, though in her tactful evasion, it is possible to read some degree of astute criticism: 'I have reason to think that, from the beginning, the financial responsibility had not been clearly defined, and that misunderstanding was the result,' she says of the Radley fiasco (*Autobiography*, p. 167). Nor does she say anything about his eight-year exile in Germany to avoid his creditors. Given the opportunity to edit his last papers in 1876, Sewell again glossed over her brother's disastrous connections with Radley: after eight years' work, she explains, 'his health broke down, and he resigned his office.' She also declines to 'bring out in detail the literary and personal characteristics of one whose life was lived for others ... but such a task can scarcely be undertaken by a sister'.[23] This seems surprising. This was surely the kind of literary task for which a sister was particularly well suited: a deferential tribute to a brother's achievements and his generosity – but presumably Sewell knew too much to be comfortable with her subject. She was well aware that some aspects of his life were too unsuccessful to document openly. All she concedes is that 'Dr Sewell's writings must be left to tell their own tale'.

More strangely, she is also largely silent about her brother Henry's political career in New Zealand, where he was very briefly that colony's first Premier, and then actively involved in several branches of government. Henry is nearly always mentioned in the *Autobiography* in relation to his marriages and motherless children, for whose upbringing the Sewell sisters took responsibility. Her brother's marriages were more significant to Sewell than their careers. She was anxious when William was engaged to an older woman (though the engagement was subsequently broken off); as for the others, 'our life was a good deal altered after our brothers married' (p. 67). For one thing, there were 'more wills to be consulted', and when her father died in 1842, the sisters lived on the 'voluntary kindness' of their brothers, rather than the natural protection which a child claims from a parent. This involved moves to two small and ugly houses at Pidford and Bonchurch, arranged for them by

William. Wherever possible, he took the elder brother role, even though the family would increasingly depend on Elizabeth's earnings as a novelist to prop up their shaky fortunes. Her reasons for avoiding discussion of William's failures are self-evident, but why she is silent on Henry's successes as a politician is less obvious. After a lifetime of being at her brothers' beck and call, she perhaps needed to focus on the family history from the sisters' point of view: to assert the primacy of their needs and struggles. Henry's political career in New Zealand was another world from her own schools on the Isle of Wight. Between the two islands were acres of incomprehension. As for William, he produced a thousand pages of reminiscences, which he declined to publish, but which he wanted his nieces and nephews to read. 'All biographies,' he declared, 'especially autobiographies, are in my own mind a delusion.' This was because complete faithfulness and truth were impossible to achieve in the reconstruction of a life. In writing her autobiography, was Elizabeth defying yet another pronouncement of her brother's she had had to accept during his lifetime? He also kept a journal, whose closing words, written shortly before his death in 1874, were 'I am weak and worthless.'[24]

Harriet and James Martineau

James Martineau managed only fifty-four pages of *Biographical Memoranda*, which, unlike his sister's *Autobiography*, has remained unpublished. The fact that he wrote it in 1877, shortly after his sister's death and posthumous publication, suggests that he did so – if not overtly – in response to hers. His note at the end says that it was written 'for an incidental purpose, away from home and all memorials'; moreover that he omitted all reference to his publications, Unitarian dissensions, and 'Many Relations with persons more or less interesting, in private or public life.'[25] The urgency implied in this statement points to a need to write what was essential and easily remembered: the construction of his career, his changing religious outlook, and his breach with his sister, which – unlike her – he is willing to discuss. In 1884, he added further information in a letter to the *Daily News*, reprinted as 'The Early Days of Harriet Martineau'. The story of their breach, and his sense of his own part in it, was a narrative he felt compelled to keep telling, while she suppressed it. Unusually, therefore, the Martineaus performed a kind of misaligned dialogue with each other; James responding only after his sister's death, making his summary of their relationship an unavoidable last word. Hers, however, was the more intense emotional dependence;

it lasted longer than his did, and her language, in recalling it, was virulent and bitter.

For Harriet Martineau, the breakdown was a more problematic narrative to reconstruct for a Victorian audience. Much of it was conducted in public, via review articles, but where she does divulge her feelings, it is largely to women friends through the medium of letters. Though details of the final collapse are omitted from her *Autobiography*, however, the early stages of their relationship are well documented, especially their shared philosophical interests. Drawn together by physical and emotional sensitivity and a shrinking from the rough treatment of their older brothers and sisters, they seem to have alternated in taking the intellectual lead, she dragging him out of bed when he could hardly walk and showing him the sunrise, talking 'very religiously to the child' (*Autobiography*, I, 17), but once he was at college, their roles were reversed, and she felt bereft without him. She was still regarding him as her 'oracle' when she was twenty (*Autobiography*, I, 108), and seeking his help on the doctrine of Necessity: 'I uttered the difficulty which had lain in my mind for so many years; and he just informed me that there was, or was held to be, a solution in that direction, and advised me to make it out for myself. I did so' (*Autobiography*, I, 109). She had already been baulked of an informative answer over ten years earlier when she asked her eldest brother Thomas about the paradox of human free will and God's foreknowledge of events – though she clearly regarded her brothers, rather than her sisters or parents as the fount of all knowledge in this respect. By encouraging her to think for herself, James was unknowingly laying the foundation of their future dissension. He certainly recognized her 'acute, rapid, and incisive advance to a conclusion upon every point', which 'pleasantly relieved my slower judgement and gave me courage to dismiss suspense'; he maintained, too, that *she* encouraged *him* into literary work, 'so that we should divide between us the proposals which editors poured in upon her, and of which, she thought, some might be handed over to me.'[26] James, however, doubted whether in their earlier childhood they had been as close as Harriet implied: 'for we naturally cared for different things and were educated on different lines' (*Biographical Memoranda*, p. 38). On the other hand, he enthused at length over the Wordsworthian walking tour of Scotland they took in 1824, while she claimed it upset her digestion (*Autobiography*, I, 128). Their inability to agree on details of their relationship is symptomatic of its increasing confusions and bad feeling, as is the mystery still surrounding her engagement to James's college friend, John Hugh Worthington.

James had performed the traditional brotherly role in bringing home a friend to meet his sister – much as Tennyson was to do with the equally doomed Hallam and his sister Emily, a few years later; but while Harriet was evasive about her feelings for him (for example denying they were anything more than good friends, then accepting his proposal the day before she asked James's advice as to whether she should or not), James himself seems to have wavered in his confidence over Worthington's suit, and subsequently denied promoting it.[27] In a characteristically mysterious passage in the *Autobiography*, Harriet refers to 'the evil offices of one who had much to answer for in what he did' (I, 126). In the event, Worthington's poor health meant that nothing could be done in a hurry, and he died the following year before the couple could be married. Harriet seems to have turned with relief back to James, whatever his role in the affair, and never fell in love again. James says nothing about it in his *Biographical Memoranda*, but in his 1884 'Early Days' admits he was surprised by his sister's engagement, and had not expected anything permanent to come of their relationship.[28]

The relationship between the siblings was, in fact, never quite the same. He married in 1828 and had numerous children, making him less available than before for intimate discussion. In turn, while he was invaluable in offering her intellectual stimulation, the success of her *Illustrations of Political Economy* (1832–4) in effect made him redundant as a mental guide, though she continued to consult him about difficult decisions. One such case arose in 1837, when she was offered the editorship of a new economics journal, but felt torn about accepting. Apart from anything else, she was tired, and wanted the mental variety of planning a novel. The 'two or three intimate friends' she had consulted for a frank opinion were all in favour, but she was still awaiting James's judgement:

> If the one remaining opinion had been in agreement with theirs, I should have followed the unanimous advice: but on the nineteenth [of December 1837], I find, 'James is altogether against the periodical plan.' I wrote my final refusal on that day; and again I was at liberty to ponder my novel.
>
> (*Autobiography*, II, 111)

On the same day, she wrote to her friend Fanny Wedgwood: 'I have just written to decline the enterprize, on James's strongly expressed opinion, which is right, I am confident.'[29] Confident she may have tried to sound, but the episode as recounted in her *Autobiography* is very much more drawn out, and expressed in gender-conscious terms. 'If I do this,' she told herself, 'I must brace myself up to do and suffer like a man... Undertaking a man's duty, I must brave a man's fate' (II, 110). Stressing the need to control her 'waywardness' and emotional vacillation, she had even drawn up a 'sheetful of subjects', before James's answer poured cold water on the plan. He also advised against accepting a government pension, though once again two other friends counselled in favour (*Autobiography*, II, 175). Successful though he was as a Unitarian theologian, he never achieved the dramatic, overnight fame of his more controversial sister, and he may have resented her entry into such a masculine sphere. As it was, most of their subsequent battles were over issues relating to periodicals and their centrality in Victorian intellectual life.

Her letters gradually reveal the growth of a mental distancing that she glosses over in her *Autobiography* – as, for instance, when she begins to joke about his complacency as a family man and theologian – 'That wonderful personage, the Revd James', as she calls him in a letter of 1837. Though this is on the whole an affectionate reference, she mentions his 'immense (loving) criticism' of her latest book which he wrote to her a week after its appearance. James was evidently still trying to keep up the teacherly stance.[30] By 1843, when she was bedridden at Tynemouth for five years and expected to die, she started writing her autobiography, but decided not to tell James: 'I wish to keep my mind clear from all family influences, & have therefore not told even James; – nor shall.'[31] The following year, in the most divisive incident of her life so far, James was 'contemptuous' of mesmerism, which she was employing as a cure for her long-standing gynaecological condition. By 1849, they were worlds apart, he having returned from Germany 'conservative, & full of religiosity', she having abandoned her religion and set up house for herself in Ambleside, beyond the reach of casual family visitors.[32] The last straw was James's insulting treatment of Henry Atkinson, Harriet's co-producer of the *Letters on the Laws of Man's Nature and Development*, their survey-discussion of phrenological and mesmeric beliefs in relation to Baconian science and necessarian philosophy. It was essentially Harriet's public disavowal of her Christian beliefs, which James, as a Unitarian theologian, was bound to resent. Moreover, Atkinson had taken over the brotherly role of intellectual sounding-board (though perhaps as James's junior by ten years, he was more like a son than a brother), guiding her through her metaphysical perplexities as James had done when they were teenagers. Harriet felt James had forced her to choose between her brother and her new friend. To her old friend Fanny Wedgwood in 1855 she grumbled about James's family not visiting her when they came to the Lake District, or cutting her over his daughter's wedding. 'The truth is that James has been injuring and wounding me in every possible way since my illness in 1839 (you know, he never went to see me all those years) and, as all my family know, I was *perfectly passive* till he compelled me to choose between him and Mr Atkinson.' Her reasons for maintaining a dignified distance were, as she told Fanny Wedgwood, 'good faith towards Mr Atkinson; and utter disesteem for James; a disesteem which every honest person would feel who duly examined that review.'[33] She wrote in similar terms to her sister-in-law Helen, with whom she kept up a sputtering correspondence until the two became exasperated with each other over the breakdown of the relationship between the siblings. 'He has lost my esteem by public conduct – not only not requiring "explanation," but so bad as to disentitle him to it,' she told Helen.[34] Nor did she intend publicly refuting him in a response to his *Prospective* review. As she indicated rather sinisterly to Helen, there were other means 'of exposing James's character as a controversialist, wh we shd use if ever the interests of truth shd require it'.[35]

Though there is no evidence that she ever put her threat into operation, she was certainly furious with this brother who had been her all-in-all in childhood. There was no way, she told Fanny Wedgwood, that James could possibly be her biographer (a false rumour spread by their youngest sister Ellen). Apart from anything else, James had in effect had little to do with her since she became famous: 'and that, considering the intervals of 4, 6, and 7 years when he has not even *seen* me, – that he despises my books, knows none of my friends, or my habits, and very few of my opinions, and has never seen me for 20 years without insulting me, – he is not exactly the person to write my life.'[36] When the *Westminster Review*, edited by John Chapman, with Marian Evans as his assistant, got into financial difficulties in 1854, and James Martineau thought of buying it, to swing it back to more acceptable religious views, Harriet stepped in with a £500 loan, partly to ensure that James was thwarted.

Meanwhile they disagreed about Comte. James found him tedious, Harriet found condensing his *Philosophie Positive* one of the most enjoyable tasks she had ever performed: 'Many a passage of my version did I write with tears falling into my lap; and many a time did I feel almost stifled for want of the presence of some genial disciple of my instructor, to whom I might speak of his achievement, with some chance of being understood' (*Autobiography*, II, 391). Perhaps she was thinking of the James of her youth, who had always been her intellectual companion;

but by 1858, James was sneering at Comte's 'puerilities', 'overbearing dogmatism and astounding self-appreciation'. He also recoiled from the way Comte paid tribute to his partner in philosophy, Madame Clotilde de Vaux, with whom he established a catechism formula for the dissemination of his ideas. Perhaps here James was thinking of the humiliating partnership between his sister and Henry Atkinson, both women humbling themselves before their male tutor. The catechism, noted James, 'is in the form of a dialogue, between himself, as sacerdotal instructor, and an "angelic interlocutrix," who is no other than Madame Clotilde'. Though Atkinson was the teacher, and Clotilde the pupil, the resonances and resemblances are too close to miss. James thought Clotilde 'converted Comte from philosophical vigour to puerile sentimentality', a sad contrast with his 'earlier genius'.[37] What seems to have upset him most about the Atkinson Letters was the spectacle of his sister bowing to the bogus wisdom of a cranky intellectual inferior. 'It seemed a kind of fascination,' James recalled, writing in his *Prospective* review: 'With grief we must say that we remember nothing in literary history more melancholy than that Harriet Martineau should be prostrated at the feet of such a master. Surely this humiliating inversion of the natural order of nobleness cannot last'.[38] Did he regard Atkinson as a grotesque replacement for himself, an insult to the memory of their own exhilarating relationship? Atkinson had certainly ousted him as the 'significant other' in Harriet's life, and unlike himself was sharing her intellectual companionship in a public and published format. For all their closeness in their twenties, the brother and sister had never actually published anything together, despite Harriet's fantasy of delegating some of her own commissions, including one from Lord Brougham: 'Let me but have something of yours to lay my finger upon against I see the Chancellor, and we will be side by side, as we have ever been. *You* shall battle with Atheism (as Lord Brougham wants me to do), while *I* fight the Poor Laws. O how glorious!' (*Biographical Memoranda*, pp. 38–9). She could not have foreseen that he would one day battle against atheism against *her*.

Whatever the complexities of what he really thought, James insisted on his own reluctance to review the book. By his own account (which his biographers have questioned), he did it only to save his sister from harsher criticism by another reviewer. Concentrating his fire on Atkinson, he tried to deal with the embarrassing book 'argument for argument'.[39] This is a somewhat disingenuous comment when juxtaposed with the review itself: for example when James jeers at the 'perpetual stream of physical miracle' in the *Letters*: 'The authors appear to live exclusively among people who see through brick walls, taste and hear across half the land; who will send you any given pain by the penny post, and write your whole biography from a bit of your old shoe.'[40] Despite this, he insisted there was no reason to fall out, and he was unaware that they had for three years after the review. 'The estrangement produced by this cause and its antecedents was all on one side,' (*Biographical Memoranda*, p.43) – a view he reiterated in his 1884 letter to the *Daily News*.

As the interests of brother and sister often coincided, they found themselves writing reviews on similar topics. Harriet tackled 'England's Foreign Policy' in the *Westminster Review* of January 1854, and James tackled 'Foreign Policy – the next campaign' in the *National Review* exactly two years later. Both contributed to the discussion of American affairs (James in his *National Review* article 'The Slave Empire of the West', 1865) and both followed the debates between science and religion; Harriet claiming that science was the 'only source of, not enlightenment, but wisdom, goodness and happiness', James arguing that 'Science discloses the Method of the world, but not its cause'. Harriet felt liberated by the loss of her belief in a personal God with human attributes, while James felt dismayed at the thought of being flung into a 'bottomless negation'.[41] Yet she twice opposed his appointment to Chairs he wanted – at Manchester New College in 1857, and the Chair of Philosophy of Mind and Logic in University College, London in 1866 – alleging that he had no just claim to the former because he no longer 'believes in Xty at all'. As far as she was concerned, he was prepared to ignore most of the New Testament, following only Paul; nor could she resist mentioning his review of the Atkinson letters again, as the place where he had implied God's defeat by man's free will.[42] There was something strangely ironic about Harriet's attack on James for not being sufficiently Unitarian, given her own triumphant abandonment of the faith: presumably she wanted him to take up a position as uncompromising as her own. The fact that he seemed to be seeking high office in the church while cherry-picking among its creeds further fuelled her indignation with him.

Nor did their feud end with Harriet's death in 1876. When her *Autobiography* was published the following year, James was offended by the way she had described their mother, whose alleged emotional undemonstrativeness he failed to recognize. His 1884 letter to the *Daily News* (his sister's old employer) was chiefly to refute this view of their mother perpetuated by Florence Fenwick Miller, Harriet's first biographer, who used the *Autobiography* as a basis for her account of Harriet's childhood. Though the breach with James had been omitted from the book by Harriet herself – to George Eliot's relief[43] – Martineau's American editor, Maria Weston Chapman, had not been so discreet, and went into considerable detail about it, under the chapter heading 'The Life Sorrow'. The fact remains, too, that Martineau must have realized there was a good chance James would read the *Autobiography* if he outlived her, and would find in it many references to their shared childhood and their strong affection for each other. His almost total absence from the second volume of her book tells its own silent story, which must have been obvious to many readers apart from George Eliot. The breach was never repaired, though at the end of their lives, both Martineaus softened, and left placatory messages. 'When you speak of my brother James, be as gentle as you can,' Harriet instructed Maria Weston Chapman (*Autobiography*, III, 322); while James decided in his autobiographical letter for the *Daily News* that despite his sister's determination to excommunicate him, it had 'in no way disenchanted the old affection, or impaired [his] estimate of her high aims, her large powers, and her noble and patient virtues'(Bosanquet, p. 241).

Why did the relationship between the two Martineaus fail so disastrously, and to what extent does it tell us anything about the complexities of gender relations within Victorian families? Constance Hassett suggests that the recurring clashes between brother and sister were 'culturally driven. The motives and authority for their contrary positions lay outside themselves'.[44] James continued to assert a brotherly hold over Harriet, performing a traditional male role, while she was responding to the destabilizing trends of the day: the American anti-slavery campaign, women's rights, alternative medicine, agnosticism and mesmerism. The Martineaus were in any case an atypical family of the period: Unitarian, intellectual, close yet rivalrous, their relationships over the years inclined to fragment. By the end of her life, it was her third brother Robert's family in Birmingham who were supplying all the emotional and practical support that one might have expected to come from James's numerous children, but no one in Robert's family was an intellectual rival. His daughter Maria actually died in Harriet's devoted service, and never seems to have challenged her aunt's authority. Harriet found her 'glorious',[45] but openly admits jealousy of her older sister Rachel (*Autobiography*, I, 19), for which she compensated by passionate devotion to Ellen, the youngest child of the family. Quarrels flared up among the family throughout her life, and the alleged mesmeric cure of 1845 alienated her eldest sister Elizabeth's family (Elizabeth's husband, Thomas Michael Greenhow, was her doctor), as well as James's. Moreover, they were a family who took their religious and philosophical positions very seriously: something that does bring them more into line with other contemporary families, such as the Rossettis, Newmans, Mozleys, Arnolds and Gladstones, riven as they were by religious differences. The most obvious difference between Harriet and James was her steady progress towards a form of agnosticism, which James, as a Unitarian theologian, could hardly be expected to condone. As Valerie Pichanick notes, 'He had moved away from necessarianism and in the direction of greater spiritualization. He was not fully sympathetic to some of his sister's more ardent personal causes: he did not condone either abolitionism or republicanism.' Hassett says he was 'aghast' when slavery was finally outlawed in America.[46]

Another major cause of disagreement between them was James's refusal to destroy her letters: she believed vehemently in the inviolable privacy of what she called 'epistolary intercourse' (*Autobiography*, I, 3); while James, who believed otherwise, had even kept shorthand summaries of the letters he had received from her in the 1820s. His unwillingness to destroy letters in itself led to a cooling off of the correspondence, since Harriet could hardly confide any intimate thoughts to someone who might subsequently publish them. Her letters became 'short, summary and dictatorial: and touched condescendingly, if at all, on the subjects of thought and work of life which remained of supreme interest to me' (*Biographical Memoranda*, p. 42). Because they quickly lost touch with each other's intellectual development, the breach, when it came, was harder to heal. His motives for keeping the letters are in themselves a complex issue. He opted to keep the ones he already had as 'memorials of a life-drama else fading and lost',[47] but presumably he also recognized her historical significance, and expected the letters to be useful and interesting to scholars. He cannot, however, have been unaware of their gossipy, mischief-making tone, and the controversies they were likely to revive.

George Eliot, who discussed the whole case with Sara Hennell, feeling that James had been wrong to review his sister's book, also felt that Harriet was the cause 'of her imputation being made public, for the statement that he was from the very beginning of her success continually moved by jealousy and envy towards her must have come readily to her lips, since she made it to a person so far from intimate with her as I was'.[48] This apparently was Harriet's often used explanation: that James was jealous and envious. If this was so, history has vindicated her rather than him, as her works are enjoying a lively reappraisal, especially among American scholars keen to reclaim her as a proto-feminist.[49]

Several of Harriet's causes have worn well: her passionate commitment to the anti-slavery campaign, for example; her achievements as a feminist role-model, fearless alike in travel and in journalism; her outspoken agnosticism and support for 'alternative' medicine, however cranky. There is no doubt that of all her female contemporaries, Harriet took the greatest risks and worked hardest, without the support of a male partner to protect her from unpleasant publicity, and that James more than once counselled against what might have been a good career-move. Whatever his real motives, which are now difficult to retrieve, his actions have the appearance of restraining a sister who had already breached the boundaries of decent femininity, while Harriet transferred her allegiance to a brother who endorsed her belief in mesmerism and lent her his daughters to make up a brotherless household of women.

As James himself indicates in his *Daily News* letter, the breakdown of their relationship was gradual, rather than sudden, and largely caused by her insistence on the destruction of their correspondence. All the signs are that despite her active life, she was more dependent on him than he was on her. After all, he married young, and had many children; his teaching and preaching were direct experiences with an audience before him, whereas hers was (except for some lectures she gave in Ambleside to the local working class) largely to an abstract readership. Her language in detailing the estrangement is bitter and scornful, whereas he goes out of his way to pay her measured tributes and demonstrate his rationality. Strongly-worded asides in her *Autobiography* often seem to target the otherwise unmentioned James: for example the suggestion that theologians were impossible to talk to about the centrality of science, 'because they avowedly give their preference to theology over the science with which it is incompatible' (*Autobiography*, II, 330), has the acidity of a sour allusion to James's stubborn theological position. What the Martineaus' disagreement illustrates is a major cultural divergence, demonstrated in the clash between the sister's anger and the brother's calm correction of the facts. As he points out in his *Daily News* letter, the Newman brothers managed to remain on good terms with one another despite their theological differences. Harriet's behaviour, unreciprocated by him, he concludes, is a further instance of her 'ability to oscillate between extremes of devotedness and antipathy' (Bosanquet, p. 241).

Conclusion

This pattern of rivalry and the rebuilding of alternative lifestyles was the common factor in all the autobiographical accounts of brother–sister breaches discussed in this chapter. In each family, the sister, born late in a long succession of children, became intellectually and economically independent in adult life, defying control; indeed, in Oliphant's case, to a degree imposing it. In each family, too, the sister's success eclipsed the brother's. Where this involved major financial mismanagement, as with the Sewells and Oliphant's brothers, reconstructing the family history to spare the brother became a difficult imperative. Most failed altogether to tackle the worst of their brothers' failures within their own autobiographies: the (usually understated) contours of their success story (which is partly the definition of autobiography) colliding with the downward plunge of their brothers' life history, and underlining their collapse. Writing about their brothers in autobiography, beyond its childhood stages, was in fact for most Victorian women an impossible task, involving them, as it must, in a narrative of masculine incompetence, or growing disillusionment. Most idealized their brothers as godlike heroes in childhood, and allowed them to fade from the later stages of their history. But their relationships with their brothers were still central to their emotional development, and another way of exploring their dual response to them had to be discovered. Most of the best- (and least-) known nineteenth-century women novelists were also sisters, whose first emotional tie to anyone other than a parent had been to a brother. From him they derived their most enduring ideas of masculinity, which in middle life were overthrown, forcing them to reconsider their original expectations. Two major patterns emerge: the idealization of the brother-figure into the perfect lover who is already domesticated and incorporated into the heroine's family; and his transformation into a forbidding father-substitute barring the way to independence and emotional fulfilment. Both of these patterns will be discussed in succeeding chapters.

4
The Brother as Lover

and my affection had indeed so engrossed me that I scarcely thought about other men except to feel that they were his inferiors.[1]

If only he were allowed to fall in love with his sister. In fact, Phil thinks he *is* in love with Brooke...[2]

In Book IX of the *Metamorphoses*, Ovid tells the story of Byblis, daughter of Miletus, who falls in love with her own brother, Caunus. Although she feels ashamed and embarrassed, she also finds it impossible to control her feelings. The relationship seems ideal, as she argues: 'Oh, if only I could change my name, and marry you, what a good daughter-in-law could I be to your father, Caunus, what a good son-in-law you could be to mine!' As she recognizes, however, 'the one thing we shall have in common is the thing which keeps us apart.' The father and father-in-law would be one and the same. Horrified by the letter Byblis sends him, her brother Caunus flees the country; Byblis, fleeing, too, weeping, and never catching up with him, is transformed into a spring of water. Ovid comments that the story 'affords a warning to other girls to love only what is permitted'.[3] Nevertheless, the story is told with some sympathy, and Byblis is given a long, emotional monologue in which she bewails the misfortune of having fallen in love with her own brother – which, however, seems to her not entirely unreasonable. The story serves as a fitting introduction to the nineteenth-century idealization of the brother as the lover most women would choose if only it were not forbidden.

In nineteenth-century fiction the strongest emotions are expressed for other members of the family, especially brothers and sisters. This was something Freud recognized when he suggested in his 'General Theory of the Neuroses' that a person's first choice of a love-object is 'regularly an incestuous one'. As the child becomes disillusioned with his parents, who were his first love-objects, he may well turn towards a sibling for consolation. A brother 'may take his sister as a love-object by way of a substitute for his faithless mother', while 'a little girl may find in her elder brother a substitute for her father who no longer takes an affectionate interest in her as he did in her earliest years'.[4] In sociological terms, too, the brother is the ideal lover. His social background is the same as his sister's, they have already lived together, but in an asexual bond, and their feelings for each other have developed from the innocence of childhood affection. For a woman, an older brother can provide both vicarious excitement and protection from danger. For a man, the younger sister is the ideal lover because she looks up to him, embodies home values, and in many ways replicates his mother, just as the brother replicates the father, but as a peer, whose rule is potentially more flexible than the father's. Jane Austen summarizes the attractions of the relationship for Fanny Price in *Mansfield Park* as 'this unchecked, equal, fearless intercourse with the brother and friend, who was opening his heart to her'.[5] Brothers and sisters enjoyed with each other an ease and freedom that was difficult to achieve in other relationships between the sexes; indeed was rarely allowed outside the family and the family home.

In the nineteenth century, family ideology saw siblings of both sexes as being more like than unlike one another, even in looks.[6] A sibling was a part of the home life, assumed to have the same fundamental values, however far their paths had diverged, and the same memories of shared experiences. As David Copperfield says of Agnes Wickfield, talking to her is 'a delightful reminder' of his 'happy life in the grave old house she had made so beautiful'.[7] Agnes is inseparable from his childhood, but also an entirely dependable guide, always there, always an inspiration and support to whom he can talk frankly without the distractions of sex-consciousness. Adrienne Rich has expressed more recently how this idea works for women in her poem 'Natural Resources' (1977), in which she describes women's search for 'The phantom of the man-who-would-understand,/the lost brother, – the twin...the comrade/twin whose palm/would bear a lifeline like our own'. This is the kind of man women want, she suggests: not the 'rapist', 'the crude pestle', 'the blind/ramrod'.[8]

Much of Victorian fiction is concerned with discovering the kind of relationship that will rescue the central characters from the isolation always threatening to engulf them in the new atomistic, industrial age, without compromising their moral integrity. Ideally the perfect lover is the closest one can come to an actual blood brother or sister, the lost comrade-twin, 'the man [or woman]-who-would-understand', in Rich's terms; but as Elizabeth Rose Gruner has argued, love for a sibling-substitute is by no means the easy option for nineteenth-century fictional heroes: 'the insistent nature–culture binary that both defines and masks the origins of family relations makes the sibling tie a complex interaction, full of desire and sublimation...'[9] What gradually emerges during the first sixty years of the nineteenth century – mainly through the work of women novelists – is a dual image of the brother as his sister's *alter ego* and his father's stern substitute. Underlying the dominant image of the brother as considerate and emotionally responsive is the notion of the brother-as-bully, the John Reed type, who stands in his sister's way and forbids access to male privilege. This type will be discussed in the next chapter, while the emotionally responsive type, the brother who is better than a husband, is discussed in this.

We normally say that a couple are 'like brother and sister' if we want to imply that they are close, but sexually uninvolved. The phrase is often used to reassure. Mrs Norris in *Mansfield Park*, for example, argues that Tom and Edmund will avoid falling in love with their cousin Fanny because they were brought up as children: 'always together like brothers and sisters? It is morally impossible...she will never be more to either than a sister' (p. 44). Couples themselves could use this tag to protect themselves from each other as well as from outside gossip (as do Gilbert Markham and Helen Graham, initially, in *The Tenant of Wildfell Hall*, while Helen's real brother, Lawrence, pretends not to be related to her), but traditionally in literature, one half of the couple begins to resent the asexual dismissal of their relationship before the other. Eliza Lynn Linton shows how troublesome this reassuring saying can be, when in her novel, *Lizzie Lorton of Greyrigg* (1866), the hero, Ainslie Forbes, tells Margaret Elcombe, the plain-featured but sensible heiress, whom he will eventually marry, '"How I wish that you were my sister instead of my cousin."' Linton, as narrator, observes that 'it was characteristic of the quality of Margaret's nature that so many men should have desired this relationship with her, and that none should have yet loved her.' No one would have wanted the tempestuous Lizzie Lorton as his sister:

> But with Margaret there was a certain stability of honour, a certain gentle nobleness of nature which form the ideal of a sister, both in relation to a man's own life, and in influence over his character. She was not a woman whom many would love in any other way than

this; but if ever she should awaken that other love, then would she be the most intensely beloved of all women.[10]

Linton's comments reveal the paradoxical nature of the ideal sister. She is someone who will exert an elevating moral influence over a man, but then that will make her, in all but exceptional cases, sexually unavailable. On the other hand, where a woman like Margaret *does* succeed in combining 'gentle nobleness' with physical appeal, Linton suggests this is the highest form of love. The male equivalent in much early to mid-Victorian fiction – the ideal brother – is honourable and noble too, but also gently assertive, sufficiently masculine to be protective, but unthreatening and easy to be with. He has his own life, but is fully capable of entering his sister's world and sharing her interests. For many Victorian writers, the nearer a couple came to this ideal of love, the happier they were likely to be.

Jane Austen and Mary Shelley

At the beginning of the nineteenth-century, in Jane Austen's gentry class, brothers and sisters helped each other to mates and married within accepted social circles. Austen's brother Henry married their cousin Eliza, daughter of the Reverend George Austen's devoted sister Philadelphia Hancock; another brother, James, married Jane's friend Mary Lloyd, whose sister Martha married another Austen brother Francis. In *Northanger Abbey*, James Morland brings to Isabella Thorpe 'the double recommendation of being her brother's friend, and her friend's brother'.[11] In turn, Catherine furthers her relationship with Henry Tilney through his sister Eleanor. The novels divide into those where marriage partners are found within a pre-existing social circle, with outsiders being discredited and driven out, and those where eligible partners (usually men) need to be imported from further afield to enliven a limited social scene. Mr Darcy is one of the more distant and exotic, introduced into the Bennets' Hertfordshire social circle by his friend Mr Bingley ('a young man of large fortune from the north of England', as Mrs Bennet describes him in the opening chapter). In *Northanger Abbey*, Henry Tilney meets Catherine at the Bath assembly rooms, and is introduced by the Master of Ceremonies: there is no way they would have met if Catherine had stayed at home, though the more socially mobile James Morland has already met Isabella Thorpe by the time Catherine encounters her. By contrast, Emma meets only family and neighbourhood connections: Frank Churchill, who is Mr Weston's son, and Mr Knightley, who is already her brother-in-law. In *Sense and Sensibility*, Elinor's husband Edward is already a family connection (brother of Mrs John Dashwood, wife of Elinor's half-brother), and they have experience of living under the same roof before they are finally united. But the novel that most strongly upholds the ideal of the sibling marriage is *Mansfield Park*, so often seen as the most problematic as well as the most 'Victorian' of Austen's novels. Part of its 'Victorianness', I will suggest, is its idealization of the brother–sister romance, which was also to enchant Dickens, Gaskell and Eliot later in the century, as well as Emily and Anne Brontë.

Almost everyone in *Mansfield Park* is a brother or a sister, and the novel seems deliberately to pit against each other three contrasting models of the relationship, as also happens in *Northanger Abbey*. In the earlier novel, all three sibling sets have a teasing relationship, mixed with family partisanship. Catherine is quickly disconcerted by John Thorpe's rudeness to his younger sisters, on whom he 'bestowed an equal portion of his fraternal tenderness, for he asked each of them how they did, and observed that they both looked very ugly' (p. 70). Henry Tilney's teasing of his sister is more subtle, in keeping with their shared taste for history and literature. In many ways, Henry Tilney is the most feminized of Austen's brother-figures – ' "my sister has often trusted me in the choice of a gown. I bought one for her the other day –" ' he tells Catherine (p. 50) – and his courtship develops under cover of a friendship between the two women. Catherine is equally delighted by the prospect of being 'sisters' with Isabella Thorpe when her engagement to James is formalized. Throughout the novel, the extension of all three families, the widening of the sibling ramifications and connections, is an exciting adjunct to the splitting into couples, but perhaps also a sign of the young people's immaturity. When Catherine does finally marry Henry, the Thorpe/Morland connection is off, and Eleanor has been suddenly spirited away by a convenient nobleman. The novel's closure implies that marriage requires concentration on the relationship itself, and the next few novels have brotherless heroines: the Dashwood and Bennet sisters, and later the three Elliot sisters.

In *Mansfield Park*, Austen seems to be revisiting the relationship between courtship and sibship, between emotional affinity with blood relatives, and the willingness to make new connections. While Catherine Morland was cheerfully open to fresh alliances, Fanny is morbidly resistant to anyone outside the family. Edmund, by contrast, seems emotionally detached from his two sisters, Maria and Julia, whose moral guardian he tries, but fails to be. Henry and Mary Crawford, on the other hand, have a flirtatious and sensual relationship, whose sexually-charged consciousness makes Fanny's friendship with her brother William look childish and innocent in its simple-hearted openness. Austen herself sees the fraternal relationship as potentially the most rewarding – greater even than the 'conjugal' but – as Harriet Martineau was to declare fifty years later in her *Autobiography* – also the most precarious. 'Fraternal love, sometimes almost every thing,' she warns in *Mansfield Park*, 'is at others worse than nothing' (p. 244). For Fanny and William, it is the only outlet for the intense emotional life they have to suppress the rest of the time. Incapable of joking about him, Fanny revels in every stage of his career progression, and perhaps celebrates his homecomings all the more because she is forbidden to show any feelings for Edmund. Ironically, there is a stronger taboo on her cousin (whom she might conceivably marry) than on her brother (whom she never could): hence the freedom with which Fanny can fuss around William, enjoying his every smile. In return, fancy-free, he dreams of spending 'all their middle and later life together' in a little cottage (p. 369): how Fanny would feel on seeing William pay court to another woman is something Austen decides not to explore, though Catherine Morland was pleased to see James and Isabella becoming friends. Meanwhile Fanny's delight in her brother's company is seen as a heartening guide to her feelings for a future lover: 'What could be more encouraging to a man who had her love in his view?' (p. 298).

Mary Crawford, taking a vicarious pleasure in seeing her brother as a sexual success, urges him to pursue Fanny, and her to enjoy 'the glory of fixing one who has been shot at by so many' (p. 358). A fit sister for one who talks of 'making a hole in Fanny Price's heart', Mary strikes the reader as being in reality the best wife for her own brother. Apart from sharing the imagery of pistol-shooting, they are both sexual adventurers for whom daring talk is at least as much fun as practical success. ' "Talk to me for ever," ' Mary urges her brother when he is in full flow about Fanny (p. 296). One reason is that she knows the marriage of one couple would assist that of the other: pairs of brother–sister marriages being especially delightful as a way of consolidating family and class alliances. Fanny herself believes, however, that Mary ' "loves nobody but herself and her brother" ' (p. 414). However shallow their talk, their relationship is easy, polished, and coquettish in a way that goes beyond the relaxed manners of the Tilneys – chiefly because the Crawfords seem to acknowledge and admire each other's sexual expertise. At the end of the novel, however, they drift apart, Henry's elopement with a married woman making it impossible even for a worldly-wise sister to live with him.

What has disturbed many readers is the way in which Edmund renews his fraternal relationship with Fanny at the end of the novel when both Crawfords, as well as Maria and Julia, have disgraced themselves. Like James Morland, who tells Catherine after his split with Isabella, '"you are my only friend; *your* love I do build upon"' (p. 203), Edmund calls Fanny '"my only sister – my only comfort now"' (p. 432), yet hopes that her '"warm and sisterly regard for him would be foundation enough for wedded love"' (p. 454). Whereas Austen conveys the sense with James that his outburst is a predictable response to his wounded trust, Edmund's words seem strange, coming as they do after many pages in which Fanny's intense love for William has been accepted with at the worst a condescending smile. The novel has touched as closely as it can on the possibility of all kinds of improper relationships: the instances occurring in the home theatricals, *Lovers' Vows*, and those in the family background – Admiral Crawford's mistress, Maria's flirtation with Henry during her engagement, her elopement with him after her marriage, Sir Thomas's dread of any developments between his sons and Fanny, and Fanny's passion for the forbidden William, coupled with her horror at the recommended match with Henry Crawford. Edmund's language jars precisely because the novel has contemplated so many imprudent matches and dismissed them: yet now the mingling of sister and wife (not to mention cousin) is being recommended as a happy ending, as it is in *Emma*, another novel with a quick turnaround from familial to sexual connection. As many commentators have also noted, the family closes in on itself, admitting Fanny as a wife and Susan as a new daughter, while driving out anyone who would significantly alter the values and ambience of the household. Whether this is a sign of family consolidation or social conservatism has been much disputed by critics.[12]

In her next novel, *Emma*, Austen demonstrates Mr Knightley's promising family qualities by showing him as brother to John and Isabella, brother-in-law to Emma, and son-substitute to Mr Woodhouse. His rival, Frank Churchill, at first seems to be Emma's natural choice because he is almost her brother. His stepmother, Mrs Weston, raised Emma for much of her childhood, and he seems, by his connection with the Westons, 'quite to belong to her'.[13] They apparently think alike about Jane Fairfax, and are soon sniggering suggestively together: 'He perfectly agreed with her: and after walking together so long, and thinking so much alike, Emma felt herself so well acquainted with him, that she could hardly believe it to be only their second meeting' (p. 214). Like other Austen heroines, she feels at home with someone who is already like a brother, but in her private fantasies, she soon imagines herself refusing him as a marriage partner. Unlike her more reliable brother, Mr Knightley, he offends in matters of taste: being at times too self-consciously gallant, or evasive about his behaviour. The point about an ideal brother is that he is unobtrusively well-bred, and after Henry Tilney, Austen's ideal brothers are rarely humorous.

Instead of seeming timid or socially conservative, the fraternal model for an Austen marriage could be seen as proposing new standards of masculinity. The best brothers/husbands have usually had a close relationship with a woman before marriage, but only with a sister: hence Mr Darcy has rescued his younger sister Georgiana from the clutches of Mr Wickham, while Colonel Brandon, Marianne's reliable middle-aged lover in *Sense and Sensibility*, failed to save his adoptive sister, Eliza (an orphaned poor relation) from a succession of bad relationships, but is drawn to Marianne because she reminds him of his 'unfortunate sister'. Mr Bingley and Edmund appear backed by two sisters, Henry Tilney by one. In each novel, the man is introduced with good domestic credentials: he already knows what women are like, but not from having had a sexual relationship with one. His manner towards his future wife is similarly diffident, considerate, respectful and unthreatening – except for Henry Tilney who teases Catherine like a younger sister. Elizabeth even shocks Georgiana by teasing Darcy, and making him loosen up: 'By Elizabeth's instructions she began to comprehend that a woman may take liberties with her husband, which a brother will not always allow in a sister more than ten years younger than himself.'[14] The ideal Austen man welcomes his wife to an extended family as well as continued connections with her own sibling group. Henry Crawford stands alone as overtly sexual in his intentions, and he is left alone at the end of the novel.

In marked contrast to Austen's novels, Mary Shelley's *Frankenstein* (1818), published the same year as *Northanger Abbey*, expresses strong reservations about sibling marriages; yet Elizabeth Lavenza, Frankenstein's bride, is not in fact his blood relation, but only an adopted sister. Victor calls her: 'my more than sister – the beautiful and adored companion of all occupations and my pleasures.'[15] He is never quite sure what to call her: regarding her as a 'possession' of his own, he calls her his 'cousin'; while Elizabeth, writing to him in chapter 22, also struggles to explain the relationship:

> We were affectionate playfellows during childhood, and, I believe, dear and valued friends to one another as we grew older. But as brother and sister often entertain a lively affection towards each

other, without desiring a more intimate union, may not such also be our case? (p. 227)

This is Elizabeth's method of accounting for Victor's evasiveness about their relationship, which his mother hoped to see cemented by marriage. Victor's blurring of his mother's and Elizabeth's images in the nightmare he has immediately after creating the monster, suggests that the incest taboo is uppermost in his mind: its graphic illustration occurring when it does connects the usurpation of God's/woman's life-creating powers with the forbidden desire for his own mother–sister. When he destroys the monster's half-built female companion, he is also, in a sense, destroying its sister (offspring of the same parent), again resisting the incest drive on behalf of another. But because incestuous relationships are at the heart of the novel (even within the De Lacey family, Felix's future wife, Safie, lives with him first like a sister, with his blood sister, Agatha), the incest taboo halts the growth of family life. Foundling, orphaned, foster-sisters/daughters who join the established families in the novel quickly become too closely enmeshed with them to marry the sons. Yet, the novel implies, the only women men *want* to marry are sister-substitutes.

The Brontë novels

Wuthering Heights takes up the problem where Mary Shelley left it, with Catherine Earnshaw's dilemma over whether to marry a brother or a stranger, Heathcliff, or Edgar Linton. Without ever revealing the truth about Heathcliff, Emily Brontë scatters just enough tantalizing clues about his origins to hint at the possibility of incest. Mr Earnshaw 'took to Heathcliff strangely' after bringing him home from Liverpool, and the child was given 'the name of a son who had died in childhood'.[16] She is also convinced that the relationship will be unchanged by her marriage: she will never be truly 'separated' from Heathcliff, and will be able to help his career with her husband's money. These are essentially the terms in which one might talk about a brother rather than a lover, or even a spiritual companion. Moreover, in denying Heathcliff's ability to feel love, Catherine behaves like a sister disbelieving in her brother's capacity for romance; yet to see Heathcliff *only* as Catherine's brother underestimates the violent affinity between the two. When Catherine insists that she *is* Heathcliff – ' "he's always, always in my mind – not as a pleasure, any more than I am always a pleasure to myself – but as my own being" ' (p. 122) – she seems to be expressing the Hegelian idea that consciousness has 'self-existence only in the self-existence of the other. Each is the mediating term to the other, through which each mediates and unites itself with itself'.[17] In sublating the other independent being, – which combines notions of destroying and preserving – the first sublates its own self too, for this other is part of itself. They can prove themselves and each other only through a continuous life-and-death struggle, which is what happens with Catherine and Heathcliff. Shadia Drury comments: 'What Hegel means by mutual recognition is to find oneself in the other and the other in oneself' – which occurred in its most idealized form in the brother–sister relationship.[18] But because one cannot marry oneself, Brontë establishes an impossible ideal as the basis for her critique of marriage.

Crucially, for Emily Brontë, the brother–sister relationship is the most perfect, but also the most totally forbidden. All the duplicated 'sibling' pairs (which include near-siblings and cousins) are drawn together and then wrested violently apart – or else, in the second generation, the process is reversed. Whereas Heathcliff and Catherine are forbidden to share a bed, the second Catherine and her cousin Linton Heathcliff are forbidden to communicate, and then forcibly married; she and her other cousin Hareton are also kept apart and then married. When Heathcliff and Catherine look into the Lintons' drawing-room ('"Edgar and his sister had it entirely to themselves; shouldn't they have been happy? We should have thought ourselves in heaven!"' p. 89), two brother-sister dyads erupt into each other and fragment. The quarrelsome Lintons fighting over a dog represent an inversion of Heathcliff's devotion to Catherine which would prevent him ever envying her. The second Catherine later wishes Linton Heathcliff were her brother; when he wants her to be his wife, she warns him that '"people hate their wives, sometimes; but not their sisters and brothers, and if you were the latter, you would live with us, and papa would be as fond of you, as he is of me"' (p. 271). Why do people hate their wives, but not their brothers and sisters? For adults, it seems, relationships are poisoned by the consciousness of sexuality, while brothers and sisters accept each other without possessiveness or jealousy, ideally under the loving guardianship of a father such as Mr Earnshaw or Edgar Linton. The second half of the novel, which has so often been excused and explained away by disappointed critics, in effect clears the way for a near-sibling pair of cousins – Catherine Linton and Hareton Earnshaw – to marry each other: something that was impossible for Catherine Earnshaw and Heathcliff, though they were not (necessarily) brother and sister, whereas Catherine II and Hareton are the *children* of a brother and sister

(Catherine and Hindley). Hindley's wife Frances is the only partner drawn from outside this shrinking gene pool, but then Hindley is the most emotionally detached of the various brother-figures of the novel. One of the novel's many mysteries is the *lack* of any strong tie between Catherine and Hindley, in a plot otherwise swarming with emotionally desperate sibling pairs.

Many of the emotions expressed in the novel seem more like those of squabbling children than of adult partners, and three of the sibling-like alliances are never consummated (Heathcliff and Catherine, Catherine II and Linton Heathcliff, and Catherine II and Hareton – though we assume this will eventually happen). Childlike resentments and anxieties abound: when Heathcliff is initially introduced into the family, Hindley resents his usurpation of Mr Earnshaw's affections; later, after Catherine's stay at the Grange, Heathcliff feels embarrassed by his lack of educational accomplishments: something Hareton also senses in front of his cousin Catherine. Heathcliff regards Isabella less as a wife and more as a means of getting back at Edgar: her blue eyes, he tells Catherine, '"detestably resemble Linton's"'; while the young Linton Heathcliff, Edgar's nephew, looks to Nelly like his 'younger brother, so strong was the resemblance' (p. 235). Even Nelly regards Hindley as a blood relation: 'my old master and foster-brother', she calls him when he dies (p. 221). Seeing Cathy and Hareton as 'in a measure, my children' (p. 351) she also condones a brother–sister marriage; while the married Isabella and Catherine, both pining for their childhood homes, long specifically to be with their brothers again: '"Inform Edgar that I'd give the world to see his face again,"' Isabella tells Nelly (p. 173). Significantly, the second generation are all only children, whereas their parents were all halves of sibling pairs. The second-generation marriages close up the loose ends of the family, until they return to the original sibling pair: Catherine and Hareton replicating their parents, Catherine and Hindley. Both the Lintons and Heathcliff – the outsiders with whom the original pair became involved, disappear. Neither sibling nor servant, never physically her lover, Heathcliff proves, in his failure to leave any permanent impact on the Earnshaw and Linton families, who close up and exclude him, the impossibility of *becoming* a brother in a novel predominantly concerned with issues of sibship and cousinship.

Though less dense than *Wuthering Heights*, Anne Brontë's *The Tenant of Wildfell Hall* also opens in a sibling society; its hero, Gilbert Markham, spoilt by his sister Rose as well as his mother, and mixing with other sibling sets: the Wilsons, and Helen Graham and her brother, Frederick

Lawrence, wrongly supposed to be her lover. Lawrence himself seems to enjoy fuelling the speculation: when Gilbert asks him if he is in love with Helen, he gives 'a tittering laugh, as if he was highly amused at the idea'.[19] As it is, Lawrence is distinctly feminized and reminds Gilbert of his sister Helen. Having first attacked him as a rival for her affections, Gilbert is then strangely drawn to him:

> partly, from his increased cordiality to me, but chiefly on account of his close connection – both in blood and affection – with my adored Helen. I loved him for it better than I liked to express; and I took a secret delight in pressing those slender, white fingers, so marvellously like her own, considering he was not a woman, and in watching the passing changes in his fair, pale features, and observing the intonations of his voice – detecting resemblances which I wondered had never struck me before. (p. 397)

This dense and embarrassed confession of inappropriate emotion makes Frederick Lawrence into a version of his sister which seems akin to the sexual confusions of Shakespeare's cross-dressed romances: only in this case, both are men. Anne Brontë introduces a new variation on the sibling as ideal lover: the woman's brother as a substitute for the woman herself (in an inversion of this idea Braddon's Robert Audley is attracted to Clara Talboys because she reminds him of his close friend George). Moreover, Gilbert soon realizes that the most direct way to influence Lawrence is via gossip about Helen. He even persuades him not to marry Jane Wilson because of the malicious rumours she has spread about Helen – again fancying her to be a rival.

Anne Brontë, in fact, uses Frederick Lawrence as a crucial linchpin in her brother–sister romance: both as his sister's fancied lover, and as a masculine version of his sister that enables Gilbert to make friends with the family and come nearer to Helen. It is not just that Brontë, like Austen, and like her own sister Emily, concentrates her story on a tightly-knit community. It is that the community itself is little more than a collection of brothers and sisters who interact only with each other: an idea repeated in Helen's inset narrative where the Hargrave siblings – Millicent, Esther and their brother, Walter, become closely involved in Helen's social life.

Charlotte Brontë's novels at first glance seem wider-ranging in their introduction of new characters drawn from outside the family; but they, too, reveal a primary concern with issues of sibling rivalry. In *Jane Eyre*, John Reed, as the fat, overindulged wastrel, seems the direct embodiment of the resented brother mentioned in chapter 12: Jane insists that women 'need exercise for their faculties, and a field for their efforts as much as their brothers do', whereas John has done nothing but squander his opportunities.[20] Moreover, Mrs Reed hated her husband's sister, Jane's mother, 'for she was my husband's only sister, and a great favourite with him' (p. 260). She prefers John to Jane, even after death, because 'John is like me and like my brothers – he is quite a Gibson' (p. 260). Sibling loyalties and jealousies are persistent into adult life in all the Brontë novels and are the main force driving the plots. When Jane hears of her uncle John's legacy, by far the best part of it is the discovery that the Riverses are her cousins. She immediately adopts them as siblings. '"You,"' she tells St John, '"cannot at all imagine the craving I have for fraternal and sisterly love."' Unlike her cousin, she does not see herself forming new ties through marriage: she does not '"want a stranger – unsympathizing, alien, different from me; I want my kindred: those with whom I have full fellow-feeling"' (p. 413). For all the Brontës, this remained the strongest proof of authentic connection.

In Mr Rochester Jane meets the ideal older brother she never had: an intellectual equal with whom she feels above all kinship: for Jane the most important of human attributes. 'I felt at times as if he were my relation, rather than my master,' she says in chapter 15, at which point she 'ceased to pine after kindred' (p. 177). At the house party, Blanche Ingram's lack of evident kinship with Rochester is what chiefly convinces Jane that they are profoundly unsuited. By 'kinship' she means that she herself has 'certain tastes and feelings in common with him' (p. 204); Blanche Ingram would make more headway with him, in effect, if she behaved more like a sister than a flirtatious lover: 'It seems to me, that she might, by merely sitting quietly at his side, saying little and looking less, get nigher his heart' (p. 216). In many Victorian novels the sister provides an attractive role model that avoids the extremes of angel or whore: in sitting by her brother's side and saying little, she intrudes the least she can on his sense of selfhood. She is as near as she can be to *being* him, but it can be a highly repressive model which largely effaces the sister as a separate being with her own identity. Ironically, of course, Jane rarely sits by Rochester's side saying little and sympathizing with him: she usually argues vigorously, forcing him to engage in logical debate, and enjoying the intellectual freedom sisters are supposed to have with their brothers.

St John Rivers poses the serious threat that he does because he is another idealized brother: a rewritten version of John Reed – earnest and hard-working, but a bully who feels he has a right to command his sisters. Unlike Rochester, he can operate emotionally *only* as a brother: he will marry Jane while feeling for her no more than for a sister. As they wrangle over the difference between brotherly and husbandly feelings, true sisters and sisters who are really cousins or wives, he assists Jane in arriving at sexual maturity. While he rejects the notion of 'adopted fraternity' (p. 431), which by his standards cannot cheat the proprieties, she insists: ' "You have hitherto been my adopted brother – and I, your adopted sister: let us continue as such: you and I had better not marry." ' Their relationship reaches crisis-point over his proposal to take her with him to India as a missionary's wife. At the time when the novel was written, it was still unusual for women to assist as missionaries in any role but as wives, though Linda Peterson has noted that by 1835 single women were being interviewed and approved for service with the Society for Promoting Female Education, 'and various sectarian groups were appointing both single and married women to go to India with missionary families and husbands.[21] Even blood-siblinghood would be too loose a tie for Rivers: an issue that is raised interestingly many years later in C. S. Forester's novel, *The African Queen* (1935). Opening with the serious illness of an English missionary, Samuel Sayer, the narrative voice comments that ill as he is, he cannot look to his sister for intimate nursing:

> Rose did not help him to undress – they were brother and sister and strictly brought up and it would have been impossible to her unless he had been quite incapable of helping himself – [22]

Unlike Jane, Rivers presumably senses that difficulties of this kind would occur: moreover, ' "a sister might any day be taken from me" ' – by marriage to another man – whereas he would have total control over a wife (p. 431). By this stage of the novel, however, Jane knows that what she feels for Rochester is more than 'kinship' in the innocent sense. When she finally returns to him, she has discovered that the ideal husband is he who combines the attributes of perfect brother with the sexual availability of a lover. Unlike her sister Emily, Charlotte distrusts the incestuous density of cousin marriages. But the brother substitute was what she discovered first, and this remains a key factor in her other novels.

In *Shirley*, Robert Moore is Caroline's cousin, the elder brother she never had in her reduced family – for whom the Yorke siblings provide a contrasting model. In *Villette*, Lucy Snowe, also without blood relatives, is brought up alongside John Graham Bretton, but so is Paulina

Home, his ideal little sister, and eventually his wife. For Paulina, the brother–sister relationship gives scope for the development of complex feelings she is too young to explain. She alternately nestles against Graham, seeming 'to feel by his feelings, to exist in his existence,' and when he comes home from school, greets him with 'a reprimand or a threat'.[23] She fantasizes about travelling abroad with him in the future: '"We intend going to Switzerland, and climbing Mount Blanck"' (p. 89). For her the older brother represents the widening of physical and emotional experience, as he also does for Lucy. Like Jane Eyre, Lucy is rescued at a point of extreme physical exhaustion and despair by a handsome and fortunate brother-figure – perhaps an ironic inversion of the hapless Branwell who had been so close a companion in childhood, but so unable to look after anyone, let alone his sisters, in adulthood – and like Paulina she finds through Dr John an extension of her pleasures: 'Under his guidance,' she says when she is recovering from her collapse, 'I saw, in that one happy fortnight, more of Villette, its environs, and its inhabitants, than I had seen in the whole eight months of my previous residence' (pp. 271–2). Perplexed himself by their connection, he calls her his '"poor little god-sister (if there be such a relationship)"' (p. 327). But she cannot be his little sister in the way Paulina can. He only ever sees her in non-sexual terms, and even suggests that if she had been a boy, '"instead of a girl – my mother's god-son instead of her god-daughter – we should have been good friends"' (p. 401).

When John is reunited with Polly, their relationship resumes in Villette largely on the basis of their childhood games of teasing and spoiling; their greatest pleasure arises from recalling the old days in Bretton, and trying to define the exact nature of their former relationship. The emotional freedom of those days is what excites them most:

> He reminded her that she had once gathered his head in her arms, caressed his leonine graces, and cried out, 'Graham, I *do* like you!' He told her how she would set a foot-stool beside him, and climb by its aid to his knee. At this day he could recall the sensation of her little hands smoothing his cheek, or burying themselves in his thick mane. He remembered the touch of her small forefinger, placed half tremblingly, half curiously, in the cleft in his chin, the lisp, the look with which she would name it 'a pretty dimple', then seek his eyes and question why they pierced so, telling him he had a 'nice, strange face – far nicer, far stranger, than either his mamma or Lucy Snowe'. (p. 519)

There is something peculiarly Victorian about this passage: the child's innocent love-making as she explores the contours of the adult male, protected by her own girlish naivety, and by the pseudo brother–sister relationship which allows them a physical freedom permitted by no other connection. In having been able to express her feelings for Graham as a child, Paulina is saved the immodesty of having to declare them as an adult. All their love-making was done when they were temporary brother and sister at home under the guardianship of Mrs Bretton and M. de Bassompierre, their 'foster' parents, when Graham partly taught her to read.

Polly and Graham/Dr John are well matched in their good looks, while Lucy and M. Paul are drawn by an affinity, which he also recognizes: their personalities may be diametric opposites, he tells her, but they look startlingly similar: '"Do you observe that your forehead is shaped like mine – that your eyes are cut like mine? Do you hear that you have some of my tones of voice? Do you know that you have many of my looks?"' (p. 457) M. Paul's offer of a closer relationship is couched in terms of siblingship: '"a lonely man like me, who has no sister,"' he explains to Lucy in the chapter headed 'Fraternity', '"must be but too glad to find in some woman's heart a sister's pure affection"' (p. 501). For M. Paul these are unthreatening conditions: the notion of the 'sister's pure affections' keeps the relationship strictly platonic. But for Lucy, initially happier than a bride, the language of sisterhood quickly becomes frustratingly ambiguous: 'I was willing to be his sister, on condition that he did not invite me to fill that relation to some future wife of his' (p. 503). Moreover, as soon as he has made this declaration, he begins to ignore her (as indeed a careless blood brother might a sister). For Lucy, whose relationship with everyone else in the novel is uncertain and shifting, the term 'sister' joins all the other imprecise titles people give her – whether 'god-sister' or 'friend'. As they draw closer, M. Paul himself is puzzled: '"I called myself your brother," he said; "I hardly know what I am – brother – friend – I cannot tell"' (p. 512). By breaking down the natural inhibitions between men and women in Villette, the term allows an easy slippage into a discreetly sexual relationship: though the fact that Paul and Lucy are prevented from marrying makes their 'siblinghood' almost literal – as well as symbolic of Brontë's sense that truly companionate marriages between people who feel like 'kin' are all but impossible to find in the real world.

Unlike Emily and Anne Brontë, who are intrigued by the convoluted connections of blood brothers and sisters, Charlotte looks for brother substitutes among men who are not actual brothers. The desirable husband – Rochester, Robert Moore, Dr John, M. Paul, and in *The Professor*, William Crimsworth – is the man who behaves most like an elder brother: teasing as well as protective, caustic, intellectual, evasive. His foreignness as a man is counterbalanced by his affinity with women: his sharing a house with a mother or sister-type; his work as clergyman, doctor or teacher bringing him into regular close contact with women. Moreover, Charlotte Brontë's heroines meet their husbands repeatedly in female settings: in drawing-rooms and school-rooms, among girls and sisters and wards, where the man must adapt to an indoors world of firesides, conversations, needlework and physical fragility.

Family sagas of the 1860s

This is very much the world, too, of Elizabeth Sewell's and Charlotte Yonge's family stories, where girls come to see their older brothers as models of male perfection which no outside suitor can match; perhaps, too, a safer option than the leap into the unknown and risky world of sexual relations in a new industrialized society, with all its fresh uncertainties. By the middle of the century, passionate attachment to a brother had become a staple feature of women's fiction: a clinging to home as a refuge from insecurity and emotional emptiness. Clara Talboys, in *Lady Audley's Secret* (1862) explains that because her father allowed her neither friends nor lovers, she has focused entirely on her brother George: '"I have had no one but my brother. All the love that my heart can hold has been centred upon him."'[24] The most extreme example of brother-worship, however, occurs in Elizabeth Sewell's novel *Ursula* (1858), which tells the story of a younger sister so devoted to her older brother Roger that she is both dismayed by his marriage to a frivolous companion of her own, and until the last few chapters of the novel, completely unable to contemplate any love-affair for herself. Roger is both a father-substitute and a kind of god to her: 'It came across me one day, when I noticed him just as he rose up from his prayers, that if I were to see him in heaven, he could scarcely be anything different.'[25] Assuming they will live together for ever and never be separated, Ursula speaks of him repeatedly as a kind of husband – shocked that he intends going to Canada without her:

> 'If God has joined us together, why are we to be put asunder?'
> 'That is said of husband and wife, not of brother and sister,' he replied.

'And if I were your wife you would take me with you?'
'I should feel it my duty,' was the answer. (p. 83)

She comments bitterly: '"A wife couldn't love you better than I do, Roger!"' Though Roger is undoubtedly fond of her, she herself recognizes the inequality of their feelings. His pet-name for her, 'Trot', is serviceable rather than romantic, and stresses her homely ordinariness: as a man he is freer to seek change in the outside world. Gradually, she comes to accept the unrealistic nature of her devotion to Roger, but she implies throughout that sexual feelings (though she never acknowledges having any) are unimportant to her in her need for male company. 'I had found in him all I needed to satisfy my imagination and my reverence; and my affection had indeed so engrossed me that I scarcely thought about other men except to feel that they were his inferior' (p. 323). Given Sewell's devotion to her own elder brother William, it is hard to know how to judge passages such as this (of which there are many in this long novel). Certainly her friends think Ursula's feelings are excessive; they gently remind her that Roger needs an emotional life of his own, and she is finally convinced by the mature adult advice of the land surveyor, John Hervey, whom she eventually marries. So much of the novel is taken up with examination of Ursula's utter dedication to her brother's welfare and willingness to sacrifice the rest of her life to him, that such feelings are not to be taken lightly. Moreover, Roger is also clearly affected by similar emotions, in that he marries a little sister substitute he can pet. It is only the constant reminder of God's providence having ordained other kinds of relationship that finally persuades Ursula of her mistaken course in life.

Charlotte Yonge's writings also glorify the brother–sister relationship as sexually purer than any heterosexual pairing. Like Sewell's they are ambivalent about the need to abandon such feelings and mature into adult relationships. In *The Pillars of the House* (1873), for example, most of the large orphaned Underwood family split off into brother–sister pairs who function like couples within the enormous sibling structure. Allegiances sometimes change within this couple-based structure, but the strength of feeling is usually mutual: brothers need sisters as much as sisters need brothers – albeit sometimes as parent substitutes. When the crippled and artistic sister Geraldine receives a marriage proposal, her feelings for her eldest brother Felix (to whom she feels 'wedded') make it impossible for her to accept – much to Felix's relief: 'She had seemed so set apart from marriage, so peculiarly dependent on him, that it had been to her that he had turned with a sort of certainty as his companion in the life of self-sacrifice that he knew to lie before him.' Geraldine fully reciprocates his feelings, as she tells him: ' "When I lean against you, I have got my home, and my rest, and all I want here. I never go away from you but I feel that I *do* want you so; and when one feels that, what's the use of looking out for somebody else?" '[26] Although Geraldine does eventually marry her suitor, Mr Grinstead, this is not until many years later, when Felix is dead.

Nor is this an isolated episode within Yonge's vast oeuvre as a writer of family sagas. Intense love between brothers and sisters is seen as so normal in her families that they rarely comment on it, except with an amused and affectionate smile. Harry and Mary of *The Daisy Chain* (1856) are well known for their passionate devotion to one another, if anything intensified when Harry begins his career as a sailor. On his returns, Mary goes wild with delight; in his absences she sleeps with his daguerreotype under her pillow; when she too gets a marriage proposal, she suffers from a conflict of loyalties, remembering that once when Harry had returned to find another sister married, he had commented: ' "Well, Molly, I'm glad it wasn't you that have married. Mind, you mustn't marry till I do." '[27] It takes another of Harry's homecomings and many outbursts of weeping for Mary to be convinced that this was not a prohibition against marriage altogether. Nevertheless, Yonge's comments as narrator imply that in marrying the dull schoolmaster, Charles Cheviot, Mary has settled for less of a man than the 'young lion', Harry, whose swashbuckling masculinity makes him the May family's hero. The wedding is 'very unexciting' (p. 252), and Charles Cheviot comes between Mary and her sister Ethel, spoiling their affectionate companionship in a way that never happened with Harry.

One further tempestuous example of the many Yonge surveys in her novels is the intense devotion of Theodora Martindale to her brother Arthur in *Heartsease* (1854), and again, a disloyal marriage is the trigger for pathological jealousy. When the story opens, Arthur has just married the sixteen-year-old Violet, whom Theodora is quick to dismiss as a frivolous and hysterical child-bride, incapable of providing any intellectual companionship. In vain, she tries to stifle her feelings for him: 'Books, lectures, conversation, dancing, could not banish that craving for her brother.'[28] Other kinds of love do occur to her, and she even becomes engaged herself for a while, but Theodora – like Sewell's Ursula, and Yonge's Geraldine – cannot persuade herself that 'normal' heterosexual love matches up to the love of brother and sister: 'There was another kind of affection,' she tells herself, 'not half so valuable in her eyes as fraternal love; it made fools of people, but then they were happy in their blindness, and could keep it to themselves' (p. 123). Theodora's dismissal of non-fraternal love implies a fear of sexuality: a sense that it risks a loss of dignity – perhaps because the emotional commitment has to be active and spontaneous, rather than part of a sibling package. Yonge's repeated emphasis on brother–sister dyads as nurturing, reassuring and safe suggests, too, a shrinking from the physical commitment to an outsider that pervades her fictional families. Yet many of these relationships are almost sexual. ' "I wish you weren't too big for rocking, Baby," ' Geraldine's older brother Edgar says in *Pillars* when sexual jealousies of various kinds threaten to upset her relationship with an older sister (II, 57).Yonge constantly teeters on the brink of acknowledging the dangerous emotions she details, while stopping short of any overt admission that they are incestuous. Treating brother–sister relationships with passionate sympathy, she nevertheless ensures that most of her sibling pairs are split up, usually by death or marriage. Family life rarely stands still for long in Yonge's novels: her children are forced to grow up and leave the idyllic world in which brothers and sisters dream of growing old and keeping house together. One of her strongest pairs, Ethel and Norman May in *The Daisy Chain*, who are intellectual as well as emotional companions, are drastically separated by Norman's marriage and emigration to New Zealand as a missionary. True to her family loyalties, however, Ethel fails to marry, but remains as her father's wifely confidante. One never entirely loses the sense in Yonge's novels that to marry is to settle for something inferior to sibling love – something coarser – however necessary it must be in a realistic world.

Dickens and George Eliot

Between the deaths of the Brontës and the rise of George Eliot, heroines of English fiction repeatedly fall in love with brother-substitutes, especially in Dickens's novels. Dickens is of course well known for his fondness for girl-brides in his fiction: specifically, however, many of them are *sister*-brides, especially Agnes Wickfield, who is a more sober and reliable character than her predecessor Dora, or David Copperfield's child/sister Little Em'ly. In *Great Expectations* (1860–1), Pip dismisses one sister-substitute, Biddy, in favour of the more glamorous Estella: like himself the foster child of Miss Havisham, but also the real child of Magwitch, who can be seen as Pip's own foster father. In *Martin Chuzzlewit* (1843–4), brother and sister Tom and Ruth Pinch set up house together like husband and wife before Ruth falls in love with Tom's friend, John Westlock – whose marriage proposal again causes a conflict of loyalties. Ruth has found excitement enough in keeping house for Tom and making him magnificent beefsteak puddings: 'She saw nothing but Tom. Tom was the first and last thing in the world.'[29] Whereas Tom is a comic character, Ruth is the idealized little sister who brings life into his bachelor existence. As they belong to different literary registers their idyllic life together can only be shortlived. Ruth, who is not the fright or the frump the Miss Pecksniffs assume any sister of Tom Pinch's to be, must be married to someone from the serious adult male world. The best that can happen to Tom is a lifelong invitation to share their domestic bliss.

In *Dombey and Son* (1847–8), Dickens's most extensive study of the brother–sister relationship, Florence Dombey, deprived of Paul, takes Walter Gay as his replacement. Symbolically, Dickens erases their class differences through the Mrs Brown episode in chapter 6, when Florence, robbed and clothed in rags, is found wandering in the street, explaining her identity as ' "my little brother's only sister" '. Taking up her dropped shoe, Walter 'put it on the little foot as the Prince in the story might have fitted Cinderella's slipper on'.[30] When he returns after being presumed drowned (the same happens with Harry May in *The Daisy Chain*), Florence 'had no thought of him but as a brother, a brother rescued from the grave; a shipwrecked brother saved and at her side; and rushed into his arms. In all the world, he seemed to be her hope, her comfort, refuge, natural protector' (p. 784). Given the ambiguous moral status of any male suitor before he has proposed and made his intentions honourable, the attractions of a brother as 'natural protector' are obvious. The brother-as-lover seems a safe alternative to the man who is unrelated to the woman, an unknown quantity, with no common memories and roots. He is above all, morally reliable, and at first, sexually neutral: Walter knows that ' "to be loved and trusted as your brother, is the next gift I could receive and prize" ' – after seeing how she spoke to him on the night they were parted (p. 804). Typically, however, as in Florence Dombey's case, the woman stubbornly goes on calling herself 'sister' and her lover 'brother' long after he would like things to be put on a different footing. Walter quietly persuades her otherwise: ' "I left a child. I find a woman," ' he tells her (p. 804). Emphasizing his continued wish to 'protect and cherish' her – the special privilege of a brother, Walter points out that this is also the husband's role, and she might give him a new name other than 'brother'. Once they are married, Walter accepts that he still has to share her affections with her dead brother Paul, and chapter 57 ends with the waves murmuring of 'Paul and Walter... of love, eternal and illimitable, not bound by the confines of this world...' (p. 908).

The most famous brother–sister novel of the nineteenth century – to which this chapter has been leading – *The Mill on the Floss* (1860) thus emerges from a context of intense interest in the theme at mid-century. It takes up the dual image of the brother as courteous, feminized man (in Philip Wakem) and as stern judge and father substitute (in Tom). It is, however, different from most of the other novels discussed in this chapter because it concerns the love of blood-siblings rather than a woman's feelings for a brother-*like* lover. Its closest parallel is with Elizabeth Sewell's *Ursula* in that both novels deal with an emotionally unequal relationship: the sister depends on the brother more than he does on her. Her life revolves around him in a way that is simply not reciprocated. On the other hand, the wider age-gap between Roger and Ursula makes him more of a father-figure, and unlike Tom Tulliver, he marries in the course of the novel. Ursula, moreover, travels to France and assists a neighbouring gentry family through their personal and financial problems, whereas Maggie is largely passive and untravelled. George Eliot strips the sibling relationship of any distractions. Tom has no lover of his own (unless we accept a few minuscule hints about Lucy), and Maggie has no natural role-models in her life other than the depressing example of 'Aunt Gritty' – another downtrodden sister alternately bullied and patronized by a heavy-handed brother.

Eliot admitted that the brother–sister relationship was always one of her 'best-loved subjects', and the novel is especially interesting in the way it explores the brother's and sister's roles in relation to each other.[31] Maggie constantly creates a nurturing role as sister-carer for her brother, only to have her offers rejected (when it comes to it, she becomes Bob Jakin's lodger rather than Tom's housekeeper as she originally planned). Her talents are always superfluous, just as Tom's are: they are mirror-images of each other's displacement from the right sphere of opportunity. Both fantasize fruitlessly about the ways in which they could impress people: Maggie with her cleverness, and Tom with his rigid fairness and physical prowess. But much as there is no call for Tom's expertise in playground-combat once he has left school, no one needs Maggie's story-telling abilities once she has grown up. In fact, although the novel was originally to be called 'Sister Maggie,' much of it is about brother Tom. It is Tom's schooldays at Mr Stelling's we witness, not Maggie's at Miss Firniss's, and Tom's quest for employment which is the later focus of the narrative, not Maggie's (until she has returned from her abortive trip with Stephen Guest). Though Maggie might have been 'a match for the lawyers' (p. 15), in Mr Tulliver's words, her articulacy is never needed. The novel, in effect, re-enacts the practices of Victorian society in seeing the man's needs as fundamental and the woman's as marginal, the man's skills as essential, and the woman's as incidental.

For her their shared childhood is the only emotional reference-point of any importance: she returns to it whenever she is in trouble. He, on the other hand, looks to a future in which he metes out harsh but fair justice: 'it seemed as if he held a glass before her to show her her own folly and weakness – as if he were a prophetic voice predicting her future fallings – '[32] The brother quickly becomes his father's representative, only without his father's soft spot for 'the little wench'. As a brother Tom functions largely as a paternalistic judge. When not judging he is earning money: something Maggie does as a teacher, only this part of the narrative is suppressed. Instead, we see her selling fancy goods at a frivolous bazaar – 'playing at shops', in effect – while Tom struggles for a place in the adult male world where men talk about 'a new market for Swedish bark' (p. 216) and 'sending out a bit of cargo to foreign ports' (p. 292). Even as a child he 'earns' more money than she does, as he harshly reminds her: ' "I always have half-sovereigns and sovereigns for my Christmas boxes, because I shall be a man, and you only have five-shilling pieces, because you're only a girl" ' (p. 30).

While the children are still young, the most complimentary way in which they can view each other is as a desired brother or sister. Whereas Tom wishes Lucy instead of Maggie were his sister (p. 78), just as Mrs Tulliver wishes Lucy were her daughter, Philip wishes he had a little sister like Maggie (p. 165). All the characters see the brother–sister relationship in terms of intensely expressed affection, but also as a place to exercise power and intellectual superiority. Maggie's fantasy is of keeping house for Tom and telling him ' "everything he doesn't know" ' (p. 34), whereas Tom 'meant always to take care of her, make her his housekeeper, and punish her when she did wrong' (p. 34). Reversing Tom's principles, Maggie later assumes that Philip would have been a more tolerant brother: ' "You would have loved me well enough to bear with me, and forgive me anything" ' (p. 308). Underlying the harsh reality of her actual relationship with Tom is the shadowy possibility of a much gentler, more emotionally responsive sibling relationship with Philip, who is also more of an intellectual equal. She subsequently looks to Philip to teach her when Tom goes out, and Philip begs to be her 'brother and teacher' when they meet again as young adults (p. 309). Their precarious relationship as 'brother and sister in secret' (p. 316) permits them to exchange self-conscious and uneasy kisses, but as in *Dombey and Son* and *Villette*, the misleading, make-believe term soon becomes problematical. What exactly *are* two unrelated people who call themselves 'brother and sister'? Two friends who have agreed to a non-sexual relationship that nevertheless allows them to kiss and be affectionate with each other? The underlying assumptions of such a pact are from the first fraught with instability, as those involved usually recognize. '"No, Maggie, I can't give you up – unless you are deceiving me – unless you really only care for me as if I were your brother,"' Philip urges Maggie at the height of his frustration with the term (p. 316). Built into the pretended relationship are elements that will immediately destabilize it.

As Joseph A. Boone and Deborah E. Nord point out, both Philip Wakem and Stephen Guest 'represent in Maggie's psychic life extensions of her brother'. While Philip reflects her own marginality, Stephen recalls Tom's 'commanding masculinity'.[33] Moreover, in her dream of the Virgin of St Ogg's (6.14), Philip turns into Tom, and Stephen drowns with her on the boat, just as Tom will do. All three want to make her act according to their own idea of what is appropriate for her nature: all recognizing her repressed sexuality, and predicting its likely outbreak. Philip predicts that she will be '"thrown into the world some day, and then every rational satisfaction of your nature that you deny now, will assault you like a savage appetite"' (p. 309); Tom puts it more cruelly as '"You would be led away to do anything"' (p. 369). In forcing her to choose between himself and Philip, he presents her with a dilemma as impossible as Catherine's over Heathcliff and Edgar: only in Eliot's novel, a third option is introduced in the form of Stephen Guest, who pushes Philip into second place as admonitory brother. All three choices are no choices at all: the Wakems are arch-enemies of the Tullivers, and Stephen Guest is all but engaged to Lucy. It would be impossible for Maggie to marry either of them, as events prove; and in returning to Tom, who has always cast a blight on her life, much as she has on his, she can only bring further destruction. So often seen as sentimental, the ending of the novel gives Maggie only a moment's moral revenge: in their embrace, they drag each other into death, much as they have dogged each other's progress in life.

In *Daniel Deronda* (1876), the last text to be discussed in this chapter, Eliot extends her study of sibling pairs to cover three types who all share what might be seen as an excessive degree of (mainly) sister-to-brother devotion. Whereas Rosamond Vincy in *Middlemarch* is dismissive of her brother Fred, all the sisters in Eliot's final novel are unashamed brother-worshippers, with (Mirah excepted) no thought of marrying a lover of their own. Hans Meyrick, who would like to marry Mirah, disqualifies himself by his jealousy of Mordecai and non-recognition of the sibling bond: according to him she has taken to worshipping him '"with such looks of loving devoutness that I am ready to wish myself in his place."'[34] Yet Hans's own sisters adore him, as does Anna Gascoigne her brother Rex. Even this late in the century, George Eliot describes a 'sibling marriage' which consoles for other disappointments, and is of uneven intensity. '[Rex] returned Anna's affection as fully as could be expected of a brother whose pleasures apart from her were more than the sum total of hers; and he had never known a stronger love' (p. 87), the narrator comments on the pair's limited experiences. Devastated by Gwendolen's rejection of his marriage proposal, Rex can only return to the grateful bosom of his sister, and a shared utopian fantasy of emigrating to Canada. '"Rex would want some one to take care of him, you know – some one to keep house. And we shall never, either of us, be married,"' Anna pleads with their father (p. 119). Coming early on in the novel, the Gascoignes' naive sibling attachment is displaced by Deronda's profounder love for Mirah: but she, too, is an ideal little sister, prepared to follow him to a distant country. At the end of her writing career, Eliot both exposes the immaturity of the woman emotionally fixated on her brother, but also makes the novel's only successful marriage a sibling type; Mordecai's death symbolically marking the transition from sister to wife which Mirah must undergo.

Conclusion

The ideal marriage in the Victorian novel adopts into the family someone who is almost a member of the family already. This is what happens with Mr Knightley, Fanny Price, Walter Gay, Daniel Deronda, and Gaskell's Molly Gibson who in *Wives and Daughters* (1866) is seen as replacing the Hamleys' dead daughter Fanny. '"I am his sister,"' Molly tells herself when she observes Cynthia's shallow love for Roger, which contrasts so strongly with her own. '"That old bond is not done away with, though he is too much absorbed by Cynthia to speak about it just now. His mother called me 'Fanny', it was almost like an adoption. I must wait and watch, and see if I can do anything for my brother."'[35] As Molly recognizes, however, not *really* being brother and sister makes their relationship strained and difficult once a consciousness of their status as potential lovers is acknowledged, and their story recaps several features of the other pseudo-sibling romances already discussed in this chapter: the initial rescue from a state of emotional self-absorption (Fanny Price, Molly Gibson, Maggie Tulliver, Jane Eyre and, Lucy

Snowe), and additional physical danger (Jane Eyre, Florence Dombey, Mirah Lapidoth); the necessary gap in age and experience, which makes the husband an ideal educator (Mr Knightley, Edmund Bertram, Rochester, Roger Hamley, Daniel Deronda); the opportunity to visit freely and become used to each other in a domestic setting; and a sharing of family concerns and problems. The misunderstandings which are so rife in these novels can be unravelled like the misunderstandings of siblings who have to go on living together. When a marriage is constructed on a different basis, and the husband is nothing like a brother – striking examples are the Helen Graham/Arthur Huntingdon match, or the disastrous marriages between Rosamond Vincy and Tertius Lydgate, Dorothea Brooke and Edward Causaubon, or Paul Dombey and Edith Granger – a solution remains elusive, and in most cases death provides the only way out.

All brother–sister plots in Victorian novels are densely constructed on the basis of a limited social range. In effect, the central characters never meet anyone who is neither a blood-sibling nor a sibling substitute; typically, relationships are thwarted by the shadow of the blood tie (or its symbolic substitute), though ultimately cousin marries cousin, Jewish man Jewish woman, social misfit, social misfit. Though the brother type may vary from the ultra-masculine Rochester and Heathcliff to the milder Roger Hamley or Walter Gay, for all its problematical status, marriage to the ideal brother confirms a concept of masculinity that is fundamentally woman-centred. Though he may be widely travelled, like Heathcliff, Rochester, Walter Gay, and Roger Hamley, he always returns and resumes the relationship with a woman who feels completely at home with him. Essentially this type of novel rewrites the male as domesticated and attuned to the distresses of disappointment and neglect, though he (like the typical brother) may also be the cause of them. The brother/husband looks inward, to the home; he cares and nurtures; he understands emotional need, if sometimes with the slowness of a brother who has taken his sister for granted. Above all, he is familiar, a man with real qualities of companionship. 'If only Hartley had been my sister,' says Charles Arrowby, hero of Iris Murdoch's novel *The Sea, The Sea* (1978), 'I could have looked after her so happily and cared for her so tenderly.'[36] This, I would suggest, is the abiding image of the brotherly husband, which most mid-Victorian novelists upheld as their ideal.

5
The Family Revenge Novel

'Now, the fact, – the painful fact, – in the history of human affections is that, of all natural relations, the least satisfactory is the fraternal.'[1]

'Why did I dream that my brother was my foe?'[2]

'A young man and his sister; the former characterized by a diseased imagination and morbid feelings; the latter beautiful and virtuous, and instilling something of her own excellence into the wild heart of her brother, but not enough to cure the deep taint of his nature.' The beginning of Hawthorne's short story, 'Alice Doane's Appeal' (1835) sounds like the opening of a fairy tale, the usual way of recounting stories of deeply ingrained sibling rivalry. In fact, Hawthorne's characters are the sole survivors of a night attack by Indians, living a life of intense attachment and 'lonely sufficiency' together, until their sibling paradise is threatened by the sister's feelings for another man, Walter Brome, Leonard Doane's counterpart, who, unlike the brother, has the right to sexual relations with the sister: 'Now, here was a man, whom Alice might love with all the strength of sisterly affection, added to that impure passion which alone engrosses all the heart.'[3] Ironically, Walter Brome turns out to be Leonard Doane's twin brother, destined by the machinations of a wizard to 'tempt his unknown sister to guilt' (p. 277) and be killed by his brother. The story weirdly incorporates all the classic ingredients of the Romantic sibling horror story: an intermingling of sex and death, incest and fratricide, frustrated desire and mistaken vengeance. The brother as ideal companion and lover quickly transforms into the jealous murderer; the virtuous sister into a sexual prize for another man. The relationship of brother and sister, which is the devotion of a couple, but a couple who cannot marry, was for many nineteenth- and twentieth-century writers a means of exploring the inherent rivalries and jealousies of a social life based on intractable family configurations.

If the brother was the ideal lover for many nineteenth-century women novelists, he was also the archetypal rival: privileged from birth by virtue of his sex, educated and planned for, the inheritor of the family fortunes and property, and in course of time, his father's substitute as lawgiver and domestic ruler. Assumed to be loyal to one another, siblings from legend, from the Bible, fairy stories and secular literature, are traditionally arch-enemies, plotting against the father's favourite: Cain against Abel, Jacob against Esau, the ugly sisters against Cinderella; in Shakespeare, Duke Frederick against Rosalind's father, the banished Duke, Oliver against Orlando, Sebastian against Prospero. The best-known examples are same-sex rivalries – usually brother against brother – with a kingdom or an inheritance as the fought-over prize.

The cross-currents of feeling in brother–sister pairs are less easy to summarize, and more complex in their operation. In the Grimms' fairy tales, for example, wicked stepmothers tend to punish the brothers more than the sisters (Hansel is fattened up for the witch's dinner in 'Hansel and Gretel'); the brothers are also more likely to be transformed into animals. In 'The Twelve Brothers,' they become ravens (swans in a similar story featuring six brothers); in 'The Brother and Sister', the brother is turned into a fawn. In each story, what complicates the plot is the sole sister's implication in her brother's misfortunes. While the sister is entirely loyal to her brothers – even prepared to risk her own life to save them – though innocent in deed, and left in human form, she plays an ambiguous role in their lives. The twelve brothers, for example, become ravens when their sister plucks twelve lilies from the garden: they had already fled their home on her birth because their father would have killed them to make her (unusually) the sole heir to his fortune. In this and 'The Six Swans', their sister can restore them to human form only by remaining dumb for several years. What we see enacted in the Grimms' tales is a dynamics of vicarious guilt and punishment involving not only wicked stepmothers and their stepchildren, but also blood-brothers and sisters caught up in the larger machinations of wilful and irrational adults. While the brothers are physically transformed into beasts and birds (symbolizing their lower natures), the sisters' family loyalty is tested by their silence and forbearance as wives and house-keepers.

Mark Poster, in his *Critical Theory of the Family* (1978), argues that the important issue in understanding how families work is not their size, but their 'emotional structures'. Steven Mintz, alternatively, refers to the 'internal dynamics' of Victorian homes, and suggests that 'much remains to be learned about the emotional and power relationships' within them. He sees sibling ties as 'a focal point for larger cultural tensions and problems'.[4] Within family histories and structures, brothers and sisters act out the wider injustices of the cultural context in which they operate: so older brothers, sent to the best public school, followed by Oxford or Cambridge, are prepared in the home for future membership of the ruling classes, while their sisters are served last at meals, or their education begrudged them, reflecting the second-class citizenship accorded to women in the outside world. As the real-life family histories discussed in Chapter 1 illustrate, many sisters were prepared to accept the inequalities inbuilt into Victorian family structures. They perhaps had little experience of anything different. Others, however, became aware that the golden boy was in reality the prodigal son; they chafed at the injustices of their family circumstances, and consciously or otherwise inscribed in their fiction the network of rivalries and resentments that underpinned the outwardly smooth-running household routines. The aim of this chapter is to examine the range of 'revenge fantasies' based on sibling rivalry that appear in nineteenth- and early twentieth-century literature, and to consider their significance as indicators of underlying tensions within the gender-balance of the family. These fantasies may extend to murder (both fear of being murdered by a sibling, as in Charles Brockden Brown's *Wieland*, and a desire to commit the murder, as in Trollope's *Can You Forgive Her?*), or may stem from a wish to see the sibling humiliated in some way.

As Juliet Mitchell argues, the role of siblings may traditionally have been downplayed by psychoanalysts, but in reality they 'haunt our social and emotional existence'. Siblings are the first people to displace us in the world and push us to one side: we are 'annihilated by someone who stands where we are'.[5] Hysterics often feel displaced: hence the crucial role played by siblings in the development of this condition. Mitchell's argument is that brothers and sisters are significant, if muted, figures in the background of the famous psychoanalytical case-histories now familiar to critics. Who, for example, remembers Dora's elder brother? Yet he figures in her first dream as shut into his bedroom by their mother and at risk from death by fire. Little Hans ('A Phobia in a Five-Year-old Boy') frequently discusses with his father and Freud his hostile feelings for his little sister: 'Hans's repressed wish was very transparent. His mother asked him if he would rather Hanna were not there, to which he said "Yes." '[6] But Freud's fullest exploration of sibling relationships occurs in his account of a lifelong struggle between an older sister and a younger brother in his 'History of an Infantile Neurosis' (the 'Wolf Man').

The analysis is recounted from the brother's point of view, and the brother is seen as the prime victim, but through Freud's discussion of the case, the sister's frustrations tell an alternative story. Two years older than her brother, she is 'lively, gifted, and precociously naughty'. As the younger brother seemed 'at first to have been a very good-natured, tractable, and even quiet child', his family used to say of him 'that he ought to have been the girl and his elder sister the boy'.[7] Beginning their childhood with the 'wrong' gendered characteristics (like Queen Victoria's first two children, the Princess Royal and the Prince of Wales), the two siblings developed a secret rivalry by which the sister tormented the brother with pictures of a wolf that terrified him; progressing from this to attempts at sexual abuse and seduction. When, under analysis, the boy began to dream, his dreams were 'concerned with aggressive actions on the boy's part against his sister or against the governess and with energetic reproofs and punishments on account of them' (p. 246). His fantasies of undressing his sister after her bath were meant to efface the memory of his own passivity under her sexual assaults, 'which later on seemed offensive to the patient's masculine self-esteem' (p. 248). As for the sister, her brilliant intellectual development, which eventually won her father's pride and approval, was destined for a premature end when she became depressed, worried that she was insufficiently good-looking, and poisoned herself abroad. Freud comments on the strained relationship between brother and sister:

> Independently of the question of seduction, our patient, while he was a child, found in his sister an inconvenient competitor for the good opinion of his parents, and he felt very much oppressed by her merciless display of superiority. Later on he especially envied her the respect which his father showed for her mental capacity and intellectual achievements, while he, intellectually inhibited as he was since his obsessional neurosis, had to be content with a lower estimation. (p. 250).

In his subsequent relationships with women, the brother sought out servants as lovers and sister-substitutes, with 'an intention of debasing his sister and of putting an end to her intellectual superiority, which he had formerly found so oppressive' (p. 251). When news arrived of his sister's death, the patient told Freud that 'he felt hardly a trace of grief.

He had to force himself to show signs of sorrow, and was able quite coolly to rejoice at having now become sole heir to the property' (p. 251). Unlike the fairy-tale stories of sibling rivalry, it is hard to tell here who was the wicked sibling and who the good. Both suffered from resentment of the other's apparently privileged position in the family, and were unable to outgrow the jealousies of their shared childhood.

Early nineteenth-century Gothic representations

Freud argues in his 'General Theory of the Neuroses' (1916–17) that children are far readier to express their feeling of wanting to get rid of brothers and sisters than they are of their parents; indeed, in dreams, siblings are symbolized as small animals or vermin.[8] Murder fantasies against rival siblings sound as if they should be commonplace (Freud thought they were[9]): the easiest and most obvious way to get rid of a hated rival. They happen constantly in the Brontë novels: for example when each of Jane Eyre's cousin-brothers, John Reed and St John Rivers, is punished with death, the first for physical, the second for psychological bullying; or when Heathcliff's enemies, Catherine's brother Hindley, and her husband Edgar, his brother-in-law, both die. In fact, however, actual brother–sister murders in fiction are rare, and when they happen, are a feature of the Gothic-Romantic tradition, rather than a later point in the nineteenth century, and more often of American literature than English; but the suggestion of them retains the power to thrill. Charles Brockden Brown's *Wieland* (1798), set in the familiar sibling society of the time (a brother and a sister become friends with another brother and sister, a sibling symmetry with which Emily Brontë plays havoc in *Wuthering Heights*), toys with the full horror of a brother contemplating murder of his sister: something that is suggested to him by the mysterious 'biloquist', Carwin, who, like Frankenstein's Monster, systematically destroys a whole family. The narrator of the story, Theodore Wieland's sister Clara, dreams of her brother beckoning her towards a pit: 'Why did I dream that my brother was my foe?' she wonders. The novel suggests that unspeakable as the husband's murder of his wife had been, the contemplated murder of a sister by her brother is too appalling to contemplate, a kind of violent incest as she considers killing him in self-defence: 'Death in this form, death from the hand of a brother, was thought upon with indescribable repugnance', Clara recalls (pp. 199–200). Even with her life in danger, Clara thinks she is being presumptuous to judge her brother, whom she continues to see as her moral superior, 'my heroic brother' (p. 206). Symbolically, she even blames herself for his suicide: 'He was stretched at my feet; and my hands were sprinkled with his blood as he fell' (p. 212). Theodore Wieland was the brilliant son of the family, the brother Clara looked to for happy companionship and moral leadership in the future. She never comes to terms with the fact that her idol has been corruptible, and might have killed her.

The question of which sibling killed which is more complex in Edgar Allan Poe's short story, 'The Fall of the House of Usher' (1839), where the brother Roderick is weakening in sympathy with his twin sister Madeline's mysterious wasting disease, and dreading an impending doom. As Leila S. May has observed, Madeline is destroyed by the 'family evil,' which can be interpreted as the nineteenth-century bourgeois domestic ideology which the selfless sister was supposed to uphold. When she breaks out of the tomb, she confirms his dread of her undisciplined desire, and brings down the structure of the whole house.[10] The point emphasized by Poe is the inextricable connectedness of the brother and sister, the sole survivors of the family: the narrator is struck by the resemblance between the two, and by the mysteriousness of the relationship between them. The climax of the story comes with Madeline's resurrection from her tomb, where her brother has buried her, and sudden appearance on the threshold of his room:

> For a moment she remained trembling and reeling to and fro upon the threshold – then, with a low moaning cry, fell heavily forward upon the person of her brother, and in her violent and now final death-agonies, bore him to the floor a corpse, and a victim to the terrors he had anticipated.[11]

Their relationship is seen as so all-engrossing that the murder is again a variation of incest: as intimate and as unnatural as the mingling of sex and death in many of these sibling revenge fantasies, best articulated by Freud's Wolf Man, suggests. No outsider has a hope of understanding the dynamics of this kind of relationship, especially mysterious in the case of twins. The fact that they are siblings exploits to the full the horrors of their mutually destructive connection which bystanders are powerless to arrest. The fact that the *sister* saps her brother's life (vampire-like) in revenge for being buried alive in the family home, opens up new possibilities for the articulating of women's frustrations with their enforced domesticity.

In nineteenth-century British fiction, the focus is more widely on issues of domestic rivalry, and the loss of equilibrium in the brother–sister relationship. Predictably, a sister's envy of a brother's advantages is more common than a brother's rancour at a sister's, with all their compensatory fantasies. Freud suggests, in 'A Child is Being Beaten', that girls usually fantasize about boys being beaten: indeed the victim is almost invariably a boy, whoever fantasizes, and often a brother.[12] In fact, sisters were usually regarded as morally superior to their brothers, who were expected to learn religious principles and notions of purity and self-denial from them. In *David Copperfield*, Betsy Trotwood often exhorts her great-nephew to acts of self-command and probity by bidding him remember what his [non-existent] sister Betsy would have done in his circumstances. In real life, Dickens resented the privileges given to his pianist sister Fanny, who was sent to the Royal Academy, while he was dismissed to the blacking factory during his father's period of imprisonment for debt at the Marshalsea. Michael Slater suggests that Fanny Dorrit is Dickens's revenge on his sister Fanny, and the Royal Academy 'degraded to a tawdry theatre putting on "leg-shows" for the delectation of such vacuous young men as Fanny's admirer, Mr Sparkler'.[13] Sisters who stay at home and keep house for their brothers (Ruth Pinch and Agnes Wickfield are good examples) are far preferred to flamboyant ones who pursue their own ambitions in a public sphere.

As one might expect, bad sisters largely occur in novels by male novelists. Even so, their wickedness is usually complicated by their brother's feelings of guilt about any violence perpetrated against them. Allon White's testimony to the devastating effect of his sister Carol's death, for which he felt responsible, at the age of five, demonstrates the deep-rootedness of these feelings, even in twentieth-century families where there were more opportunities for other relationships. Recounting a 'false memory' of remaining still and silent while his sister walked towards her drowning, he admits that he 'wanted her dead. I hated her'. According to his mother, he was elsewhere, playing with a friend in another garden; yet he continued for most of his life to feel somehow responsible for his sister's death, for not stopping her when he knew she was in danger. When he himself contracted leukaemia in his thirties, he was convinced that his illness was caused by identification with his drowned sister: 'Carol actually constituted a part of my being, she was me. Not as a part of my personality, but as something much more physical, an hysterical body, a violence which terrifies me even when expressed as mere words here on the page.'[14] The idea of the sister contained within as 'an hysterical body' is well exemplified in Poe's

Madeline, Dickens's Mrs Joe, and Charlotte Brontë's Bertha Rochester: all sisters who perform violent attacks on home and family on behalf of the other meeker characters, especially their sensitive brothers – Roderick Usher, Pip, and Richard Mason – but who themselves are ritually exorcized from the text by the end, victims of their brothers' vengeful wish-fulfilment.

Dickens and L. P Hartley: sisters in wheelchairs

Dickens's Pip in *Great Expectations*, battered through his childhood by his only surviving sibling, Mrs Joe, feels after her murder that he must be in some way to blame: all the more as she was clubbed to death with the leg iron he helped Magwitch to saw off with Joe's file. Though Mrs Joe never showed him a moment's kindness until she was a chair-bound invalid, Pip feels guilty for unconsciously wishing her death. When Orlick insists: '"It was you as did for your shrew sister,"' he articulates Pip's own repressed culpability – complicated by Orlick's sense of the sibling rivalry operating between himself and Pip: '"You was favoured, and [I] was bullied and beat."'[15] Moreover, the assault deprives her of sight, hearing and speech, and greatly improves her temper – much as Pip's pseudo-sister Estella will later be chastened by a brutal marriage to the bully Bentley Drummle. Though Mrs Joe (who has no name of her own) is a marginal character in the novel, she becomes one of those figures that people Pip's overcrowded mind and torment him with a sense of his own latent callousness: 'The figure of my sister in her chair by the kitchen fire, haunted me night and day' (p. 297). Mrs Joe, a helpless figure in her chair, duplicated in the trapped Estella, seems to reappear as Hilda in L. P. Hartley's story of a lifelong younger-brother–older-sister obsessional feud, *Eustace and Hilda* (1944), when Eustace is nearly tempted to tip his tormentor over a cliff edge.

Another older sister entrusted with moral responsibility for her younger brother's upbringing, Hilda Cherrington employs a succession of manipulative and sadistic strategies to humble her brother Eustace and destroy his confidence. As Eustace later recalls, 'she was a taskmistress, leading the chorus, undefined, unrecognised, but clearly felt, of those who thought he ought to try more, do more, be more, than he had it in him to try, or do, or be.'[16] In 'The Sixth Heaven', the novel is self-consciously in dialogue with the ending of *The Mill on the Floss*, when Maggie, intending to rescue her brother Tom, actually paddles him towards a death by drowning. Eustace, watching a boat while he is out walking, imagines Hilda in a boat with him: 'they were together, like

Tom and Maggie Tulliver in the "Mill on the Floss"' (p. 384). Imagining a melodramatic end for both of them, he laughs, but this is not the last of his revenge fantasies against his sister. Having given her a red dress, he dreams of her crying 'red tears like drops of blood' (p. 520) – perhaps recalling the time when he called her a murderer for letting the shrimp die in *The Shrimp and the Anemone*. By the final section of the novel, she has, like Mrs Joe, been reduced to speechlessness and paralysis, struck down by a form of sexual jealousy or hysteria, as she hears her supposed lover has become engaged to another woman. Again, Eustace's reaction is as complex as Pip's: a mixture of guilt and triumph as their roles are reversed and the younger brother becomes the carer with all the power. 'The calamity had given them to each other; this helpless, moveless, speechless Hilda was more his than the Sovereign of Highcross Hill' (the convalescent home which Hilda ran before she was taken ill) (p. 668). It is at this point in their lives that Eustace thinks of pushing her in her bath chair to the very edge of the cliff, in order to shock her out of her passive and silent state: only an inner voice tells him 'he would not stop at the cliff's edge; he had a subconscious wish to get rid of Hilda, the albatross that was hung around his neck' (p. 686).

Hilda's image in fact merges with Miss Fothergill's, the strangely terrifying woman in a wheelchair whom Hilda urged him to befriend in childhood, and who in turn took such a fancy to Eustace that she left him money in her will. She is the Miss Havisham figure of Eustace's childhood, intense and pervasive: a benefactress he must humour without understanding her. Twice over in the novel, therefore, Eustace is haunted by images of wheelchair-bound women – one old and with a disgusting deformity, the other young and beautiful, as much Estella as Mrs Joe: both of them in his power, yet both all-powerful over his destiny. Emotionally paralysed by his contact with them, Eustace is never free to hate them. The wheelchair is always a symbol of their helplessness and his own guilt at being free and mobile. On the occasion of the cliff-top experiment, which finally happens, he collapses, and swaps places with Hilda in the wheelchair, as if his moral weakness has become a physical deformity. His final image of her, in a dream before he dies, is of the anemone he had seen in the rock pool during their childhood, apparently dying of hunger. In pushing his finger into its mouth, he is killed by its greed and its icy coldness: 'The water was bitterly cold; but colder still were the lips of the anemone as they closed around his finger' (p. 735) – a disturbingly sexual image which reflects the many suggestions of incestuous fantasy earlier in the novel. In turning Hilda into the glamorous red-dressed woman weeping blood, the engulfing mother, the tyrannical cripple, the fatally ambiguous Maggie Tulliver, and the anemone who will swallow him in the icy water and stop his heart, Eustace makes of her a composite evil fairy tale sister whose battle to control him finally triumphs over his battle to control her. The other characters in the novel remain insignificant background figures in the intense fight to the death which the brother and sister enact throughout the three volumes of this trilogy.

Bertha Rochester: the mad sister in the attic

Perhaps the best-known violent sister in nineteenth century literature, however, was created by a woman, Charlotte Brontë, in Bertha Rochester, the mad wife in *Jane Eyre*. While much is said by feminist critics about Bertha as an abused and abusing wife, her role as a sister plays a central part in Brontë's study of contorted sibling relationships in the novel. Her fury against Richard Mason parallels Jane's against her cousin John Reed, when she flies at him like a fury in the opening chapter. 'I don't very well know what I did with my hands,' Jane recalls, 'but he called me "Rat! Rat!" and bellowed out loud' (p. 43). The state of panic she brings on the household anticipates the terror that will break out in chapter 20, when Bertha Rochester attacks her brother, biting him like a 'tigress' (p. 241). '"She sucked the blood: she said she'd drain my heart,"' Mason explains (p. 242). Local rumours around Thornfield in fact assumed that the mysterious lunatic kept in the house was Rochester's 'bastard half-sister', as he tells his accusers at the aborted wedding-ceremony (p. 320). Like Poe's Madeline, Bertha – banished to the attic, as Madeline was to the vaults – destroys the fabric of the household in the act of destroying herself.

The third variation in sibling caretaking occurs in the Moor House section of the novel, when St John Rivers cautiously offers the exhausted Jane food and drink in his kitchen, but orders the women to '"restrain her"... And he withdrew the cup of milk and the plate of bread' (p. 363) – like a jailer or doctor controlling a mad patient. Mad and vagrant sisters in Brontë's novel fight their real or pseudo-brothers for a mastery they can achieve only through outbreaks of physical or verbal violence which threaten the continuum of household life. Unable to fight St John physically, Jane lashes out with words that appal him: words he finds '"violent, unfeminine, and untrue"' (p. 438). Neither his house nor her schoolhouse is finally able to contain her passion, which finds a home only in the buried seclusion of Ferndean.

Bad brothers: an introduction

In other nineteenth-century novels the bad brother functions either as an immovable judge or as an idle wastrel, and in both cases he is egotistic and entirely unable to understand his sister's point of view. Extending the idea to include other relationships, Freud observed that 'in many families, the men are healthy, but from a social point of view immoral to an undesirable degree, while the women are high-minded and over-refined, but severely neurotic' – a pattern that with variations reappears in much Victorian literature, where the overbearing, self-important brother contrasts with the more honest and unhappy self-sacrificing sister.[17] Dickens shows that such behavioural patterns can be established from childhood. Both Tom Gradgrind (*Hard Times*) and Charley Hexam (*Our Mutual Friend*) assume that their older sisters will marry so as to advance their brothers' careers (an aspiration shared by Eustace Cherrington, who wants Hilda to marry his glamorous friend and protector, Dick Staveley). Both sisters look into the fire on the hearth and dream of happier times which they are powerless to restore, except by giving themselves to masterful husbands. Tom tells his sister, Louisa, '"It would do me a great deal of good if you were to make up your mind to I know what, Loo. It would be a splendid thing for me"' – and no great sacrifice for her as she has no other lover.[18] Similarly, in *Our Mutual Friend*, Charley Hexam sees no reason why his sister Lizzie should not marry Bradley Headstone, the schoolmaster; only this time, the sister refuses. In his list of reasons why she should oblige him and accept the proposal, Lizzie's own needs come last, after his own and Headstone's. In each novel, a breach between the siblings, begun by the brother, leaves the sister sorrowful and forgiving. *Hard Times* closes with a picture of a 'lonely brother, many thousands of miles away, writing, on paper blotted with tears, that her words had too soon come true, and that all the treasures in the world would be cheaply bartered for a sight of her dear face' (p. 313).

The spectacle of a brother interfering with his sister's marriage plans, and assuming the father's role in running the family, is recurrent in Victorian literature. While Tom Tulliver forbids his sister Maggie to meet Philip Wakem, another Maggie, in Elizabeth Gaskell's *The Moorland Cottage* (1850), is ordered by her Tom-like brother Edward, to give up her engagement to Frank Buxton, whose father will otherwise prosecute him for forgery. As it happens, this is the second generation of Buxtons to experience this kind of brotherly bullying: Mr Buxton himself disapproved of his own sister's marriage, and now repentant, raises his niece as a future bride for Frank. Gaskell presents Edward as the apple of his mother's eye, like Tom Tulliver: lazy, indulged and patronizing. Like Tom Gradgrind, he takes to financial misdealing in his adult life; then reappears in his sister's life, asking for help. His return is also reminiscent of Charlotte Brontë's Henry Hastings story, from her Angrian sagas, discussed in Chapter 2. Both sisters are willing to hide their brothers and cover up for them, despite knowing they have broken the law. Gaskell herself uses a similar plot in *North and South* (1855), when Margaret Hale's long-lost brother Frederick returns, a proscribed man after leading a mutiny on board his ship. While, though, Frederick is seen as having acted from noble principles, however rashly, Maggie Browne and Louisa Gradgrind have to live with their brother's disgrace and sacrifice their own needs for his. Maggie may insist on keeping to her engagement, but she agrees to accompany Edward in his escape to America (a plot device also used to whisk Tom Gradgrind out of the country). In each case, the novelist seems to accept that a sister's loyalty to a brother will override the law, even if the brother's unworthiness is evident to both sister and reader. What she does is legitimate emotionally, if not legally, though the claims of law are also vindicated when the brother ultimately dies (Edward before the ship has sailed further than the Welsh coast). The sister can thus be saved without compromising her loyalty, which is her most dependable quality.

Victorian novelists recognize and explore the various worldly temptations to which brothers are exposed while their sisters stay safely at home, concerned only to balance their lovers' claims with their brothers'. The range of ways in which a brother could go wrong was much wider than the limited choice of temptations offered to a sister, though in neither case is sexual lapse often used as the prime cause of estrangement and disappointment. Perhaps because unchastity was such a terrible possibility to contemplate in a sister, wicked sisters in nineteenth-century novels tend to be harsh and cruel, like Mrs Joe, rather than voluptuous and sensual. Nor are wicked brothers often seen in sexual terms, though their susceptibility to other kinds of worldly temptation unavailable to their sisters perhaps becomes an emblem of this. Though George Vavasor in Trollope's *Can You Forgive Her?* has a discarded mistress, she is not seen as the true cause of his wickedness, and his sister knows nothing about her. George's weakness is his constant need for money, and his willingness to use any woman in his way as a source of funds.

Trollope and Oliphant

The privileged brother in fiction often feels he owes nothing to anyone. He regards himself as entirely free of family demands, while the sister is doubly burdened with them, and more often than not, condemned to inactivity. Her options are limited, while the brother typically moves to another town, another country, or goes out every evening to drink and gamble. The novelists who best represent this gap in outlook and expectations are Anthony Trollope and Margaret Oliphant. In *Can You Forgive Her?* (1864–5), George Vavasor goes about the country hunting, raising money to finance his election, and entering Parliament, while his sister Kate looks after their grandfather and half-heartedly waits for husbands ('"The truth is, I'm married to George"'), while trying to persuade George to marry their cousin Alice.[19] George spends money lavishly, and Kate gains it as a reward for her family loyalty and patience in the £500 a year she is left by her disillusioned grandfather. The novel's plot traces Kate's mounting repugnance for her brother who does little but try to extort money from her. As far as Kate is concerned, the money itself is unimportant: the key issue is his sickening moral decline, culminating in his insistence that she should perjure herself in court to contest their grandfather's will. When she refuses, he threatens to murder her: '"Say that you will do as I desire you, or I will be the death of you"' (p. 593). Though he stops short of murder, George causes Kate to break her arm in what must be one of few instances of sibling violence directed by a brother against his sister, in Victorian fiction. For Kate this is the culminating moment of disillusionment; yet even at this stage, she can imagine forgiving him:

> My whole life has been at his service. I have been his creature, to do his bidding, just as he might tell me. He made me do things that I knew to be wrong – things that were foreign to my own nature; and yet I almost worshipped him. Even now, if he were to come back, I believe that I should forgive him everything. (pp. 666–7)

Trollope himself is clear about where a sister's duties to her brother end and her loyalty to her best friend begins. Though the title of the novel refers to Alice Vavasor's treatment of her lover John Grey, Kate has to share some of her cousin's blame for moral shortsightedness. 'To risk herself for her brother was noble,' Trollope states. 'But when she used her cunning in inducing her cousin to share that risk she was ignoble' (p. 572). Besotted as she is by her brother, she fails to acknowledge that a wife lacks the special disinterestedness of a sister, and has far more to lose by such a match. Though she knows she would become redundant if George ever married ('"If George ever married, I should have nothing to do in the world"', p. 96), her plan is to marry him off to Alice, who, in turn, envies Kate her brother's political career: 'Kate could, as his sister, attach herself on to George's political career, and obtain from it all that excitement of life which Alice desired for herself.' (p. 143). The novel crucially explores the differences between a sister's involvement in a brother's career and a wife's role in a husband's. With the brother–sister relationship, the ground is prepared and the sharing assumed. While George is relaxed with Kate and can talk freely to her, the sexual awareness between himself and Alice always puts a strain on their relations, even when they are discussing money and politics. Alice, in turn, finds him physically repugnant (something Kate overlooks), and uses the money to keep him at a businesslike distance. Where Kate's love is blind and instinctive, Alice's is full of self-doubt and reservations. Kate's love for her brother is the only real purpose in her life. When Trollope dooms her to disappointment, he shows such irrational feelings to be understandable, in the face of women's directionless lives, but something to be recognized and controlled. With her aunt's discarded suitor, the wealthy farmer Mr Cheesacre as her only romantic option, however, Kate has little choice but to continue channelling her emotional energies into her brother's life and career. In the end, she is left with nothing but an undisclosed future, her youthful energies and affections wasted on a brother who never appreciates her finer qualities, while she has always seen them in him, when no one else does.

Close to Trollope in her study of Victorian social connections and small town life, Margaret Oliphant is also an expert at showing how sisters try to live vicariously through their brothers who go out into the world while they themselves stay at home with little to think about except the running of the household affairs. Oliphant was herself a younger sister with one brother who drank (Willie) and another who was an economic failure (Frank), quite apart from finding other kinds of ineptitude at living reappear in her husband Frank (who was also her cousin) and her sons, Cyril and Francis (known as Cecco). One of Oliphant's earlier and now little read novels is *Harry Muir: A Story of Scottish Life* (1853). A married man with three sisters who earn a living by fancy needlework, Harry is lazy, good-humoured, and mysteriously unsuccessful at everything he undertakes. Nevertheless, his sisters are proud of him and devoted to his welfare. 'Darkest and saddest of all domestic calamities,' Oliphant reports, 'these women, to whom he was so very dear, could not *trust* the man in whom all their hopes and wishes centred.'[20] His older sister, Martha, seven years his senior, has in him 'something of the mother's pride' (I, 32); emotionally, he compensates her for her fading hopes of marriage, even though Harry has a wife and two sons of his own. To her, perhaps, this propping up of a useless brother is only the norm: the Muirs lodge in a house owned by a Mrs Rodgers, whose three daughters also work hard to support their brother Johnnie – 'a shabby and not very young man, with shuffling indolent limbs stretched across the hearth' – incapable, 'between his rheumatism and his false shame' of any strenuous endeavour on his family's behalf (I, 123–4). When Harry inherits a family estate, the Muirs' fortunes seem to be permanently recovered: the brother who was their secret shame becomes what he should be, their source of salvation, and all goes well for a while as they establish themselves in their new home. The normal structures are restored as the sisters become their brother's dependants: something that Martha, for one, finds difficult: having always imagined herself as the guardian and protector of her orphan siblings, Martha's natural pride takes a knock as she realizes she is Harry's 'dependant sister, curbing and burdening his hands, and restraining the harmless indulgences he longed for' (II, 74–5). When Harry, predictably, gets into bad company and neglects his responsibilities for weeks at a time, the reader senses that Martha's energies will soon be called upon to resume her protection of the family. Oliphant gives her the moral satisfaction of finding him unconscious in the road one night: 'And now she lifts him up into her own arms, up to the fierce heart which has throbbed with passionate love for him all his life'(III, 143). Moreover, when Harry dies, his will leaves everything to Martha: she in turn, preserves it in trust for his wife and son, and defends his honour to all who challenge it. Not only does Martha put the estate back on a sound financial footing; her youngest sister, Violet, shames the torpid Johnnie Rodgers into finding work as a clerk: '"When I hear a little thing like you speaking about work, and helping to keep a house, it makes me think shame of myself, Lettie"' (III, 270).

Oliphant's novel clearly implies that women are better managers than men: not least because they are never exposed to the temptations of drinking and gambling, which their weak brother is unable to resist. Even with money in their hands, Harry's sisters never abandon their natural instinct for work; they therefore have no difficulty in returning to it when Harry's death creates another crisis in their lives. Indeed Oliphant's comments on Martha's humiliation at being her brother's dependant, make it clear that women enjoy the call on their energies.

This was to remain the favourite pattern of many subsequent Oliphant plots, of which the best known is probably her early Carlingford novella, *The Doctor's Family* (1863). Here the idle brother–active sister theme is carried across two families, as the conscientious doctor, Edward Rider, acquires through his wastrel brother Fred, a tornado of self-effacing energy in his Australian sister-in-law, Nettie. What Edward cannot understand (as his own and Fred's sister, briefly mentioned, was the same) is why women are so ready to forgive their dissipated brothers: 'The more worthless a fellow is,' he muses, 'the more all the women connected with him cling to him and make excuses for him... Mother and sister in the past – wife and Nettie now – to think how Fred had secured for himself such perpetual ministrations, by neglecting all the duties of life!'[21] Again, Nettie is given the responsibility of attending to everything when Fred drowns – duly punished, as useless brothers generally are in Oliphant's novels – yet she is conscious of being the only one with any real pity for him: '*Her* heart alone was heavy with regret over the ruined man – the now for ever unredeemable life –' (p. 124). Yet as so often happens in Oliphant novels, no one seems to appreciate her efforts. Resigning her own emotional needs, Nettie is prepared to sacrifice herself to her sister's family, much as Edward Rider was prepared to do everything he could for Fred; yet her sacrifices – and Edward's – soon prove to be fruitless. Her sister Susan, Fred's widow, quickly consoles herself with another man, who offers to escort them all back to Australia: 'In the bitterness of the moment it was not the sudden deliverance, but the heartlessness and domestic treachery that struck Nettie' (p. 177). Oliphant shows in this, and many of her other novels, how much harder it is for her heroic characters to abandon their heroism and accept the prospect of an easier life. Nettie takes much of the story to be persuaded that she can leave her sister's family to another protector, and marry her brother-in-law's brother – though not without taking one of Fred's children with her, at the boy's own request: a continuing symbol of the troublesome dead brother, perhaps.

In *Phoebe Junior* (1876), more sisters chafe at the uselessness of privileged brothers. The Miss Dorsets are expected to look after their brother John's children, sent home from India, much to Sophy Dorset's disgust. '"You think I ought to be fond of them because they are my brother's children? We are not always very fond even of our brothers, Ursula,"' she tells her young guest, Ursula May.[22] Oliphant, who herself looked after her brother Frank's children when he became incapable, narrates that John Dorset had been married at a time when Sophy was herself due to be married – only her engagement was broken. Ursula, meanwhile, goes home to find her brother Reginald hesitating over whether to accept a sinecure in the church: a wardenship worth an annual fee of £250, normally offered to elderly men (Trollope's *The Warden*, 1855, builds its plot round the controversy generated by an elderly man's accepting a disproportionately high fee for a similar sinecure). Ursula, desperate to earn some money, but offered only housework for her widowed father, 'wished with a sigh that there were sinecures which could be held by girls. But no, in that as in other things, "gentlemen" kept all that was good to themselves' (p. 73). For Oliphant, much of the joke derives from the ludicrous notion of 'sinecures for girls', which everyone knows is impossible. Sophy Dorset's older sister Anne insists, in a way that few if any men do in Oliphant's novels: '"I think we have only a right to our existence when we are doing something...Nobody is of any consequence who does not do something"' (p. 57). Through the twists of the plot, Reginald seems to pay dearly for his unwanted sinecure, in that he is left at the end without a wife, but with a houseful of orphaned siblings.'It is not thought in the family that Reginald will ever marry,' Oliphant concludes (p. 341).

This is often the pattern of Oliphant's novels, which are full of privileged brothers idling through life with their hands in their trousers pockets, while their sisters agitate for movement and progress of some kind in their societies and households. In *Hester* (1883), Oliphant's cynicism about sibling households is pushed one stage further, in two other variations on the theme. While the young rebellious socialites, Ellen and Harry Vernon, embody the self-indulgent frivolity of a brother–sister 'marriage' (which hardly changes when Ellen actually marries), the Ashton siblings, Emma and Roland, merely make the best of a bad job. As the youngest of seven, Emma accepts that she has to move from house to house and be taken care of in turn by her older siblings, until such time as she can marry. Literary precedent does nothing to reassure her: '"It might be cheerful for me if Roland were to spend his evenings at home as Tom Pinch in Dickens did with his sister. But then Roland is not a bit like Tom Pinch,"' Emma grumbles more than once in the novel.[23] All Emma learns from her experience is that '"nobody wants you, and that you must just do the best you can for yourself"' (p. 274). Having failed to hook a husband at the tea dances she has conscientiously attended, Emma meets her match on the train back to her brother's, and disappears from the story.

Protective rivalry: Mary Cholmondeley and William Hamilton

Close female friendships are the ideal alternative to the frustrations of the brother–sister relationship. Based on conditions of equality, they offer unconditional emotional support when the gender-based rivalry of the sibling relationship has failed. The novel that best chronicles the contrast between these two types of relationship is Mary Cholmondeley's *Red Pottage* (1899), the story of a brother's attempted destruction of his sister's literary career. According to Elaine Showalter, 'In the story of the brilliant novelist Hester Gresley, whose narrow-minded clergyman brother cannot understand her irony or her profundity, Cholmondeley dramatized her smouldering personal sense of the woman writer's oppression.'[24] By making the brother a narrow-minded clergyman and family man with a sanctimonious wife, living in a dull part of the country ('Middleshire,' watered by the River Drone), Cholmondeley intensifies her attack on all aspects of the male-dominated establishment, not just the literary. James Gresley, who himself has pretensions to literary success (in the form of theological articles, which he patronizingly asks Hester to check for spelling and grammar), embodies the pursed-lipped narrow-mindedness of the world beyond Hester's warm relationship with her friend Rachel. The description of his physical appearance reads like a caricature of St John Rivers:

> Mr Gresley's suspicious eye and thin compressed lips hinted that both fanatic and saint were fighting for predominance in the kingdom of that pinched brain, the narrowness of which the sloping forehead betokened with such cruel plainness. He looked as if he would fling himself as hard against a truth without perceiving it, as a hunted hare against a stone wall. He was unmistakably of those who only see side issues. (p. 52)

Appropriately enough, he writes under the pseudonym 'Veritas', telling his sister: '"I merely place before the public forcibly and in a novel manner a few great truths"' (p. 60). Though James is willing to give her a home, and she enjoys the favour of his young children, Hester embodies everything that is modern and rebellious, while he stands for the settled and unsympathetic outlook of the church. As the perceptive Bishop of Southminster comments: '"He has been kind to her according to his lights, and if she could write little goody-goody books he would admire her immensely, and so would half the neighbourhood"' (p. 87).

But Hester, instead of throwing herself into parish work, has written a novel called *An Idyll of East London*; her second novel, *Husks*, is the one her brother violates, reads, corrects, and finally burns, appalled by its religious views.

Cholmondeley stresses the unbridgeable gap in their two visions of life, so that when James begins surreptitiously reading his sister's manuscript, returned by the publishers for minor alterations, he simultaneously registers its visionary quality, and his own lack of imagination. James flatly disbelieves in any emotions he has never experienced for himself. Tellingly, he classes his sister's book with George Eliot's, as 'profane', 'immoral', and 'coarse' (p. 263). Yet the act of authorship sanctifies her, while James is described in increasingly comic and prosaic terms. While James is juxtaposed with a bed of brussels sprouts, 'Hester, standing in a white gown under the veiled trees in a glade of silver and trembling opal, which surely mortal foot had never trod, seemed infinitely removed from him' (pp. 155–6). Everything that James does in relation to his sister's manuscript is furtive and cowardly. Having opened his sister's parcel and read the manuscript without her permission, he seeks advice from the Archdeacon by inventing a hypothetical case about a letter, is advised to burn it, and does so. The burning of his sister's manuscript is the climactic moment of betrayal in the novel, like Hedda Gabler's destruction of Eilert Lovborg's manuscript in Ibsen's *Hedda Gabler* (1890): the destruction of an important work by a jealous rival. As in Ibsen's play, the manuscript is seen as a symbolic child. Before James destroyed her book, Hester was nursing his sick child, Regie. The parallels between the two cases are obvious to her: '"I did not let your child die,"' she tells him. '"Why have you killed mine?"' (p. 276). Though she is perfectly clear about the differences in their behaviour, Hester succumbs to the inevitable attack of brain fever, during which her chief obsession and worry is that she has killed Regie, her brother's son; the equivalent of her manuscript, the thing that was most dear to him. Psychologically, it is hard not to read this as a displaced, repressed wish to murder her brother in revenge for his destruction of the thing that was most dear to her. A relationship such as this is impossible to heal, and Hester ends the novel travelling abroad with her friend Rachel: the mutual supportiveness of female friendship replacing the rivalrous competition between irreconcilable brother and sister.

Questions inevitably arise about the strength of Cholmondeley's feelings, and the reasons for her anger. The obvious place to look for answers seems to be her collective family autobiography, *Under One*

Roof: A Family Record, published nearly twenty years after *Red Pottage*, in 1918; but though the book is dedicated 'To My Brother Tom', Tom and her other brothers hardly feature in it. The book focuses instead on just four people: the father she wholeheartedly loved and admired, the mother who was a perpetual invalid, 'Ninny', the family nanny; and finally her younger sister Hester, who died in 1893 in her twenties, leaving Mary her literary executrix. Cholmondeley worried that 'those two excellent men', her surviving brothers, would accuse her of disloyalty for her 'character drawing' of the four, expecting them instead to be 'portrayed as perfect characters'.[25]

Linda Peterson discusses Mary's dilemma over the publication of her sister's work in her latest study of women's autobiography, contrasting Mary's failure to publish and extol her dead sister's work with Charlotte Brontë's efforts to safeguard Emily and Anne's posthumous reputations.[26] Mary was shocked to discover how critical Hester had been of her family: 'Perhaps it was just as well we did not realize it, had not the remotest suspicion of the critical attitude of her mind towards every one of us, except Father.'[27] Hester the sister becomes the surprising, disturbing member of Cholmondeley's real-life family, just as Hester Gresley shocks and disturbs her brother James, on to whom Mary seems to project her own unease about her sister Hester's potential genius. Privately, Cholmondeley felt her sister's work was still immature and of patchy quality, and her very existence hardly known outside the Hodnet parsonage where they had lived: 'She died a quarter of a century ago, and it is doubtful whether any creature exists who still vividly remembers her, except her brothers and sisters, and the kind sister-in-law to whom she owed so much' (p. xv). In taking command of her sister's posthumous reputation, Mary was behaving like James Gresley, deciding what was fit for public consumption, irrespective of the author's own wishes. Additionally, Mary removes all her brothers from the family chronicle, and sees them as not requiring historical commemoration, though curiously, one brother Reginald returns, in *Red Pottage* as the sick child 'Regie', Hester's nephew, who nearly dies. The family configurations were further complicated by Cholmondeley's admission that 'there is a good deal of me in Hester, tho' I had hardly realized it. I think the character is entirely opposed to mine, but of course I have put in my own feelings exactly about "writing," or at least a small portion of them.'[28]

Cholmondeley's novel and family history together represent her attempts to reorder her family life, so that she herself controls the survival and reputation of her parents and especially her siblings.

A Hester's literary pretensions are cut down to size in both texts, but the sister Mary who made the decisions in the Cholmondeley family becomes a brother James in the fictional version. Did Cholmondeley find it easier to imagine a brother, rather than a sister – and a caricatured clergyman brother at that – suppressing a sister's ambitions? Did that make more sense, culturally and ideologically? Cholmondeley seems to have projected her own guilt about replacing Hester as the family novelist, on to the stock brotherly villain James Gresley, and intensified it through the near death of another vulnerable member of the family, the little nephew Regie (himself named after another Cholmondeley brother). By a weird twist of fate, stranger than anything Cholmondeley wrote in her novels, another brother, Dick, died of heart failure many years later after sitting on the verandah reading *Red Pottage*.[29]

It was, of course, fairly common for surviving siblings to make decisions about the preservation of manuscripts and reputations, the construction of lives to be offered to the public. Apart from the Brontës, the best-known examples are Henry and James Austen's control, together with their nephew, James Austen-Leigh, of their sister Jane's posthumous reputation, William Michael Rossetti's of his siblings Dante Gabriel and Christina, and the Pater sisters' – Clara and Hester – of their brother Walter's literary remains. One of the most curious, however, which serves as a fitting conclusion to this chapter, in that it encompasses all the suppressed rivalry over ownership of a sibling's achievements, is the case of the eminent scientist and mathematician, William Rowan Hamilton, and his poet sister Eliza.[30] Hamilton (1805–65), who was Professor of Astronomy at the Dunsink Observatory in Dublin, had tried in vain to interest his four sisters in astronomy, but enjoyed a close relationship with Eliza (1807–51) with whom he shared a passion for poetry. They both visited Wordsworth in 1830, and discussed her poetry with him. When Eliza died, she left her brother

> the most entire control over her papers, which were many, with power to preserve or *destroy*. To some extent – indeed to a large one – I have used the *latter* power, by putting into the flames, after reading them, a great number of the sheets of a journal which, I am convinced, would have brought me in some hundreds of pounds if I could have borne to publish it, but which was written for *herself alone*, though in her dying hours she gave *me* permission to read it, and which described too freely, as I judged, though without any

particle of malice, our many visitors of long ago to this Observatory.[31]

Hamilton's unctuous use of italics makes his declaration of conquered self-interest something akin to James Gresley's pretences over his sister's manuscript in *Red Pottage*: in each case the brother finds what sound like good reasons for suppressing work that might have enhanced his sister's reputation or at least left the public with more information about her and the life she led. Hamilton, in fact, took four years to open 'what she considered her *pet box of letters*', which contained a good many letters written by himself. 'We loved each other to the last,' Hamilton told a correspondent, 'and I had the satisfaction of being – *useful* to her. Indeed I have burned a great number of letters of hers to me, because I did not like to preserve records of the *gratitude* of one who deserved *all*, and *more* than all, which it was in my power to do' (*Life*, III, 28). To scholars now trying to piece together more information about Eliza Hamilton and her poetry, her brother's apparently well-intentioned destruction of her papers is to say the least frustrating; his reasons for doing so still harder to understand by today's standards. His explanations twist and writhe in a way that suggests more complex motives for suppressing his sister's personality as manifested in her private writing, and even in her choice of what letters of other people's to keep in her '*pet box*'. Eliza, for her part, feared, in their youth, that 'he might be heading for a terrible fall some day'. Hamilton's most recent biographer, Thomas L. Hankins, reprints a poem Eliza wrote in 1832, which worries about her eagle-like brother eventually crashing to the ground if he fails to reverence God and heed his wrath. 'Is there around the lofty habitation,/Of thy bright spirit, any guard from Him?' Eliza asks her brother. 'Canst thou defy the inward desolation/With which his wrath all brilliant thoughts can dim?'[32] This perhaps was the ultimate act of revenge: the invoking of God's anger on a sibling who was heedlessly carving out a brilliant career for himself. When Hamilton twenty years later destroyed her journal and letters, not from revenge, but to protect her from seeming too lively and too grateful, thereby depriving himself of 'some hundreds of pounds', his actions, and still more his reasons for them, reveal the psychological intricacy of his feelings about her, and about himself in relation to their lifelong friendship. Hamilton claimed that their attachment to each other was 'more like that of twins than of a brother and sister' (*Life*, III, 28), yet they clearly had secrets from each other, and Hamilton occasionally passed on to Eliza Wordsworth's critical comments on her poems.[33] Eliza had disappointed him in not turning out to be another Caroline Herschel: 'You know I have set my heart on having *one* of my sisters an astronomer,' he complained to Sydney, the next sister down (Hankins, p. 57). During their lifetimes, Hamilton ultimately failed to control any of his sisters – Sydney even emigrated to Nicaragua with his elder son, ending her days in New Zealand – so his destruction of Eliza's journals acquires an additional resonance. There is no evidence that Hamilton was motivated by any desire for revenge on his sister (after all, his own career was, at the time, more successful than hers, though he had himself wanted to be poet); what this story suggests, however, is a degree of emotional obsessiveness and self-deception which links him with Mary Cholmondeley and her unease about Hester's remains. While Hamilton felt the need to justify his destruction of his sister's papers, Cholmondeley displaced her own complex feelings about Hester on to her fictional character James Gresley and allowed him to act out her disloyal instincts. In both families, a sibling was simultaneously honoured and erased as the survivors struggled to reconcile themselves with a talent they both respected and disparaged.

Sibling rivalry is in many ways an expression of self-doubt, a sense that someone else – a peer, who sprang from the same parents – is more successful, more privileged than oneself. For many Victorian novelists, the brother–sister competition went to the heart of the social inequalities faced by both sexes. It allowed them to express guilt at getting on, resentment at being left behind. The childhood faithfulness of sisters, moreover, was often disregarded when other options (especially a wife) subsequently offered. In the novels discussed in this chapter, brothers are exiled and killed, sisters tamed, subdued, or humiliated. Violent fantasies are immediately punished by sensations of shame, which remind the surviving sibling of the tabooed nature of injury to bloodbrothers and sisters.

Allon White's autobiographical essay about his sister Carol, cited earlier, suggests what was for him a recuperative way out of this impasse of guilt and shame. Carol's 'good' half was her twin, Debbie, a suitable bone marrow match for her brother: 'Debbie would give me life just as Carol had threatened to take my life away. Carol had made me ill, Debbie would make me well again'(p. 43). Though a text of the 1990s, White's essay says much that is relevant to the double-faced image of the nineteenth-century sibling as hated second-self or saviour, the 'hysterical body' within, which Juliet Mitchell also acknowledges. Claiming, like Catherine Earnshaw of Heathcliff, that his sibling *was* himself, White articulates another idea that several Victorian writers sought to explore: the indivisibility of brothers and sisters, the possibility of *being* one's own sibling, and experiencing the same life from another perspective. The next logical step from rivalry is a supplanting of the rival by total absorption: *becoming* the rival 'other', and living the other person's life. This is the subject of the next chapter.

6
Changing Places: Siblings and Cross-Gendering

> And he said he was *tired* of being a boy and he wanted to be a girl now. And I said, "But you can't be a girl if you're a boy," and he said, "Yes I can. If I want to, I can."[1]

> ... for Peter was a lady then.[2]

Elizabeth Gaskell sounds an unlikely person to be writing about crossdressing, and *Cranford* (1853) an improbable place to find it, but here, in fact, is one of the best examples in Victorian literature of a brother dressing up as his sister. Peter Jenkyns, a successful 'hoaxer', emboldened by his success in disguising himself as a lady visitor who admires the Rector's sermons, goes one step too far and walks up and down the garden dressed in his sister Deborah's clothes, apparently nursing a baby. His father is so appalled at the disrespect shown to Deborah, that he strips and publicly flogs him: an act which breaks up the family as he flees abroad until his parents and Deborah are dead, and his surviving sister, Miss Matty, well into middle age. As for Miss Matty herself, retelling the story to Mary Brown, she becomes momentarily confused as to whether she should call Peter a man or a woman: 'Peter said, he was awfully frightened himself when he saw how my father took it all in, and even offered to copy out all his Napoleon Buonaparte sermons for her – him, I mean – no, her, for Peter was a lady then.'

Why does he do it? And twice? For a joke? To shock his family and the neighbours? To get revenge on Deborah? Miss Matty is unsure ('What possessed our poor Peter I don't know'), but hints at rivalry between the two for their father's approval, adding that Deborah 'never laughed at his jokes, and thought him ungenteel, and not careful enough about improving his mind; and that vexed him' (p. 52) Or does he do it because he wants to know what it feels like to be his sister? Though the last reason may sound the least convincing, according to two historians of cross-dressing, it was not uncommon in the nineteenth century for men to find the 'feminine life-style more attractive'. Women, too, experimented with cross-dressing in order to fight in wars or go to sea; in Russia, especially, according to some estimates, 'hundreds of Russian women disguised as men fought in World War I'.[3] Judith Halberstam's study of *Female Masculinities* (1998) similarly testifies to the historical and contemporary existence of 'women who feel themselves to be more masculine than feminine', and dress and behave accordingly.[4] Cross-dressing as a means of escape from the constraints of female gentility was something even the fragile Elizabeth Barrett fantasized about. In 1842, when she was thirty-six, she told Mary Mitford that as a child she had been indignant with nature for making her a woman, and was resolved to 'dress up in men's clothes as soon as ever I was free of the nursery, and go into the world "to seek my fortune". "*How*", was not decided; but I rather leant towards being poor Lord Byron's *page*.'[5] Though she never cross-dressed, Emily Dickinson occasionally signed herself 'Brother Emily' in writing to her cousins Louise and Frances Norcross.[6] For brothers and sisters growing up in the same house together, aware of each other's opportunities and restrictions, curiosity about the partially-concealed secret lives of siblings seems to have been rife. The mystery that grew up around boys' boarding schools has already been discussed in Chapter I, but boys, too, were absent from their sisters for many weeks at a time, and must have had only a hazy idea of what it was like to be a girl, and how they spent their days. Yet this degree of gender-separation is, according to some theorists, neither tenable nor true. Judith Butler's interrogation of the fixed relations between sex and gender, together with Freud's notions of the inherent bisexuality of children, provide a constructive framework for the issues to be discussed in this chapter, which will show how the brother–sister dyad offered opportunities to escape the restrictive ties involved in being a sibling of either sex.

Judith Butler's project is concerned with what she terms the 'indeterminacy of gender', the separation of biological sex from artificially constructed gender, which she sees as a performance, 'an incessant and repeated action of some sort'. Gender therefore becomes a matter of choice, as we construct ourselves according to our own needs at the time.[7] The cover illustration of her book shows two sisters, Agnes and Inez Albright, dressed to look like a girl and a boy, though both sporting quantities of frills and ruffles. In the nineteenth century, gender was indeed ambiguous in young children. Victorian male and female babies were dressed alike, and boys wore 'long clothes' until they were able to move about. Tennyson's sons continued to wear long hair and frilly clothes well into their boyhood. Even the notion that 'pink is for girls and blue for boys' is historically unstable, according to Marjorie Garber, who notes that this idea came into vogue only after the Second World War.[8] In fact, going on photographic evidence, while most Victorian babies were dressed to look like girls, Freud's theories initially proceeded on the supposition that children of both sexes experienced a similar psycho-sexual development, and could be regarded as boys. They both, in early infancy, shared a passionate love for their mother, and experienced no significant psychological differences in the pre-Oedipal stage. One of his most famous and controversial statements for feminists is his pronouncement in 'Femininity' (1932) that 'with their entry into the phallic phase the differences between the sexes are completely eclipsed by their agreements. We are now obliged to recognize that the little girl is a little man'.[9]

Though Freud constantly reassessed his theories, and modified them in accordance with his shifting impressions of human behaviour, one of his abiding interests was in the notion of bisexuality, of which he felt women were more acutely aware than men. 'Dora' is a classic example of a woman closely identified in childhood with her older brother. As Juliet Mitchell points out, Dora tried to compete and merge with Otto, for example by copying his childhood illnesses and getting them more severely than he did, and in her narrative to Freud confusing her own age at a key point in her life with her brother's. 'The Oedipal story,' according to Mitchell, 'is the result of Dora's failure to be like, as good as, or just *be* her brother.'[10] By the end of his life, Freud believed that 'no individual is limited to the modes of reaction of a single sex but always finds some room for those of the opposite one'; he saw the necessity of sexual division as a difficult fact both for men and for women. Juliet Mitchell comments that for Freud, 'in the unconscious and preconscious of men and women alike was echoed the great problem of this original duality.' Bisexuality remains, for Freud, 'the irreducible nub of the practical exposition of personality.'[11]

As Chapter 4 suggested, Victorian siblings in literature were regarded as being more alike than different; hence their appeal as idealized sexual partners or 'second selves'. Catherine Earnshaw's impassioned cry that she *'is'* Heathcliff is one of the most poignant moments in *Wuthering Heights*; while in *The Mystery of Edwin Drood*, the twins Neville and Helena Landless are so alike that each time they ran away from their stepfather in Ceylon, she always dressed as a boy. In Dinah M. Craik's novel of sibling relations, *The Head of the Family* (1852), which is rather like Charlotte Yonge's *Pillars of the House* in its focus on older brothers and sisters as parent-substitutes for an orphaned family, the eldest two Graeme children, Ninian and Lindsay, meld together as a scarcely differentiated couple: 'The brother and sister – very like one another always, and growing liker every day – sat thus, as they sat night after night keeping quiet vigil together, old bachelor and old maid.'[12] After the death of one sibling, the sameness can actually intensify, as Conrad suggests in *Under Western Eyes* (1911), when Nathalie Haldin starts to acquire more masculine characteristics following her brother's loss. Joseph A. Boone and Deborah E. Nord suggest that this emphasis on 'sameness' in Victorian sibling relations actually points to 'a breakdown of sexual roles and a blurring of gender distinctions that further unsettle the familial status quo of which, ironically, brother and sister are part'.[13] The argument of this chapter is that Victorian writers were intensely aware of this inherent sameness within difference, with its concomitant difference within sameness, and used the brother–sister duality to open up their exploration of the paradoxes between them. Gender as something accidental, that in Judith Butler's terminology is 'a free-floating artifice' (Butler, p. 6), is central to the suggestion that for many nineteenth-century writers it was not seen as final, but as something symbolically negotiable within the text, if not within life itself. The text therefore becomes a place of free play, where the possibility of gender inversion can be entertained, and its implications followed through, whether within a single poem (as in Branwell Brontë's 'Caroline'), a short story (as in Lamb's three contributions to *Mrs Leicester's School*), an episode in a troubled life (as in Sarah Grand's novel of 1893, *The Heavenly Twins*), or through an entire life history (as in Eliza Lynn Linton's *Autobiography of Christopher Kirkland*).

There was also an underlying fascination with blurred gender differences in society at large, which Linton's novel is not alone in exemplifying. Evidence of this is particularly strong in texts such as Poe's 'Fall of the House of Usher', where Roderick's looks are feminized, and he has caught his sister's languorous disease, suffering, like her, from a heightened acuteness of the senses which sounds like a form of neurasthenia (before the term was regularly applied to women in the 1890s). In Mary Elizabeth Braddon's *Lady Audley's Secret* (1862), Robert Audley falls in love with Clara Talboys partly because she closely resembles her brother George, Robert's best friend. In texts where there is a suggestion of homosexual attraction, the sister provides a more acceptable object for the men's homoerotic feelings: so at the end of *Lady Audley*, Robert is able to share his house with his wife *and* her brother, having offered, in his marriage proposal, to look for George ('our brother', p. 372) in Australia. Less happy is the conclusion to a similar dual relationship with a brother and sister in *Brideshead Revisited* (1945), where Charles Ryder sees Sebastian Flyte as a 'forerunner' of Julia. Though she too was curious about him, Charles maintains his interest was 'keener, for there was always the physical likeness between brother and sister, which, caught repeatedly in different poses, under different lights, each time pierced me anew'. Julia's appearance is initially boyish and 'flat-chested'.[14] Later disturbed that Charles can so easily have forgotten Sebastian, Julia discusses with him what he meant by seeing her brother as a 'forerunner'; Charles confesses inwardly: 'I had not forgotten Sebastian. He was with me daily in Julia; or rather it was Julia I had known in him, in those distant Arcadian days' (p. 288). In many ways, the blurring of gender characteristics opened up new possibilities for relationships – to which Eve Kosofsky Sedgwick's notions of 'homosocial desire' and the homoerotic love-triangle – offer a useful guide.[15] In Waugh's case the fought-over love-object is not a woman, but Sebastian, for whom both he and Julia have strong feelings. In Braddon's, too a common devotion to George is what draws Clara and Robert together emotionally.

At the same time, the frustrations of rigid gender demarcations in the family and society are never forgotten. There is a strong sense that what would be normal and acceptable for one sex would be outrageous for the other. Because brothers and sisters begin life scarcely differentiated, the widening of the gap between them exposes the extent of the frustrated desire which is at the heart of the brother–sister relationship.

Even so conservative a novelist as Charlotte Yonge alludes to the inappropriate or even accidental distribution of genders among the numerous brothers and sisters of her large fictional families. Mrs May, writing to her sister in *The Daisy Chain* (1856), and describing her children, remarks:

> It is a common saying that Tom and Mary made a mistake, that he is the girl and she the boy, for she is a rough, merry creature, the noisiest in the house, always skirmishing with Harry in defence of Tom, and yet devoted to him, and wanting to do everything he does. Those two, Harry and Mary, are exactly alike, except for Harry's curly mane of lion-coloured wig. (p. 44)

As it is, Harry, Mary and Tom are known in the family as 'the boys' (p. 4); yet it soon becomes obvious that their paths in life will dramatically diverge. While Harry goes to sea, and Tom trains as a doctor, Mary stays at home, helping in the parish until she marries a dull schoolmaster, afraid that Harry will blame her for marrying first and 'betraying' their relationship. In *The Pillars of the House* (1873), Robina, a girl with an adapted boy's name, is 'comically like a boy and like her brothers' (I, 147): her siblings, especially her brothers, often call her 'Robin', while their religious and effeminate brother Clement is known as 'Tina'. Yonge comments that Clement 'looked so much as if he ought to have been a girl, that Tina, short for Clementina, was his school name' (I, 7). When the eldest brother Felix finds him irritating, he says: ' "Don't be such a girl, Tina" ' (I, 200), and gives him a lecture on 'manliness'. Yonge is an expert chronicler of the tensions within large families doomed to follow the paths laid down for them by masculine and feminine tradition, as they struggle with the intense emotional loyalties across the full sibling range. Their emotional needs as girls and boys, in fact, often run counter to what their society expects of them, and many resist the career choices already made on their behalf. Tom May initially hates the idea of being a doctor, while Angela Underwood, in *Pillars*, longs to be a nurse; Felix abandons all hope of going to university in order to support his family of orphaned siblings by working on the local newspaper; Edgar has the freedom to leave home and become an artist, while for Cherry (crippled anyway), the same opportunity has to be carefully negotiated and permitted only on a short-term basis. Career choices apart, Yonge's families of brothers and sisters often query the broader gender assumptions their societies attribute to them. In each large family, there is usually at least one child who seems to have been born into the wrong sex: something Ibsen takes up in *Hedda Gabler* (1890) and *Little Eyolf* (1894). In the later play, Allmers remembers calling his half-sister Asta 'Eyolf', which is what she would have been called had she been a boy. She, in turn, dressed up in the blue Sunday suit he had worn as a child. Gender boundaries can be seen as this easy to cross, but only within the home, and never for long. All the time he is dressed as a 'lady', Peter Jenkyns is terrified by his father's gullibility. As we have seen, the punishment for being found out could be severe and humiliating.

Moreover, there is much more to gender than a change of clothes, or the coining of a nickname. Many nineteenth-century writers were intrigued by the possibility of living as a member of the opposite sex; of experiencing a woman's emotions rather than a man's, or vice-versa; in the broadest sense, of having other choices, or different perspectives.

Being a brother in a family where one had grown up as a sister, being a sister instead of a brother, were options that could at least be pursued in fiction or poetry, and made to extend the boundaries of an individual life: hence the use of plots tracing the parallel adventures of brothers and sisters, as, for example, in *Nicholas Nickleby, Dombey and Son, Hard Times, North and South, Wuthering Heights, Can You Forgive Her?* and F. D. Maurice's now largely forgotten novel, *Eustace Conway: or, The Brother and Sister* (1834). Conrad continues the theme, in a modified form which emphasizes the sister's role, in *The Secret Agent* (1907) and *Under Western Eyes* (1911). This fictional pattern not only widens access to forbidden feelings and experiences normally unavailable to the opposite sex, it also allows writers to displace on to brother or sister figures experiences that would be inappropriate to their opposite sexed siblings. A classic example of this occurs in Gaskell's *North and South* (1855), when Margaret Hale's brother Frederick (who led a mutiny) reappears in the novel at a point where Margaret's own behaviour has become particularly transgressive. She has flung herself against John Thornton to protect him from missiles thrown at him by his striking factory-workers, and now appears to be meeting her lover at the railway station by night. This 'lover' is, of course, her brother, the only man she should be able to meet secretly and kiss in public without forfeiting her reputation as a chaste middle-class woman. At the same time, Frederick symbolically bears the blame for his sister's transgression, while she symbolically atones for his. While she has defended an unpopular master and tried to save him from injury, Frederick has led a mutiny against his. His appearance at this stage in the novel distracts attention from Margaret's actual indiscretions, by placing them in a larger, 'masculine' perspective, while also creating new ones, which only the reader knows to be untrue. The novel seems to be suggesting that although ultimately a sister's transgressions are lesser than a brother's, in that her life is not at stake, as his is, within the narrow world of a sister's domestic life, they can be magnified into a type of mutiny. Frederick becomes a scapegoat for his sister's disobedience, carrying her act of rebellion against accepted standards of behaviour into the wider world of life at sea as a serving member of the merchant navy.

Like most Victorian novelists who write about sibling pairs, Gaskell stresses the similarities between the brother and sister. Even though they have been separated for years, Margaret feels drawn to Frederick, whose femininity within his masculinity is mentioned more than once. Mrs Hale recalls that as a baby Frederick was 'much prettier' than Margaret. As an adult he has 'delicate features, redeemed from effeminacy by the swarthiness of his complexion, and his quick intensity of expression'.[16] Margaret, in turn, wishes she had a man's power of free and frank speech, so that she could discuss her behaviour with Mr Thornton: '"I wish I were a man, that I could go and force him to express his disapprobation, and tell him honestly that I knew I deserved it"' (p. 385). Brother and sister are both rebels against what they consider to be harsh authority; both stand up for people they think are too weak to defend themselves; both act impulsively and both are driven into hiding – Frederick in Cadiz, Margaret at home with her parents. Because this is in some ways an unnecessary subplot of the text (a further example of Gaskell's melodrama, like another family-based plot element in *Mary Barton*, the return of Aunt Esther), its significance as a commentary on Margaret's experiences – like Kate Nickleby's on her brother Nicholas's – needs to be carefully re-evaluated.

Margaret's position is further complicated by the fact that she cannot clear her own name without implicating her brother. Either Frederick must be regarded as her lover, or she must reveal his identity as a returned mutineer, now accused of manslaughter at the local station. Frederick is also caught in an intractable double-bind in that he cannot clear himself through a court martial except by endangering his own life. '"But how must I make them know?"' he asks Margaret in words that anticipate the impossibility of clearing her own reputation. '"I can't send a bellman about, to cry aloud and proclaim in the streets what you are pleased to call my heroism"' (p. 326). For both siblings, issues of patient obedience, or the risks of speaking out are at stake. Margaret tells Mr Bell that what she did was '"wrong, disobedient, faithless"' (p. 485), but it was not for herself that she told lies: '"I had no conscience or thought but to save Frederick"' (p. 484). Similarly, according to Mrs Hale's account of the mutiny, '"It was not for himself, or his own injuries, he rebelled"' (p. 154). While the brother's rebellion makes him a permanent exile, the sister's makes her lie, blush, and lose her chaste reputation. While Frederick is always passionate and impatient, Margaret, instinctively emotional like her brother, has to confess and wait. She never has the opportunity to run away to a foreign country and start a new life, as her brother does. In summarizing Margaret's moral dilemma towards the end of the novel, Gaskell uses a vocabulary similar to that applied to Frederick's experiences, but repositioned in a domestic context. Remembering how she had vowed to live 'as brave and noble and life as any heroine she had ever read or heard of in romance', Margaret learns that 'not only to will, but also to pray, was a necessary condition in the truly heroic' (p. 502). Rewritten for a sister, the notion of heroism still concerns speaking out, as it does for Frederick, but ultimately a woman has to speak in defence of her own sexual innocence, rather than of another person's rights.

This, too, is what Kate Nickleby has to do, when she defends herself against Sir Mulberry Hawk at her uncle's all-male dinner-party, while her brother Nicholas stands up for Smike at Dotheboys Hall. Here, too, as in other Victorian novels that follow the parallel fortunes of a separated brother and sister, the challenges both face reflect the different gender expectations of the societies they inhabit. While Nicholas is the victim of Fanny Squeers's wounded sexual pride, Kate is allowed, in her workplace, only to offend another woman, Miss Knagg, and at a comic level. Nevertheless, their sameness is noted even by Ralph Nickleby, who has some grudging respect for his niece, if not for his nephew. '"There is some of that boy's blood in you, I see,"' he grumbles, when Kate come to complain about the behaviour of Sir Mulberry Hawk, and 'something in the flashing eye reminded him of Nicholas at their last meeting'.[17] Once Sir Mulberry's attentions have become too dangerous for Kate, and she is moved back into safety with Nicholas and her mother, the girl-in-distress plot is passed to Madeline Bray, with Nicholas as rescuer. Dickens comments, of Kate, that 'Living under the same roof with the beloved brother from whom she had been so suddenly and hardly separated... she seemed to have passed into a new state of being' (p. 571). From now on, their reactions to events are largely alike. They both love and protect Smike, they are both fond of the Cheerybles, they both fall in love, but feel they are too poor to live with anyone except each other. Only Nicholas has the power to be proactive – taking Smike away to be nursed towards a peaceful end, or saving Madeline Bray from her marriage to Arthur Gride.

Most commonly, however, nineteenth-century writers keen to explore the implications of belonging to the opposite sex, adopted a first-person narrative that told their history from within. In itself, this was nothing new. Two of the best-known eighteenth-century male novelists, Defoe and Richardson, had successfully produced full-length narratives written in a female voice, and Dickens sustains Esther Summerson's voice through half of *Bleak House*, alternating with the more cynical worldly-wise voice of the omniscient (assumed male) narrator. Moreover, cross-gendered verse had been written since (at least) the *Wife of Bath's Prologue*, and as the editors of an anthology specifically of this kind of poetry explain, the poets 'dramatize gender itself, bringing to the fore the ways in which a society standardizes social behaviour'.[18] What was different about the Victorians' use of the cross-dressed voice was its specific application, in several key instances, to the issue of sibling relations within the family, making their work an interrogation of how their experiences would have been different had they been of the opposite sex. In each case, the swapping of sexual identity allows them to express an aspect of themselves which was forbidden or less available to them from their gendered position within the family.

The Brontës

This is true of all four Brontës. At the beginning of *The Professor* (1856), its narrator, William Crimsworth, identifies himself specifically as a younger brother with feminized features. Compared with the successful Edward, ten years his senior, he is 'inferior' in form, 'thinner, slighter, not so tall. As an animal, Edward excelled me far'.[19] William remains intensely interested in women throughout the narrative. He recalls that their mother, whose portrait on Edward's wall he admires for its gentle thoughtfulness, was left destitute after her husband's death, 'unhelped by her aristocratic brothers, whom she had mortally offended by her union with Crimsworth' (p. 7). He rejects his sister-in-law's infantile and unintelligent femininity, much as Jane Eyre deplores the brainless sensuousness of the women at Rochester's house-party; while at Mlle Reuter's school, he studies the fleshly girl pupils with unusual intensity: in effect, the intensity of a woman who knows her own shape and is comparing her own smallness with the solidity of the less sensitive pupils, half proud and half ashamed of herself as an inferior specimen. Anne Brontë, in *The Tenant of Wildfell Hall*, also studies her women characters with the 'insider knowledge' of another woman, but initially plays with Gilbert Markham's role as an annoying brother who comes in late for tea, refuses to fall in love where his sister wishes, and in turn, feels irritated with the women of his domestic circle. Anne, as Gilbert, uses a self-consciously 'masculine' dialect, combining slang and uncouth language, as when he gives his younger brother Felix a 'resounding whack over the sconce', for collaring him in the passageway (p. 10). By the end of chapter 4, Gilbert wonders whether his masculinity has possibly been compromised by his family: 'Perhaps, too, I was a little bit spoiled by my mother and sister, and some other ladies of my acquaintance; – and yet, I was by no means a fop – of that I am fully convinced, whether *you* are or not' (p. 32). All three of the Brontë sisters' male first-person narrators – William Crimsworth, Gilbert Markham, and Lockwood – two of them specifically brothers – are seen as partly feminized, drawn awkwardly to women, yet not entirely at ease with them, and inclined to compensate by shows of masculine bluster (easily exposed as little more than an act). Though Gilbert and Crimsworth eventually become more sympathetic characters, their masculinity is constantly problematized in the text. Their pride is easily wounded, and they seem defensive and vulnerable, even ridiculous in the way they take themselves so seriously. As men they are ill-at-ease with their masculinity, and indeed with other men.

In his fullest 'Caroline' poem (1845), however, Branwell adopts the voice of a young girl (Harriet), who mourns the death of her sister Caroline, a Maria Brontë type. Like his sisters, Branwell sets up a layered narrative structure for this nostalgic poem, one of several preoccupied with a sister's death. A neutral, omniscient narrator sets the scene until Harriet is introduced, remembering 'thoughts of "Long Ago"'. The poem recalls in painful detail the aftermath of Caroline's death – not the death itself, but the sealing of the coffin and its burial, the surreal presence of her parents and the juxtaposition of the funeral rites with images of their shared childhood. In many ways, the poem's emotional identification with the buried body, and stage-by-stage narrative of the funeral ritual anticipates Emily Dickinson's 'I felt a funeral in my brain': 'Down, down, they lowered her, sad and slow,/Into her narrow house below.... And wild my sob, when hollow rung/The first cold clod above her flung.'[20] Harriet both longs to join her sister, and dreads similar exile to 'yonder dismal tomb' (line 270); she merges memories of the nightmare burial with their peaceful nights together in a shared bed:

> And thus it brought me back the hours
> When we, at rest together,
> Used to lie listening to the showers
> Of wild December weather. (ll. 283–6)

As a female narrator, Branwell can achieve more complete intimacy with his sister than he could as a mere brother (it was Charlotte and Emily who shared their special 'bed plays' as children: presumably stories they told each other in their shared bed). Moreover, like William Crimsworth, Harriet feels closer to her mother, and to female patterns of emotion than she does to the more self-contained style of her father's mourning. While her 'father's stern eye dropt a tear' (127), her 'mother mild' presses her 'to her aching breast/As if her heart would break' (177–8); the father, in any case, plays a minimal role in the poem, while the emotional burden passes from both parents to the surviving sister, Harriet. Caroline becomes 'my Caroline' as Harriet claims the right to mourn her with unreserved passion, building the poem to a terrifying nightmare of the crucifixion and Judgement Day, which culminates in Jesus's cry of 'My God! – my God! – hast Thou forsaken me!' (320). Harriet pleads for Caroline's protection from the terrible images of ghosts and 'glistening charnel damps' (331), only to realize she has been dreaming, and Caroline has gone for ever:

> 'Twas day – and I, alone, was laid
> In that great room and stately bed;
> No Caroline beside me! (347–9)

Above all else, the poem confronts the finality of death and the permanent separation of the dead and the living by a wide and 'unrelenting' (350) tide, while the nightmare about the crucifixion and Jesus's cry of betrayal, allows Branwell (by then an unsuccessful man of twenty-eight) to explore the sense of being abandoned by the sister who gave him most comfort and security in childhood; herself a substitute for the mother who had died when Branwell was four.

In an earlier 'Caroline' poem, 'Caroline's Prayer. On the Change from Childhood to Womanhood', published in the *Bradford Herald* and the *Halifax Guardian* in June 1842, Branwell uses Caroline's voice to pray for guidance in her adult life as she leaves childhood behind. The poem also appears in the much longer narrative poem, 'Sir Henry Tunstall', as an inscription in a book. In another published poem of 1842, 'On Caroline', signed 'Northangerland' (an Angrian pseudonym often used by Branwell), the narrative voice asks 'Why beats thy breast when hers is still?/Why lingerest thou when she is gone?' Though Branwell buried his guilty poems inside other, longer poems, and, like his sisters, inscribed narratives within narratives, one of his clearest, most recurrent themes, is the mourning for a dead older sister by a younger one, equally terrified of dying herself, and of facing life alone. Writing as a sister, rather than a brother, Branwell could employ a richer, more poignant emotional range; writing as a child rather than an adult, he could take his grief still further into the realms of the unregulated raw emotion he clearly wanted to express in these poems. While his sisters used the male voice largely for comic effect (this is especially true of Gilbert Markham's and Lockwood's clumsier attempts to ingratiate themselves with women), Branwell relied on the younger sister's voice for tragic expression of an unhealed emotional wound.

Ultimately, all the Brontës valued the uses of androgyny for what they wanted to say about themselves. Quite apart from their choice of sexually unspecific first names (Currer, Ellis and Acton – names, like their brother's – not to mention Lockwood's and Heathcliff's – which could be first name or surname), Anne made a point of stressing in her Preface to the second edition of *The Tenant* that the author's sex was unimportant: 'All novels are or should be written for both men and women to read...' (p. 5). Such was the confusion over the sex and number of the various Bell 'brothers,' that E. P. Whipple, reviewing *Jane Eyre* for the *North American Review*, believed 'Currer Bell'

> divides the authorship, if we are not misinformed, with a brother and sister. The work bears the marks of more than one mind and one sex, and has more variety than either of the novels which claim to have been written by Acton Bell. The family mind is strikingly peculiar, giving a strong impression of unity, but it is still male and female.[21]

Ironically, of course, Branwell was the one family member who had no direct hand in the writing of any of the Brontë novels.

Walter Pater

For Victorian men raised to feel they must support the women in their family, and subordinate their own emotional needs to the wider good of the household, the possibility of being a woman and a sister was an opportunity to view the same household and its circumstances from the position of someone who was assumed to be innocent, helpless, and emotionally repressed, rather than active, worldly-minded and practical. In one of his *Imaginary Portraits* (1887), 'A Prince of Court Painters', Walter Pater adopts the voice of Marie-Marguerite Pater, daughter of Antony Watteau's godfather, and sister of Jean-Baptiste, on to whom she projects much of her thwarted feelings for the painter. 'He is greatly taken with Antony, clings to him almost too attentively, and will be nothing but a painter, though my father would have trained him to follow his own profession,' Marie- Marguerite reports of Jean-Baptiste.[22] Her devotion to her brother allows her to disguise her feelings for Watteau: in vicariously living with Jean-Baptiste in Paris, she can also live with Watteau; and when Watteau rejects Jean-Baptiste, Marie-Marguerite can share his sense of hurt: 'It makes our friendship and fraternal sympathy closer' (p. 26). With no engrossing interests to occupy her in Valenciennes, her life revolves entirely around this double focus of her brother and his hero who is also her own. She records her thoughts in her journal, sealing still further the privacy of her feelings, and, as Pater was aware, reinforcing her own helplessness in the process: 'One's journal,' she admits, 'here in one's solitude, is of service at least in this, that it affords an escape for vain regrets, angers, impatience. One puts this and that angry spasm into it, and is delivered from it so' (p.39). For all her vicarious living with the two artists, Marie-Marguerite feels permanently separated from them and their world. Not only do they leave home and go to Paris, but there they also experience a world of sights and emotions that will never be open to her. 'There are good things, attractive things, in life, meant for one and not for another,' she tries to persuade herself, '– not meant perhaps for me; as there are pretty clothes which are not suitable for everyone' (p.28). In the end, religion offers her the peace of mind she finds nowhere else: 'And one *lives* also most reasonably so. – With women, at least, it is thus, quite certainly' (p.43). David Dolan has suggested that Pater uses Marie-Marguerite's aesthetic preferences to indicate his own changing views on art and morality.[23] Jean-Baptiste, on the other hand, is reconciled with Watteau, and will become heir to his unfinished work, while Marie-Marguerite will share only in Watteau's search for 'something in the world that is there in no satisfying measure, or not at all' (p. 44).

Within his own family, Pater (1839–94) was sandwiched between an older sister, Hester (1837–1922), and a younger, Clara (1841–1910), with whom he lived for much of his adult life, and who after his death opposed the writing of an official biography. Michael Levey suggests that Pater was much closer emotionally to Clara than to Hester, and that they lived together as an isolated family group with no other ties, though there was also an older brother, William (1835–87).[24] In narrating a male artist's career in 'The Prince of Court Painters', from the viewpoint of a female bystander who was excluded from such a life herself, Pater gave himself the opportunity to reflect on the frustrations of being an outsider, of not being allowed to participate in an aesthetic life as a practising artist. Marie-Marguerite is fully aware of her exclusion: in fact, her sense of not being allowed to paint is at least as important a part of the narrative as the adventures of the two men who are. Her personality and her frustrations are allowed to push Watteau's life and her brother's experiences into the background, though it seems as if their careers have sidelined her. Even her portrait, started by Watteau, remains unfinished. As William E. Buckler suggests, it is never entirely clear whose story this is: 'it is alone [in *Imaginary Portraits*] in using the autobiography of one person to relate the biography of another so as to pose in a fascinating way the question of who is the told of and who the teller, or who is the portrait's real protagonist and what is its real subject.'[25] Like Branwell Brontë in his 'Caroline' poems, Pater uses an outer female narrator, who feels her identity has been overshadowed by stronger personalities and presences, to dwell on the emptiness of her own life while deploring the absence of a loved sibling. For other critics, such as Gerald Monsman, Pater's use of both a brother and a sister who are lesser than the great painter, is a way of expressing both his own removal from direct artistic production, and the loss of his father, as a key male role model, in early childhood: 'By projecting himself into both brother and sister,' argues Monsman, 'Pater can suggest simultaneously his frustration at being a mere belated imitator of original genius, like Jean-Baptiste, and also his impatience at being condemned to living without companionship of a high artistic order, like Marie-Marguerite.'[26]

Like most of the other Victorian writers discussed in this chapter, Pater was intrigued by the opportunities offered for self-exploration by androgynous images or brother–sister pairings. A classic example is his essay on *Measure for Measure*, written for the *Fortnightly Review* in 1874, which argues that the main interest of the play is not, as in its source, Whetstone's *Promos and Cassandra*, the relationship between Isabella and Angelo, but that between the brother and sister, Claudio and Isabella – as it is, notes Pater, in Greek tragedy. Characterizing a sister's love as 'a sentiment unimpassioned indeed, purifying by the very spectacle of its passionlessness, but capable of a fierce and almost animal strength if informed for a moment by pity and regret', Pater goes on to evoke Isabella's initial tranquillizing effect when she first appears on the stage, followed by her eruption into violent and unexpected anger: 'The swift, vindictive anger leaps, like a white flame, into this white spirit, and, stripped in a moment of all convention, she stands before us clear, detached, columnar, among the tender frailties of the piece.'[27] Closer to home, Charles and Mary Lamb, with their brother–sister 'marriage', also acquired symbolic importance for Pater, who wrote about them in the *Fortnightly Review* of 1878. Pater noted Lamb's taste for what he called 'household warmth,' and his contentment with his sister's love, rather than any stronger passion: 'The yearning for mere warmth against him in another, makes him content all through life, with pure brotherliness, "the most kindly and natural species of love", as he says, in place of the *passion* of love.'[28] In both pieces, what appeals to Pater is the unimpassioned nature of sibling love, which nevertheless has the potential to flame into protective fury when the rights of the brother are threatened in any way. By seeing the sister, rather than the brother, as the strong protector, the column of white flame, and assigning her the active role, he reverses the usual expectations of the brother–sister balance of power.

The portrait of the Mona Lisa, in its mysteriousness like much else that Leonardo da Vinci painted, appealed to Pater for other reasons: this time its ability to combine both sexes in one. Pater had already seen signs of this in a red chalk drawing of Leonardo's in the Louvre, noting: 'It is a face of doubtful sex, set in the shadow of its own hair, the cheek-line in high light against it, with something voluptuous and full in the eye- lids and lips.'[29] Though this portrait eventually resolves itself into a female face, Leonardo's John the Baptist has 'delicate brown flesh and woman's hair' (p. 118), while the Mona Lisa itself contains all the experiences of both sexes: 'the animalism of Greece, the lust of Rome, the mysticism of the middle age with its spiritual ambition and imaginative loves...' (p. 125). As Jennifer Uglow has observed, Pater's critical work is essentially concerned with the identifying of balance and harmony: 'His aim, in criticism and later philosophical fiction,' she suggests, 'was to reconcile opposing elements: scientific "fact" with the truth of art, intellectual honesty with human compassion and imaginative vision, the Hellenic ideal of form with Romantic "soul".'[30] The reconciliation of male and female can be seen as another aspect of this aim, the brother–sister relationship providing a better model than the husband and wife, because of the absence of passion, and the closer approximation to a state of androgyny.

Sarah Grand's *Heavenly Twins*

The final texts to be discussed in this chapter were written by women exploring what it was like to be a brother. Sarah Grand's *The Heavenly Twins* (1893) follows the paths of three young women embarking on unsatisfactory marriages, one of whom is Angelica Hamilton-Wells, twin sister of Theodore, known as 'Diavolo'. Everything about the twins inverts conventional expectations of them, in that all the stronger characteristics belong to the sister rather than the brother: 'Angelica was the dark one, and she was also the elder, taller, stronger, and wickeder of the two, the organizer and commander of every expedition.'[31] Fiercely loyal to one another, the twins refuse to be educated along differing lines according to their gender, and simply swap teachers, so that Angelica gets the male tutor and Diavolo the governess. Angelica implies, however, that there is more to their rebellion than her desire to learn mathematics and the classics: the twins' very bodies are a site of gendered confusion: '"Diavolo and I find that we were mixed somehow wrong, and I got his mind and he got mine"' (p. 124). No wonder, then, that as Angelica grows up (and both twins view with alarm the signs of her physical maturity, as signalling the end of their close bond), she finds herself increasingly ill-at-ease with her own femininity.

She and Diavolo exchange clothes at an early point in the novel when they are respectively bridesmaid and pageboy at the wedding of their friend Evadne. The whole of Book IV, however, is taken up with the story of 'The Tenor and the Boy', a somewhat surreal interlude of cross-dressing, which Grand wrote before the rest of the novel, and published as a separate work in 1899. Though the reader guesses the truth long before the final revelation is made, the 'Boy' (in reality Angelica disguised in her brother's clothes) completely deceives the sensitive Tenor, an Orsino-like character who has already noticed 'how like in feature the brother and sister were' (p. 384) and relishes the many hours of relaxation he spends with his feminine young companion. At the same time, he is attracted to Angelica, whom he sees (in her own clothes) as a distant and unattainable ideal. One of the pleasures of the relationship, as far as Angelica is concerned, is noting 'the tender reverence of his face when her own name was mentioned' (p. 447), though she also enjoys the 'tolerant loving glance' she receives as the 'Boy'. Her disguise thus enables her to experience the simultaneous, but subtly differing pleasures of being loved both as a male and as a female; but for Angelica, the real purpose of the disguise is something much larger than the pursuit of a particular relationship, important though this is to her. Once her real identity is discovered (via a boating accident), the inevitable questions are asked by her dismayed family (she is even, at this stage, married to an older man whom she calls 'Daddy' and who lets her do more or less what she wants). Frustrated by every aspect of her femininity, but especially her clothes, Angelica simply wanted to be free, like her brother. When she put on his clothes, she did her best to become him:

> I assumed his manner and habits when I put these things on, imitated him in everything, tried to think his thoughts, and looked at myself from his point of view; in fact my difficulty was to remember that I was not him. I used to forget sometimes and think I was. (p. 452)

As a twin who has had an especially close relationship with her brother, Angelica finds it all too easy to assume his identity: '"I tell you I was a genuine boy. I moved like a boy, I felt like a boy; I was my own brother in very truth"' (p. 456). Apart from enjoying the personal release accorded her by her disguise, she tells the Tenor how she particularly relishes the 'free intercourse with your masculine mind undiluted by your masculine prejudices and proclivities with regard to my sex"' (p. 458).

The Heavenly Twins is a strange novel, combining outspoken criticism of the *fin-de-siècle* marriage market with episodes that are patently surreal and quasi-Gothic, much as its tone veers from sentimentality about friendship to plain speaking on issues such as syphilis and infidelity. Equally, the episodes involving Angelica's cross-dressing and ultimately successful attempt to 'become' her brother, at least for some weeks, are difficult to judge in terms of Grand's position as a 'New Woman' writer. The reader is so used to the comic relief provided by the Heavenly Twins' mischievous charm, that when what starts as a childish prank (the clothes-swapping at Evadne's wedding) becomes a serious bid for personal freedom from the disadvantages of being a woman, it can be hard to know whether or not Grand applauds her flouting of conventions. She certainly has more energy than the other two women in the novel, Evadne and Edith, who both suffer deeply from the hardships of bad marriages, and she seems to finish with the best compromise (given that all the marriages in the novel require at least some degree of compromise). But once Angelica is found out – first by the Tenor (who soon afterwards dies of pneumonia after his ducking in the river), and then by her uncle (who also momentarily mistakes her for Diavolo), her further opportunities for disguise are numbered. Grand does, however, give her one final celebratory fling. For one last time she puts on Diavolo's clothes and revels in the sheer physical delight of being able to run away from her uncle's house: 'Then she threw up her arms and stretched every limb in the joy of perfect freedom from restraint; and then with strong bounds she cleared the grassy space, dashed down a rocky step, and found herself a substance amongst the shadows out in the murmuring woods' (p. 530). By the end of the novel, having already caused one man's death by her determination to be her brother, Angelica has accepted the constraints of marriage, and is even 'grateful for the blessing of a good man's love' (p. 551).

Eliza Lynn Linton's *Christopher Kirkland*

No Victorian author suggests that cross-dressing, or any other cross-gendering practice, can lead to permanently satisfying freedom, however thrilling its temporary effects. Eliza Lynn Linton's *Autobiography of Christopher Kirkland* (1885), which also surveys the many different paradigms of love available, searches hard for marriage-substitutes, and concludes that a man is ultimately no freer, and no more successful than a woman in finding happiness through marriage. Linton's novel, uniquely in Victorian fiction, is largely her autobiography with the sexes changed round, so that she becomes a brother, and several (though not all) of her brothers and sisters swap genders. The germ for this seems to lie in Linton's own sense of having been born into the wrong sex. Her first biographer, George Somes Layard, reports her saying 'more than once... with something of gravity, that when she was born, a boy was due in the family, and it was only the top-coating that had miscarried.' Her family, apparently responding, looked on her 'rather in the light of a naughty boy than a weak and defenceless little girl, naughty or otherwise'.[32] Her androgynous nature was something critics continued to remark on well into her old age. However feminine Linton liked to appear, in terms of enjoying needlework and keeping herself and her house in perfect order, interviewers who were impressed by her underlying 'gentleness', still felt, with Mrs Alec Tweedie, that she had 'a man's brain coupled with a woman's tenderness'.[33] Less tactfully, Geraldine Jewsbury implied she was 'a ramping raging Man woman, a *homasse* as the French say', without a womanly trait in her.[34] Linton was discussed by others in the kind of essentialist, sexually polarised language she herself used to describe the way society divided along 'masculine' and 'feminine' lines. Despite the weakness of many of her male characters, who appear in her novels as vain, selfish, materialistic and cruel, Linton theoretically associated 'masculinity' with a largeness of outlook, personal courage, and constancy, whereas 'femininity' for her means emotionality, timidity and obedience. Yet the whole of society, as Linton depicts it in this novel, seems to be wrongly gendered or sexually skewed, beginning with Christopher's brother Edwin, 'the most beautiful of us all,' based on Linton's sister Lucy, and a pet of their older sisters.[35]

Edwin is a kind of Cherubino figure whom women adore as a pretty boy, but when he goes to London to write his first novel (as Linton herself did, with her father's grudging blessing), Christopher finds himself in a widely gender-ambivalent world. In this loosely-structured novel, which for pages lists the characteristics of the scores of people he meets on his travels in London and Paris, apparently for the sake of constructing an impression of bohemian society, almost everyone, however minor their role in the plot, seems to be androgynous or inhabiting the wrong body. His first landlady in London has 'a magnificent contralto voice, formidable eyebrows, a decided beard and moustache, and hands as large and strong as a man's' (I, 249); later, he marries Esther Lambert (the William James Linton character), a woman who hates housekeeping and would rather be out on the campaign trail, while her children are difficult to tell apart in their 'queer epicene costume, which left it doubtful whether they were girls Bloomerized or boys in feminine tunics' (III, 18). Pure 'masculine' or 'feminine' characters are few and far between in the novel, the most perfect being Cordelia Gilchrist, whose devout Catholicism eventually prevents them from marrying (and even she was based on the Catholic doctor, Edward MacDermot, with whom Linton fell in love in 1848, but never married because of the insuperable differences in their beliefs).

The gender ambivalence of Kirkland's capital cities directly affects the kinds of relationship his friends can form. Several times in the novel, men and women who want something more than mere friendship, have to invent a variation of the brother–sister relationship to meet freely, go about together, and express their strong feelings for each other within acceptable parameters. 'Cordelia had taken the habit of calling me brother, and wished that I should call her sister,' Christopher recalls of the woman he wanted to call 'wife' (II, 236), summarizing both the attractions and frustrations of this designation. 'Sister Cordelia' is a name that 'seemed to keep us together in the invisible bond which we could neither break nor draw closer' (237) – its nunlike associations unspoken, but difficult to ignore as a reminder, both of Edward MacDermot's Catholicism, and of Cordelia's unbreakable chastity. While the brother–sister fantasy serves its purpose of deflecting curiosity and criticism away from their relationship, it also arrests its development into anything more passionate and sensual. Perhaps for the same reason, another of his women friends, Althea Cartwright, is 'one of those women who have always on hand a "brother" or "son" or "uncle," according to relative age, with whom they go about' (II, 118). Again, no one initially comments on their situation as they go around together, 'as if we had the right of close companionship by blood-relationship' (II, 133). As Christopher ages, failing to establish any permanent relationships, he begins to take on son and daughter substitutes, his last meaningful relationship being with the aunt and nephew, Felicia Barry and Arthur Ronalds:

> As my regret with Arthur was that he had not been my son, so my sorrow with Mrs Barry was that she had not been my sister, seeing that she could never have been my wife. To have lived with her would have been to have lived in such intellectual and emotional opulence as would have compensated me for all I had lost. (III, 302)

Why is it so impossible for Christopher to make a successful marriage? Why can he think of permanent relationships only in terms of sisters, sons and daughters, aunts, uncles and mothers? The novel suggests either that he loves where marriage would be impossible for religious and moral reasons (as with Cordelia Gilchrist), or for temperamental ones (as with Esther Lambert, who is too disorganized for him to live with); the underlying psychological reason was probably that as a masculine-identified lesbian (before such terms were openly used), Linton found the whole concept of marriage unworkable. Women and men in this society are equally afraid of committing themselves to a socially-sanctioned institution that they personally distrust, whereas sibling relationships permit intimacy without sexuality, or clearly defined rules. Moreover, this is an essentially gender-transgressive society, where the most exciting relationships cross the usual socially-sanctioned boundaries. In the course of his adventures, Christopher becomes intimate with several sister-substitutes whom he never marries, with women who are older and women who are younger, with his niece, with an aunt of his friend, and most ambiguously of all, with a beautiful young androgynous man who dies after sharing his life's philosophy with him. In one of the novel's most complex passages, from a gender perspective, Christopher reflects on his enjoyment of a woman's presence in the house:

> And I confess I like to hear the frou-frou of a woman's dress about me... The sense of her softness, sweetness, and dainty smallness compared to my own sinewy bulk, and the feeling that I can protect her if need be, soothe what I suppose is my masculine vanity. And I feel more at home with her now, in my old age, than I do with my own sex. Men often rasp me, while women never fatigue. (III, 207)

Like Charlotte and Anne Brontë, writing as William Crimsworth and Gilbert Markham, Linton as Kirkland homes in closely on the bodies of women, their physicality, their presence as flesh and blood; but whereas the Brontës feel a certain disgust for their own sex when women are anything other than small and neat, Linton seems to revel in the variety of women's bodies and facial features, as well as the rustle of their voluminous clothes. As written, in fact, by a woman with lesbian inclinations and a taste for daughter-substitutes, this passage takes on additional resonances which allow Linton to express her physical attraction to younger women, and what was ultimately a wish for them to remain (unlike herself) dainty, soft and gentle – characteristics for which her other novels often reveal an underlying contempt.[36] Linton spent all her life trying to reconcile an outward profession of anti-feminism with an inward knowledge that she was herself unable to occupy the traditional woman's role of wife and mother. The best she could manage was a brief second marriage to W. J. Linton and stepmotherhood of his children by a previous marriage, before entering into a permanent separation from him. Even her daughter substitutes left her to get married, as does Christopher's adopted niece Claudia Hamilton.

Linton's preoccupation with gender roles in turn leads Christopher to keep defining what he means by 'masculine' and 'feminine' characteristics, terms that were under critical scrutiny in the 1880s, with Linton herself fighting a traditionalist, rearguard action on behalf of gentle, maternal womanhood while personally transgressing every boundary placed in her path. One of Christopher's favourite words in this text is 'virile', which he associates primarily with physical and moral courage, whether in a man or a woman. Among the first people Christopher meets in London is a Miss King, the eldest sister at his solicitor's house, who has 'certain virile characteristics – witness her personal courage and her constancy...'. She also has 'the most ultra-feminine notions of propriety' (I, 248). Also 'virile' is the self-respect Christopher feels is a vital component of anyone's makeup (III, 320), as well as the strength possessed by men who find going to church irksome (III, 159). A freethinker herself, Linton recognized that the mental characteristics agnosticism developed, such as a general independence of outlook, would be considered by the family and society she lived in inappropriate in women.

One of the most important influences in Linton's life was her elder brother Arthur, ten years her senior, brave and handsome in a way that was legendary. At the age of eighteen he left home to fight in the Polish army against Russia, was captured, but escaped hanging because a Russian officer was moved by his good looks. 'He was and remains ever in my mind as the perfect embodiment of manly power and moral greatness,' she told Mrs Tweedie, 'for he had not a trace of meanness, vice, or deception. He was, and is, the great ideal of my life.'[37] Unsurprisingly, one of Linton's youthful blueprints for society, at a time when she had been more concerned with the rights than the duties of women, involved a 'community of pursuits' between the sexes, bringing about 'a fine fraternal condition of things, where all men would be like big brothers and no woman need fear' (Layard, p. 139). When her vision of a society governed by benevolent Arthurs collapsed under her conviction that the sexes were becoming too much alike under a regime of equality, and sharing their vices rather than their virtues, she fell back on gendered stereotypes: strong, heroic men, gentle virtuous women. By the time she wrote *Kirkland*, however, this too was looking untenable. There are far more women in the novel than men, and all of them have distinctive, strong personalities which usually prove too much for Christopher and his old-fashioned ideals. However hard Linton strove to see women as meek and gentle, even her own characters proved to her that they were otherwise. The quietest and most ladylike, such as Kirkland's niece, Claudia Hamilton, disappear from the novel soon after they are introduced, because there is nothing to say about them. They get married and slip out of the plot. The feisty, unconventional ones, like Kirkland's wife, Esther Lambert, reappear and talk and try to impose their philosophy on him. Ultimately, he is left looking to an androgynous ideal as the only way out of the impasse caused by sexual incompatibility. Arthur Ronalds is Kirkland's ideal because his character 'combined the strength of a man with the purity of a woman. He was essentially a measure of the highest standard to which humanity can attain under its present conditions' (III, 250). Significantly, however, these ideal attributes are combined in a man, rather than a woman, and a young man who dies after a marathon exposition of his philosophy.

As Nancy Fix Anderson has suggested, Linton inverted the sexes in her novel 'ostensibly as a veil but in fact as an unconscious means of maintaining psychological veritude' (p. 178). Christopher Kirkland's raging rebellion against the family and religion, his determination to break free and go to London, would have been harder to depict in a female character, even though Linton had done all these things herself, without alienating her readers and even risking charges of implausibility. As a woman whose fiercest loyalties were to men safely removed from the marriage market (her father substitute, W. S. Landor, her heroic brother) or to women she could pet as sisters or substitute daughters (Lucy Lynn, Beatrice Sichel, the original of Claudia Hamilton), Linton used the novel to explore the impossibility of marriage for a man whose relationships are all with substitute family members – pseudo siblings and children above all. As a woman, going defiantly through life in vain pursuit of one hopeless relationship after another (which was essentially what Linton did), she would have seemed unbelievably immoral and isolated; pitiable, too, as a woman who had failed to sustain any lasting loving relationships. Growing up with the image of a brother as a free spirit, Linton experimentally swapped genders – only to find that the brother-figure, Christopher Kirkland, is as trapped as she was, unable to find himself a permanently satisfying *modus vivendi*. When it came to it, Linton either knew of no other way of living (in which case gender was immaterial), or felt society would defeat men as fully as it defeated women who wanted to live unconventionally. The irony is that by volume III of the novel, Kirkland *does* want to live conventionally, with a tidy wife who has abandoned her outside activities. Esther's refusal to be a Victorian housewife, on which Christopher's hopes are now pinned, causes the collapse of their marriage, and the end of his domestic fantasies.

This chapter has discussed the way Victorian brothers explored the implications of being their own sister, and sisters the implications of being their own brother. As Sandra Gilbert and Susan Gubar suggest, the 'plot of sex-change' is by no means the same for both sexes. Whereas for the male writer 'female impersonation has always been both thrillingly transgressive and dangerously debilitating,' for the female, male impersonation is 'never so threatening'.[38] Although Gilbert and Gubar attribute the latter to what Freud sees as the girl's greater bisexuality, while the male impersonator of women has to deal with the implications of the castration complex, the risks and thrills of sibling cross-gendering need not be seen entirely in psychoanalytical terms. Male impersonators of women generally have more to lose in abandoning the sex with more social and political power for that with fewer choices, though perhaps a richer emotional life. The examples discussed in this chapter suggest that Branwell Brontë and Walter Pater used sisterly personae to explore positions of stasis within families where their real needs, emotional and in (Marie-Marguerite) Pater's case, vocational, were underestimated; while the two women who used fraternal identities as an alternative medium for viewing the marriage market, were attracted to the notion of greater freedom, only to discover that this was, in fact, illusory. While being a sister might at first seem to offer emotional release (as a sister, Branwell Brontë can mourn Maria more openly), female introspection, in both texts, is seen as something of a cul-de-sac, a renewal of the psychological impasse with which each text begins, and which therefore offers its male author little permanent relief. For sisters impersonating their brothers, the promise of escape from the constraints of femininity proves equally empty, as Angelica has to abandon her brother's clothes and be a good wife, while Christopher Kirkland finds that all the wives, in refusing to be good, have left him without a wife at all. As Elaine Showalter has observed, 'transgressive desires in women seem to have led to guilt, inner conflict, and neurotic self-punishment, rather than to fantasies or realities of criminal acting out.'[39] Along the way, moreover, close companions have died and marriages failed, demonstrating the impossibility of improving social arrangements by a change of gender; the only really positive relationships emerging, at least from Grand's, Pater's and Linton's work, being the touchingly ephemeral friendships between older and younger men (the Tenor and the Boy, Watteau and Jean-Baptiste, Christopher and Arthur Ronalds). These Shakespearean relationships are also, of course, in tune with the times: the growing awareness of homosexual instincts which writers of both sexes were increasingly acknowledging in their work. Though all these relationships in the texts discussed here were short-lived, they seemed to provide an appealing alternative to the mercenary or otherwise hypocritical marriage so widely deplored in late nineteenth-century writing. Sibling 'sexchanges' can be seen as part of this wider pattern: a pattern which openly confronted all kinds of dissatisfaction with given gendered characteristics and expectations.

By the close of the century, the sexes were, in many respects, coming closer together, as men appeared more effeminate, women 'harder', and more masculine. Linton (ironically, in view of *Christopher Kirkland*) was among those who deplored the sexual indeterminacy of the age, and noted how the lines of demarcation between the sexes were becoming 'blurred and obliterated'.[40] Within the first twenty years of the next century, however, the sharp divisions between male and female experience were to be renewed with a violence few could have anticipated. As the next chapter will show, for brothers and sisters, the First World War mounted the fiercest threat yet to the stability and survival of their relationship after the many challenges it had faced in the nineteenth century.

7
'Most Unwillingly Alive': Brothers and Sisters in the First World War

How can one believe it, that it should be the *object* to kill Yvo?[1]

By the turn of the century, sisters apparently no longer needed to feel disadvantaged alongside their brothers. Oxford and Cambridge now had women's colleges, and several other universities, including the medical schools, were prepared to accept women on degree courses; serious school examinations had been available to girls since the reform of the Cambridge examinations system in the 1860s; employment opportunities were gradually widening, following pressure from organizations such as the 'Langham Place' set, and influential articles in the press.[2] Gender crises, of the type discussed in the previous chapter, threw into question the precise nature of male identity and masculinity in ways that should have made relations between men and women more equal. The reality for the brother and sister relationship in middle-class families, however, is that things went on in much the same fashion, at least until the First World War, when tight-knit sibling groups were shattered as never before.

Evidence gathered from memoirs written at the end of the nineteenth century and the beginning of the twentieth suggests that in middle-class families the old patterns of envy and admiration over brothers' schooling and sisters' subservience persisted as if little had changed. Although Vera Brittain attended a school that was by no means inadequate, she had to prepare for the Oxford entrance examination on her own, knowing that her brother Edward was receiving a superior education at Uppingham, and indeed that he had been the privileged sibling throughout their childhood. 'I asked if it were not equally important that I should have a career too,' she recalls telling her father in 1915, when Edward was already in the army. 'He answered very decidedly,

"No, Edward was the one who must be given an occupation & the means to provide for himself."' Considering herself the more intellectual of the two, Brittain was furious, and vowed: 'But I will show them.'[3] Nor was she an exceptional case, if Virginia Woolf's anger over 'Arthur's Education Fund' is anything to go by. Although the name comes from Thackeray's novel, *The History of Pendennis* (1848–50), Woolf felt that sisters had been paying into that fund, and making sacrifices on their brothers' behalf, from 1262 to 1870. Nor were they formally released from the family home until 1919, when the professions were opened up to women after the war by the Sex Disqualification (Removal) Act. Even by the approach of the Second World War Woolf felt the private house was still 'a going concern', with more daughters staying at home to look after their mothers than sons staying at home to look after their fathers.[4] This had certainly been Woolf's own experience between 1895 and 1903, after her mother had died and all the responsibility of looking after her ailing and grief-stricken father had devolved upon her older sisters Stella (until she also died) and Vanessa. Fiction of the time continued focusing on the plight of the daughter who either failed to marry, or was expected to stay at home: Arnold Bennett's *Anna of the Five Towns* (1903) and May Sinclair's *Mary Olivier: A Life* (1919) are good examples.

As Woolf noted, the expense of sending girls to school and university was often seen as the first place to start economizing if a family wanted to cut down on expenditure. Moreover, as she observed in her essay-novel version of *The Years*, *The Pargiters* (1932), there was considerable prejudice against higher education for girls.[5] Even in a privileged family such as the Potters, Beatrice Webb's extended family of sisters and brothers-in-law, girls' education was viewed as a less urgent issue than boys'. 'The difference in attitude to the education of sons as compared with daughters,' observes Barbara Caine, 'could not be more marked. The schooling of sons was a matter of immense importance and every step was taken to ensure their adequate preparation for the entrance examination of the desired schools and colleges.' Caine cites the figures spent on Stephen Hobhouse and his brother Arthur, the eldest sons of Margaret and Henry Hobhouse, Beatrice Webb's elder sister and her husband. In 1899, Stephen's private school fees came to £132 per annum, while the second son, Arthur, at Eton, cost the Hobhouses £150. The eldest daughter Rachel, and three other children, all lumped together for accounting purposes, cost only £103 between them.[6] When Arthur and Stephen grew up, their mother wanted them to live with their sister Eleanor, who kept house for them.

In other families, such as Gwen Raverat's, granddaughter of Charles Darwin, it was simply not the norm for girls to attend day schools in the 1890s and early 1900s. 'The upper classes did not approve of day schools, though boarding schools for older girls might sometimes be allowed,' recalled Raverat, who was born in 1885, and had two brothers and a sister. Instead, she was kept at home with a governess, while her brother Charles went 'fairly young' to St Faith's, followed by Marlborough. Gwen herself finally escaped to school when she was sixteen, having managed to learn Latin with Charles, 'which they thought most unfeminine, and really indecent'.[7]

Memoirs such as Raverat's testify to a continuing preoccupation with sibling attachments even at the end of the old century and the beginning of the next. Among middle- and upper-class siblings, traditional relationships persisted, with sisters enjoying the comradeship of their brothers when they came home for the holidays, and as they grew older, appreciating their protection at balls and parties. For girls who stayed at home to be educated, or went to girls' schools, brothers were still the best means of meeting suitable husbands, as Vera Brittain's *Testament of Youth* so clearly illustrates. Older unmarried siblings might continue living together and depending on each other emotionally, as happened with Edith and Osbert Sitwell, and Gertrude and Leo Stein. In fiction, old patterns of possessiveness and jealousy persisted. In Conrad's *The Secret Agent* (1907), Winnie Verloc's intense, maternal love for her younger, feeble-minded brother Stevie turns her into a murderess when Stevie is accidentally blown up by an anarchist bomb. Even in Lawrence's *Lady Chatterley's Lover* (1928), an intense brother–sister relationship – between Clifford Chatterley, and his sister Emma, who helps him with his writing – partly contributes to the marital problems of the Chatterleys: 'She would never forgive Connie for ousting her from her union in consciousness with her brother,' Lawrence says of Emma. 'It was she, Emma, who should be bringing forth the stories, these books, with him.'[8] For women who failed to marry or find another purpose in their lives, the brother – married or single – remained an emotional centre, whereas we start to hear less about brothers intensely dependent on their sisters. Brothers' lives were becoming fuller and busier with increasing calls to action: administration in India, the Boer War, even at school the Officers' Training Corps, and in boyhood, Baden-Powell's scouting movement: all were tempting brothers away from their sisters, even if only in spirit, and sisters were often still left feeling like bystanders. In May Sinclair's *Mary Olivier*, Mary, an only sister, broods over the departure of her brother Mark for the Royal Field Artillery in India, though at his coming-of-age and farewell party, she shares his reflected glory: 'She was Sub-Lieutenant Mark Olivier's sister. His only one.' The gunner's Latin motto thrills her and becomes part of her consciousness: 'All through the excitement of the evening it went on sounding in her head.'[9]

Despite the opening up of higher education opportunities, it was still the exceptional few – mostly from the middle- and upper middle classes – who went to Oxford, Cambridge or London universities. Fiction found a new subject in the narrating of battles to be allowed to leave home and pursue higher education – of which the best known is perhaps H. G. Wells's *Ann Veronica* (1909). The persistence of old family living styles is marked in the novel by the fact that Ann Veronica's aunt lives with her widowed brother, the family's father. Ann Veronica's own brother, Roddy, urges her to abandon her bid for independence in London and return home, however constraining she finds it: ' "A home *may* be a sort of cage, but still – it's a home," ' he argues, adding: ' "You go home and live on the G. V. [governor], and get some other man to live on as soon as possible." '[10] No one requires this of Roddy himself, who works in the motor trade, and perhaps Wells's own later heroine, Joan, of *Joan and Peter* (1918), has greater freedom than Ann Veronica because she is an illegitimate child raised unconventionally as a foster-sister with her cousin Peter. Though they both go to Cambridge, their Uncle Oswald wonders at the general absence of women at the university. 'Where were the girls of the peerage, the county-family girls and the like?' he muses. 'Their brothers were up, but they stayed at home...'[11] Nor do Forster's Margaret and Helen Schlegel, intellectuals though they are, seem surprised that they should stay at home while their young brother Tibby goes to Oxford. Despite his effeminacy, the sisters still look to him for advice when they discover Margaret's husband, Mr Wilcox, has had an affair with Jacky Bast. Helen employs Tibby to arrange financial compensation for the Basts, though they ultimately refuse it.[12]

In Virginia Woolf's *The Years* (1937), which begins with a snapshot of the Pargiter family in 1880, the gap between male and female experience is further emphasized, as the eldest sister Eleanor muses over her brother Morris's career and wishes she could understand his life more fully. At the same time, she keeps back details of her own poor-visiting, doubting whether he will understand. 'That was the worst of growing up, she thought; they couldn't share things as they used to share them.'[13] As the eldest, Eleanor regards it as her duty to superintend the boys' careers, write letters to those who are away from home, and if necessary, plead with their father for one of them to be allowed to pursue his chosen course in life. Morris is her favourite brother, as Woolf indicates in *The Pargiters*: 'the grown man looked up to, the Lord Chancellor, or Lord Chief Justice whom she [respected] literally, devotedly; but he was also the little boy who used to come to her and say that everybody liked Ned better than they liked him...' (p. 30). This seems to have been the special appeal of sibling memories to Woolf: the timeless juxtaposition of the often insecure child's consciousness with the mature adult's. Other sibling pairs in the novel continually revert to old brother-and-sister rituals of mutual teasing when they are long past their childhood. Rose and Martin still argue when they are middle-aged, while Peggy, their niece, watching them in the 'Present Day', finds herself succumbing to a similar instinct with her own brother, North. 'They had to fall back on childish slang, on childish memories, to cover their distance, their hostility' (p. 301). They still know exactly how to hurt each other, though Peggy suddenly remembers something that was good about their shared childhood: 'And he used to read her his poetry in the apple-loft, he remembered, and as they walked up and down by the rose bushes' (p. 301). Peggy, now a doctor and a fully professional woman, unlike her aunt Eleanor, nevertheless feels emotionally adrift without a husband or family of her own. However deeply she resents it and feels out of sympathy with her brother, her relationship with North is an inescapable link with the past, an emblem of childhood. It was this emblematic quality, resonant of timeless summer days, that became such a poignant theme of post-War reminiscence among women writers who had lost brothers in the trenches.

The First World War restored to English middle-class families an extreme notion of 'separate spheres', which took the male world into unknown regions of training camps and foreign fields. This was an unimaginable version of the mysterious boarding school into which sisters were given only glimpses in letters or on gala days such as the Uppingham Speech Day which Vera Brittain describes in *Testament of Youth*. The male world became literally a foreign country – Flanders fields, Italy, Gallipoli; brothers grew up and became unrecognizable in their army uniforms, subjected to a discipline their sisters could scarcely imagine; and the letters sisters had craved from boys' boarding schools became letters from the battlefront, describing officers and colleagues, rather than masters and fellow-pupils (in some cases their comrades in arms had been schoolfriends). The letters were more willingly sent, and answers more eagerly awaited than before, but they were also more evasive about the experiences they discussed. The war truly defamiliarized many brothers for their sisters, just at a point in the evolution of family history when their relations were becoming more comradely. A recurrent trope in much memoir-writing of the time, which symbolizes this change, is the first sight of a brother in his army uniform. When Edward Brittain returned home for his first wartime Christmas, Vera commented: 'He seems so tall & absolutely grown up; I shall be proud for anyone to see him, he really is a fit object for devotion. He has never looked so well as he does in his military clothes.'[14] Though Vera was the elder of the siblings by two years, Edward's experience in the war, in which he won the Military Cross, gave him sudden seniority. In his later correspondence, he addresses her as 'dear child'.

More seems to have been written about lost brothers than about lost husbands and sons, even lost fiancés in the First World War. It was, after all, essentially a young men's war, the initial call-up being for men aged 18 to 30, and a brother, once lost, was irreplaceable. Whereas Vera Brittain was willing to marry her brother's friend Victor Richardson after the death of her fiancé, Roland Leighton, there was nothing she could do to replace Edward – except, as she hoped, have a son who would look like him.[15] Storm Jameson bluntly confessed, when her brother Harold was killed, that she would sooner her husband had died. 'This had nothing to do with love,' she admitted. 'I loved K. more warmly than I loved my brother. But – I realized it then, . . . love is a paltry emotion compared with the ties of blood.' She at last understood the meaning of Antigone's tragedy.[16] The language of adoration, which was the staple of Victorian schoolgirl vocabulary, returned – if it had ever entirely gone away. Roland Leighton's sister, Clare, for example, was convinced that her love for her brother would even protect him from flying bullets: 'It was as though my adoration of him must act as a charm.' Cynthia Asquith, who lost two brothers in the war, and many friends and relatives, mourned 'Darling, darling little Yvo' and her 'beautiful brother' Hugo, as well as 'Darling, brilliant, magically charming Raymond', her husband's brother.[17] After their deaths, it was, of course, impossible for any sister to write dispassionately about her brother. Equally, she was no longer free to resent his advantages, when his so-called 'duties' had taken him to the Front to be killed. For sisters left behind at home, bewildered by their own alarm, as well as by their desire to see brothers enlist and serve their country, the war did more than any previous event in the last century to restore a romantic intensity to brother–sister relationships. It also intensified their sense of guilt and uncertainty about their own roles in the war and after. What could they do to help their brothers? And what happened to the relationship once their brothers were killed? What were they supposed to do with the surplus, redundant emotions, their survivors' guilt, when the war ended? As Vera Brittain's heroine Ruth Alleyndene of *Honourable Estate* (1936) observes, women 'apparently no longer counted unless they could fill subordinate roles in the Army auxiliary services, or hurriedly raise sons to young husbands whose drastically shortened expectation of life left little opportunity for begetting children'.[18]

Two kinds of brother emerge as recurring types in the autobiographies and novels of women who survived the war. The easier to understand is the young and charming baby brother, the darling of the family, whom no one regards as fully grown up until he appears in army uniform and is sent to the battlefields within a year of leaving school. Those most tragically affected by the war were those on the brink of their university career: the men born in 1895–6, with places at Oxford and Cambridge: some, like Edward Brittain, with sisters looking forward to being college students with them. For sisters who felt their brothers were artistic and intellectual, rather than military men, the waste of life and opportunity when their brothers enlisted was acutely painful – even though the necessity of enlisting was something they themselves acknowledged. Vera Brittain urged her brother Edward to join the army, and in the early stages of the war, at least, even envied him his direct involvement: 'don't you feel you wouldn't miss it for anything?' she asked him in April 1915, before anyone she cared about had been killed.[19] Significantly, her autobiographical persona, Ruth Alleyndene, feels nothing but apprehension when her favourite brother Richard joins the Chelsea Rifles, and takes no part in persuading him to enlist. Unlike Vera Brittain herself, she is already away at Oxford when the war begins, and unable to influence her brother's decision.

For Lady Cynthia Asquith, married to Herbert Asquith, the Prime Minister's son, the death of her youngest brother Yvo (1896–1915) impressed on her for the first time the full horror of the war. Yvo, for her, stood for youth, innocence, and charm: she had even looked forward to the 'fun' of having him home with a 'slight wound' (*Diaries*, p. 90): 'One looked *forward* to him always as an ever-increasing joy...' The sudden cancellation of Yvo's future, the knowledge that they could look only *backwards* at his short life, also horrified her younger sisters Mary and Irene: the latter 'simply idolized Yvo. His photograph was always under her pillow' (p. 91). The adored younger brother, inevitably doomed to die in battle, was also a recurrent character in novels about the war. In Irene Rathbone's *We That Were Young* (1932), the heroine Joan Seddon is deeply devoted to her younger brother Jimmy (whom she calls 'Jumbles'), aged sixteen at the start of the novel. Though Joan is courted by other men, and is even engaged to be married, the love of her life is clearly Jimmy. They are entirely relaxed with each other; warm, affectionate, even sexually aware (in the opening sequence he watches her dress). There are many references to his heart-stopping good looks: 'Beautiful eyes. Luminous. A saint's eyes, or a seer's.' She sits on his knee, 'her cheek against his hair'.[20] Like many devoted sisters of the time, Joan becomes a Voluntary Aid Detachment nurse as the best way of being close to her brother: each time they meet up again, she admires his increasing manliness: his ability to lift her up when they play charades (p. 120), the strength of his arms: 'those arms which only yesterday had been the thin little arms of the Preparatory School-boy' (p. 121). Her happiness in Jimmy's company is essentially a delight in the perfection of his young man's body, with its remaining suggestions of childlike innocence: real adult men, like Colin Paley, who is in love with her, never excite her in the same way. Indeed her one clear image of marriage is of having a home into which Jimmy can call whenever he likes (p. 133). She finds it difficult to visualize him doing a man's job: 'Guns, horses, men, billeting. In the ordinary way he would be just leaving school' (p. 369). Ironically, Jimmy survives all this, and dies of influenza when the war is over, leaving her totally bereft: 'With him she had lost a brother, a son, and half herself...' (p. 430).

Relationships with younger brothers seemed to be even more acutely painful than those with elders: after all, the sister's role with a baby brother had usually been maternal and protective – hence Joan's feeling of having lost a son as well as a brother in Jimmy's death. Among the Imperial War Museum's many collections of First World War brother–sister correspondence is that of Norman Austin Taylor (1895–1918) with his older sister Joyce (1889–1979), who wrote to him as 'My dear little boy'. When Taylor, who served in the 1st Battalion, 1st Surrey Rifles, and was awarded the Military Cross, was killed in the final year of the war by a machine-gun bullet, Joyce lamented in her diary the loss of:

> Five foot ten of a beautiful young Englishman under French soil. Never a joke, never a look, never a word more to add to my store of memories. The book is shut up for ever & as the years pass I shall remember less & less, till he becomes a vague personality, a stereotyped photograph.[21]

Though their correspondence during the war had been largely humorous, and Taylor had sent his father, rather than his sister, 'a lurid blood and thunder description' of 'affairs in our vicinity', Joyce writes of

Norman after his death in much the same way as the novelists commemorated their younger brothers. On the rare occasions when a brother was too daunted by battle to fight on, the sister's involvement became more problematic. It was one thing to rejoice over a brother brought home with an honourable 'blighty wound' ('I'm still looking for that cushy wound which will bring me home on the wounded hero touch,' Norman Taylor joked with his sister Joyce), another to discover that he had been psychologically crushed by battle. Rose Macaulay's Wartime novel, *Non-Combatants and Others* (1916) (dedicated 'To my brother and other combatants') recounts a close and protective relationship between the heroine Alix and her younger brother Paul – 'rather a brilliant boy,' who had 'just obtained a particularly satisfactory Oxford scholarship'.[22] When he is supposedly killed in action, Alix discovers that in fact he went to pieces in the trenches and shot himself. ' "He was such a *little* boy," ' she protests, rejecting the hollow comfort of friends: 'Paul was insistent; she pressed her hands against her eyes and saw him on the darkness, her little brother, white-faced, with the nervous smile she knew' (p. 104). Older sisters in novels like this never recover from their brothers' deaths. All they can do to assuage their bitterness and grief is find war work that will give them some sense of helping them, even posthumously. With thirty-eight the upper age-limit for VAD enrolment, sisters clearly had a more obvious role here than mothers. They could go to the Front and nurse; they could play the part of 'sister' to someone else's brother.

The other kind of brother who appears in memoirs and novels about the war is the mysterious, opaque, unknown character who died before anyone could really understand who he was. Even before the war started, however, heroic brothers – unusually handsome, intelligent or adventurous – who died before they reached adulthood, became ghosts who haunted their sisters' memories. Eglantyne Jebb, founder of the Save the Children Fund, dreamed of her brother Gamul who died of pneumonia at Marlborough in 1896, while she, with her sisters, stayed at home and was taught by governesses. 'Twenty years later,' claims Jebb's biographer, 'Gamul came back to her in dreams so vividly that she felt he was still living, though on a different plane, and needed her help.'[23] Ironically, Gamul was to have been a doctor; raised by their father's unmarried sister. However, the girls of the family made it to Oxford, where another brother, Dick, was able to meet Eglantyne for walks, bicycle rides and other social events – much as Vera Brittain had hoped to do with her brother Edward and his school friend Roland Leighton, had not the war interrupted their careers. Another legendary dead brother was Ivy Compton-Burnett's Guy, who survived a narrow brush with pneumonia at the age of fourteen, only to die of influenza as a Cambridge undergraduate in 1905. Though Ivy immediately sought consolation from her next nearest brother Noel (who was to die in the war in 1916), Guy's loss, according to Hilary Spurling, 'remained a source of almost unfaceable pain to the end of her life'.[24] Intense sibling relationships became a regular feature of her writing, and are highlighted particularly in her novel of 1929, *Brothers and Sisters*, which recreates an entire sibling society in the fashion of mid-nineteenth century literature.

Virginia Woolf

The most legendary of the legendary dead brothers before the war, however, was Thoby Stephen, Virginia Woolf's elder brother: handsome, aloof, slightly melancholy (Henry James referred to him as 'poor dear mild able gigantic Thoby'[25]), and ultimately unknowable because of his premature death from typhoid at the age of twenty-six in 1906. Woolf's early diaries and letters show that Thoby featured as a companion and playmate who often preferred to spend his time with other males, while Virginia was thrown more into the company of her sister Vanessa. In the gloomy years following their mother's death, and then their half-sister Stella's, Thoby's promise was one of their few consolations. Woolf, aged fifteen, noted in her diary a compliment from Leslie Stephen's sister-in-law, the novelist Anne Thackeray Ritchie: 'As soon as she was out of the door after lunch, she said to father in a loud voice – "Oh Leslie what a noble boy Thoby is!"'[26] Though he lacked Woolf's own cleverness, she recalls his dominance over the family group when they were all at home living with their widowed father. She says several times in her 'Sketch of the Past' that 'he was not clever' (though she learnt about the Greeks from him, and they discussed Shakespeare);[27] instead he was shy, distinguished-looking, mysteriously adult, reserved, biding his time without realizing that time was the one thing that would be withheld from him. Liking to sketch people in terms of memorable scenes in which she could remember them, Woolf was able to produce only one significant picture of Thoby: on a boat, 'steering us round the point without letting the sail flap' (*Moments*, p. 136): a picture which subsequently suggested the scene in *To the Lighthouse* where James Ramsay steers the boat and wins his father's approval.[28] Woolf was convinced that had he lived, he would have been a great judge: 'Publicly, he would have been, had he been put on, a judge certainly. Mr Justice Stephen he would be today;

with several books to his credit... By this time, aged sixty, he would have been a distinguished figure; but not prominent; for he was too melancholy, too independent, unconforming, to take any ready made mould' (p. 140). She wanted him to be both stately and slightly dangerous, like Percival in *The Waves*: 'Percival whom I wanted to lose his hair, to shock the authorities, to grow old with me.'

Thoby perhaps stands out all the more in Woolf's memory for being so unlike the other Stephen men: Sir Leslie, querulous and self-pitying after his wife's death; Adrian, the all-too-human younger brother, with whom Woolf never had such an intense relationship, though she lived with him after Thoby's death and Vanessa's marriage; their half-brothers, George and Gerald Duckworth, who in private sexually abused the sisters, and in public wanted the Stephen girls to go into society and become conformist upper middle-class women. Thoby's appeal to Woolf lay in his aborted life-span, his permanent youth combined with a sense of his middle-aged gravitas as a potential pillar of the establishment. His life was over and complete, yet it left many questions unanswered. It could be made the subject of endless speculation over the ideal of a masculine life, a life very different from their bookish father's.

In fact Woolf began fictionalizing Thoby as soon as he was dead. In order to protect her friend, Violet Dickinson, who had been on the fatal trip to Greece where both she and Thoby had picked up the infection, Woolf pretended Thoby was still alive for a month after his actual death. Her depiction of Thoby as a decidedly masculine invalid demanding solid food and beginning to 'curse a good deal' stresses his frustrated vigour in a caricatured style: 'He is very cross with his nurses, because they wont [sic] give him mutton chops and beer; and he asks why he cant [sic] go for a ride with [Clive] Bell, and look for wild geese,' she told Violet five days after the death. At times, she sounds to be trying too hard: 'The d[octo]r. says his brain is the strongest he knows; and his heart is fit to do the work of two men.' When the truth finally broke, Woolf had turned him into a virile hero, 'splendid to the end': 'I can feel happy about him' she decided; 'he was so brave and strong, and his life was perfect.'[29]

While Woolf's older male characters, such as Mr Ramsay and Peter Walsh, are fully knowable with all their quirks and peculiarities, her younger ones remain shadowy. Most critics agree that Jacob, of *Jacob's Room* (1922) is modelled on Thoby, especially in terms of his shadowy reserve, but also his judge-like authority. Overheard arguing with his friend Bonamy, Thoby pronounces in a loud, overbearing voice words such as 'good', 'absolute', 'justice' and 'punishment'.[30] Fanny Elmer sees

Jacob as part of a different race: 'She thought how young men are dignified and aloof, and how unconscious they are, and how quietly one might sit beside Jacob and look at him' (p. 113). Young men appear to her oddly childlike and commanding. When he goes to Greece at the end of the novel, and she has only his postcards with which to construct his image, Fanny forms an even more heroic impression of him as 'statuesque, noble, and eyeless' (p. 166); the battered Ulysses in the British Museum gives her a 'fresh shock of Jacob's presence' (p. 166). Fanny's experience of the absent Jacob replicates Woolf's attempts to reconstruct her dead brother from isolated memories of him. He is 'eyeless': a strange word whose many resonances build up her abiding, monumental image of Thoby. 'Eyeless' suggests blind justice, appropriate to one she saw as a judge; but also Milton's hero, Samson Agonistes, 'eyeless in Gaza', a doomed hero, deprived of his strength (symbolically castrated, perhaps). Like Ulysses, he is a wanderer, and indeed a sailor (Woolf's abiding image of Thoby). Unlike Thoby, however, Jacob dies in the war (as his surname, 'Flanders,' foretells) – as if Woolf felt that someone as heroic as Thoby should have died in action, rather than as a typhoid victim after a holiday in Greece. His being 'splendid to the end' prefigures the language of First World War battlefield heroism.

Thoby's mystery in many ways encapsulated – perhaps helped originate – Woolf's theory of the ultimate unknowability of any one individual, and drove her strenuous efforts to find a new way of describing personality while recognizing that this was in itself impossible. Sara Ruddick, however, is unconvinced by suggestions that Thoby also appears as Percival in *The Waves*, one of Woolf's most monumental absentees around whom the others build their ideas of heroism. She prefers to generalize the image of Percival as 'the common longing for and fear of the warrior; the unanswerably, indifferently strong'.[31] Percival is undoubtedly a striking presence, even at school. Neville's early description of him, however, suggests that he is a potential law-giver, like Thoby, and that he is 'eyeless' like Jacob: 'He should have a birch and beat little boys for misdemeanours. He is allied with the Latin phrases on the memorial brasses. He sees nothing; he hears nothing. He is remote from us all in a pagan universe' (pp. 29–30). A giant among pygmies, Percival is godlike in his inhuman indifference. Building on Ruddick's suggestion, I would see Percival as Woolf's attempt to merge Thoby's image with that of the First World War soldier killed in battle. Neither Thoby nor Percival dies this way, and indeed Woolf was unusual for a woman of her generation in not having any close male relatives killed in the war (her friends were more likely to be conscientious objectors). Sometimes accused of ignoring the war in her concentration on upper middle-class family life, Woolf has now been recovered as someone intensely interested in it, especially in her characterization of the shell-shocked Septimus Warren Smith in *Mrs Dalloway*, as well as allusions to Andrew Ramsay being killed by an exploding shell in *To the Lighthouse*, and the zeppelin raids in *The Years*. As Hermione Lee puts it, Woolf's books are actually 'full of images of war: armies, battles, guns, bombs, air-raids, battleships, shell-shock victims, war reports, photographs of war-victims, voices of dictators'.[32]

Bernard believes Percival is quite simply 'a hero' (p. 105) round whom the others gather like soldiers round their captain. His departure in a taxi after their farewell meal together as he sets out for India, has all the finality of death, which his friends are powerless to stop. 'What can we do to keep him?' Neville wonders. 'How bridge the distance between us?' (p. 126). Percival dies in the next section of the novel, but (like Thoby) not heroically, by an avoidable accident: 'He fell. His horse tripped' (p. 128). Neville tries to envisage exactly what happened, and how Percival felt as he hit the ground: Bernard imagines the 'bandaged head, the men with ropes' (p. 133) – very much as surviving sisters tried to call up what had happened to their brothers killed in the war. As Bernard says later in the novel, still haunted by Percival's pain, 'What torments one is the horrible activity of the mind's eye – how he fell, how he looked, where they carried him' (p. 227). Neville responds to the news with the telegram still in his hands: the usual means of receiving bad news from the Front. Like Vera Brittain, who lost an entire generation of friends in the War, Neville feels like a solitary survivor: 'From this moment I am solitary. No one will know me now' (p. 129). He needs to be convinced, like many War widows and brotherless sisters, including Brittain herself, that the death was worth something, and not just a meaningless accident that could have happened to anyone. He believes that if someone had only tightened Percival's stirrup by three holes, 'he would have done justice for fifty years, and sat in Court and ridden alone at the head of troops and denounced some monstrous tyranny, and come back to us' (p. 129).

Bernard's reaction articulates many of the feelings survivors had about those who were dead in battle. The dead were both lucky to be missing life's further tragedies; on the other hand, they were arrested in midflow, eternally young, but relatively inexperienced in the maturer pleasures of family life and professional success. Bernard feels both: 'You are well out of it' and 'But this is better than one had dared to hope' (p. 131). Percival will never father a child or know the mixed pleasures of becoming a middle-aged man. As a 'judge' (the way Woolf repeatedly sees brother-figures), Percival must be an invisible arbiter somewhere, but no one knows how to communicate with him. The longing for Percival as someone to laugh with, to treat as a normal brotherly friend, continues to haunt the sibling-like set of friends whose changing relationship Woolf charts in *The Waves*.

Vera Brittain and Rebecca West

For Vera Brittain, too, the sense of a relationship being unfinished, a brother being unknown, is what dominates her writing about her younger brother, Edward, who survived until the last year of the War, only to be killed in Italy in June 1918. Even before the War started, Edward had always been something of a sealed, self-contained character, whose real feelings were difficult to fathom. Vera's intended mother-in-law, Mrs Leighton, certainly found him enigmatic, and not altogether likeable: 'She thinks him rather prim, & wonders very much how he can be so musical & yet possess no temperament at all, which is what I have often wondered myself.'[33] She even felt he resembled George Eliot's Tom Tulliver in his tendency to priggishness.[34] Neither of them was particularly relaxed with women, and as they admitted to each other in their wartime correspondence, their upbringing by a 'totally inadequate father and mother' had drawn them closer together. Vera added that they were also alike in not being interested in sex, 'unless it is united with brains & personality'.[35] All the more disturbing was it, then, when Vera discovered after Edward's death that he had been about to face a military enquiry into his alleged homosexual relations with men in his company. As the editors of Vera Brittain's correspondence with her brother and his three friends, Roland Leighton, Geoffrey Thurlow and Victor Richardson comment, 'It seems a possibility that, faced with the disgrace of a courtmartial, Edward went into battle deliberately seeking to be killed.'[36] This is something she explores in her third novel, *Honourable Estate* (1936), where she invents the letter Edward might have written if he had wanted to explain his actions to his family. In this case, the homosexual soldier, Richard Alleyndene, who, like Edward Brittain, has a particular talent for forming romantic friendships with other men, finally tells his sister the horrors of the battlefield, especially the waste and disfigurement of men's bodies, and what war does to their minds. He especially loathes the degradation of their tastes, their dehumanization into bayonet-wielding thugs who seek solace in prostitutes and the whisky bottle. Richard turned instead to his aptly named friend Valentine, with whom he formed a relationship he can hardly describe to his sister, Ruth: 'You will know what I mean if you remember a conversation we had in the bicycle shed years ago about Val having to leave Ludborough'. What he seems to fear more than the probable court martial, once their relationship has been exposed by some 'swinish fellows', is the reaction of his parents: 'Knowing so well what the Alleyndenes are I can't confront Father and Mother with the fact that their son is what they would call vicious and immoral instead of a virtuous patriotic hero.'[37]

However supportive sisters could be with their letters and small comforts from home, they could never supply the solace of immediate bodily intimacy from one who had been through exactly the same experiences. Hence the wide margin of their incomplete brothers' lives in which sisters could insert episodes that seemed fitting. While Woolf reinvented Thoby first as a jolly masculine invalid, then as a military or imperialistic hero round whom his friends cluster with their memories, and Brittain filled in the gaps of her brother's unknown homosexual army life by clarifying what happened to Richard Alleyndene, Rebecca West, who was one of three sisters, created a brother she never had: Richard Quin, the adored only brother of the twins Mary and Rose, their sister Cordelia, and their Cousin Rosamund in her novels *The Fountain Overflows* (1957) and *This Real Night* (1984). Though written long after the War, they recreate in detail the family's struggle for survival in the early years of the century, following their father's financial failure and his disappearance. As the only male Richard Quin is especially valued (in *The Fountain Overflows*, he is worshipped on Christmas morning like a kind of Christ child[38]), but the family is essentially self-contained, feeling the need only for a few eccentric choices of friends from the outside world. Even in the later novel, when the girls have grown up, they are reluctant to meet new people: as Mary, one of the twins says, 'we need not fear loneliness, for there were enough of us at home to give us all the companionship we needed.' When they are still children, they assume naively that their parents can hardly feel strongly for each other because they are unrelated by blood. The other twin, Rose, comes even closer, and entirely loses her sense of separateness from him for a moment: 'When I put out my hand and ran my finger along the fine line of his jaw it was as if I had touched myself. We were more or less the same person.'[39] Their mother, who was a concert pianist, significantly abandoned her career when she was 'handed a telegram which told her that her favourite brother had died of sunstroke in India'.[40] Out of sympathy for him, she falls ill with a fever that lasts for weeks, ending her professional life.

Richard Quin, regarded by the twins and Rosamund as 'much the nicest of us four children' (*Fountain*, p. 2) is somehow girlish and masculine at the same time, making him the ideal sisters' brother. His masculinity is unthreatening – partly by virtue of his youth, partly because it is seen as there to protect his sisters. Everything about him is romantic: his natural charm and calm, his purity and goodness. When they find him asleep in his room at a point in the later novel when the eldest sister, and least likeable, Cordelia, has been worrying about his chances of making a living, he lies in a kind of masculine bower of promise, his room 'hung with his musical instruments, his boxing-gloves and his fencing foils, his rackets and bats' (*Real Night*, pp. 208–9). Like many of the young men who go to war in these novels and memoirs, there is nothing innately warlike about him. Debonair, idle, and cultured, he goes uncomplainingly to the Front, where they know he is doomed: even as a small child, he had seemed to be warning them of the brevity of life, the lack of time to be what they wanted. Like Jacob and Percival, he soon becomes nothing but a memory, an evanescent presence. 'As I stood in the darkness,' Rose recalls of their farewell kiss, 'his mouth came down on mine; and then he was not there' (*Real Night*, p. 241). The worst part of his death, as far as his sisters are concerned, is not knowing what to do about him. Even the sounds of their piano-playing 'affirmed our knowledge that Richard Quin was everywhere, was nowhere, was failing us, had been failed by us' (p. 248). Not that there is anything historically unique about the experience, as the sisters recognize: 'The occasion of our grief was classically decorous, our brother had died for his country. But our grief was useless' (p. 249).

Katherine Mansfield

Where the lost brother is an only son in a family of sisters, and the youngest child – the long-awaited heir – his death acquires a deeper resonance. For Katherine Mansfield, unlike Rebecca West, there was no need to invent an adored baby brother. She already had one: Leslie Heron Beauchamp (1894–1915), killed demonstrating hand grenades in Ploegsteert Wood. The fact that he was killed, in a sense, by his own hand, and when instructing his own side (his sergeant also died in the accident) must have made his death seem all the more futile. In fact, the signs are that the closeness of the relationship was invoked posthumously. Although the two had always got on well, they had never been particularly close in childhood, Katherine being six years older than her brother. They were separated when Katherine, with two of her sisters, came to London in 1903 to be educated at Queen's College, Harley Street. Though the relationship resumed on Katherine's return to New Zealand in 1906, she was back in London again in 1908, and saw him only for a short while in 1915, the year he was killed, when he was training as an army officer in England. It was at best a patchy relationship, but like Dorothy Wordsworth, separated for most of her childhood from William, she talked of living with him when they grew up: 'he and I mean to live together – later on,' she told Sylvia Payne, her cousin and Queen's College school friend, in 1908.[41] She even persuaded her friend Ida Baker, known as 'L.M.', with whom she chose a professional name for their intended musical careers, to call herself 'Lesley' after her brother. Once he was dead, Mansfield rediscovered his presence in her childhood, and his importance to her as an adult, to the extent that she began to shut out John Middleton Murry, her lover and future husband. In her private papers she noted that she could never be 'Jack's' lover again: 'You have me,' she told her brother, to whom she spoke aloud in her writing, 'you're in my flesh as well as in my soul. I give Jack my "surplus" love but to you I hold and to you I give my deepest love.'[42] No wonder Murry felt that Leslie's death had 'cast a shadow' between them: 'He, though dead, was far more real and near to her than I was now; and that was anguish to me.'[43]

Initially, her brother's death made Mansfield feel she was as good as dead herself, and had nothing to live for other than the reconstruction in her fiction of their childhood life together. It seemed to crystallize all her confused feelings about her father, her dissent from the more conventional of her family's values, her separation from the family, and their overall worth to her as an isolated, childless semi-married invalid living in the south of France during wartime. Mansfield became gradually steeped in the consciousness of war, however little it appears overtly in her writing. In February 1918, she described the war as 'never out of my mind & everything is poisoned by it. Its [sic] *here in me* the whole time, eating me away – and I am simply terrified by it – Its at the root of my homesickness & anxiety & panic – I think.'[44] Like many women writers of the time with younger brothers killed in the war, she associated her soldier brother not with violence, but with the lost innocence of their shared childhood. Writing about New Zealand now became a sacred debt to him, a 'duty' that replaced all other duties. It was the one thing, she claimed, that prevented her from committing suicide at that point (*Notebooks*, p. 16). She felt he wanted her to write about their childhood, and that he must continue being her companion, even now he was dead; she wanted to co-opt him into her consciousness, to see things with his eyes, as she was still doing towards the close of the War in 1918. To Murry she described a dream she had had for two nights of her brother, whose nickname was 'Chummie', correcting her spelling of a French street name. After seeing an exhibition of paintings in her dream, three of them by him, they 'idled down the street... arm in arm. It was very hot – He fanned himself with the catalogue. And he kept saying: "Look, dear", and then we stopped, as one person, & looked for about 100 years and then went on again' (*Letters*, I, 195). If the dream is anything to go by, Leslie was associated for her with ideas of looking and representation. He appears in her dreams and other recorded fantasies as telling her how to see and what to say. 'It is with you that I see, and that is why I see so clearly', she told him through her journal.[45]

Above all else, he is associated with the urge to remembrance. '"Do you remember, Katie?" I hear his voice in trees and flowers, in scents and light and shadow' (*Notebooks*, p. 16). Soon after his death in October 1915, she promised to join him as soon as she had completed her commemoration of their shared childhood. She immediately began recording small incidents from their family life in New Zealand – their picking up of fallen pears in the garden of Acacia Road, where Mansfield lived with Murry in London, triggering their memory of the fallen pears in their Wellington back garden: an Edenic memory, typical of a lost childhood, like the story 'The Apple Tree,' written in 1915, which recalls their shared smile over a floury apple their father thought would be perfect. 'We were almost like one child,' Mansfield remembered. 'I always see us walking about together, looking at things together with the same eyes, discussing.'[46] Another dream, recorded this time in a poem, showed them walking beside a stream back home, fringed with poisonous berry bushes. His determination to eat them, despite her warning, culminates in his transformation into a Christ figure, waiting for her with the berries in his hand: 'These are my body, Sister, take and eat.'[47] On another occasion she 'saw' her brother 'dotted all over the field – now on his back, now on his face, now huddled up, now half-pressed into the earth'. The night before, she 'saw' him in bed, where she was expecting Middleton Murry; then she woke 'and was he, for quite a long time. I felt my face was his serious, sleepy face' (*Journal*, p.46).

The iconography of Mansfield's dreams about Leslie is never entirely straightforward; nor can her commemoration of him be classed as a predictably sentimental tribute to a dead soldier brother. Sometimes he appears in Murry's place, sometimes he merges indissolubly with herself; on other occasions he is dispersed, or Christ-like; as she fails to start writing she senses him waiting for her to start, looking at her with 'thoughtful eyes' (*Journal*, p. 49). His presence tends to be admonitory, perhaps reviving old memories of jealousy. Her poems about his childhood suggest that she was jealous of his special position in the family as the only son and youngest child. As the third girl, she must have been conscious that her birth was something of a disappointment, as it postponed once again the arrival of an only son. 'The Grandmother' describes a young sister wanting to see the baby brother her grandmother is carrying round the garden:

> 'Beautiful,' said Grandmother, nodding and smiling.
> But my lips quivered.
> And looking at her kind face
> I wanted to be in the place of Little Brother
> To put my arms round her neck
> And kiss the two tears that shone in her eyes.

The poem suggests that the sister would have liked to be as special to her grandmother as the brother is: to have had that additional access to her private emotions. In 'Little Brother's Story', she suggests that she and her grandmother collude in his undeserved praise, which they automatically accept is due to him. When they both tell their grandmother a story, the brother's seems to be directed against his sister:

> 'Once upon a time there was a bad little girl
> And her Mummy gave her the slipper – and that's all.'
> It was not a very special story.
> But we pretended to be very pleased –
> And Grandmother gave him jumps on her lap.

Her own story, which was about a spotted tiger with a knot in his tail, is received without comment, despite its imaginative superiority. The brother is rewarded with an extra demonstration of love for telling a story about his sister's spanking.

Several of her stories are about family configurations like her own: a succession of girls, followed by a treasured only son. In 'New Dresses' (1910), Helen Carsfield used to frighten her baby brother, and 'take away his bottle to see what he would do'; while in 'Six Years After' (1921), a bereaved mother remembers in detail her soldier son's first leave, but '[f]or some reason there is no place for the girls in this memory; they might be unborn.'[48] In 'At the Bay' (1922), the sister's confused feelings about the birth of the baby brother are projected on to the mother, Linda, who claims to feel complete indifference to him: 'As to the boy – well, thank Heaven, mother had taken him; he was mother's, or Beryl's or anybody's who wanted him. She had hardly held him in her arms.'[49] The baby, on the other hand, rejects her indifference and smiles so beguilingly that she has to acknowledge his confidence of being liked. When she was first planning an earlier version of 'Prelude', 'The Aloe', she intended the last chapter to be a tribute to Leslie's birth and beauty: 'And you must mean the world to Linda,' she added (*Journal*, p. 50). All the stranger, then, is Linda's struggle to accept the baby. She remains, throughout the Burnell series, emotionally detached from all her children: she appears relaxed and comfortable only with her brother-in-law Jonathan in a way that she can never be with her husband Stanley. The absence of sexual fear in the brother–sister relationship allows her to respond cheerfully to his language of pseudo-courtship ('Greeting, my Fair One! Greeting, my Celestial Peach Blossom!'), and notice afresh 'how attractive he was' (pp. 235–6). Lying beside her, he rolls over on the grass, just as the baby had done, and, complaining about his office drudgery, compares himself with a fly dashing against the walls in a hopeless effort to escape from a room: ' "it's against the insect law, to stop banging and flopping and crawling up the pane even for an instant" ' (p. 238). A similar image appears in another story of 1922, 'The Fly', which was published just two months after 'At the Bay'. It was, in fact, a favourite image of Mansfield's, as Gillian Boddy's collection of drowning fly references shows;[50] here, it appears in a story about two fathers, a boss and an old employee, mourning the deaths of their only sons, killed in the War. Shattered though he was by his son's death six years earlier, and the collapse of all his dreams about building up the business for him, the boss nevertheless senses that his feelings are wrong. 'He decided to get up and have a look at the boy's photograph. But it wasn't a favourite photograph of his; the expression was unnatural.'[51] Feeling alienated by the picture of his son, the father turns instead to a fly that has fallen into his inkpot. Having rescued it once, he then becomes fascinated by its attempts to struggle back to life, until after three attempts to shake itself free of further ink blots, the fly gives up and dies. The image of the struggling fly overwhelmed by external circumstances is sufficiently broad to apply either to the bereaved father, or to the lost son. It also articulates a more general sense of hopelessness which the War and her brother's death seemed to encapsulate, until it becomes an emblem for the futility of human effort. However hard the fly tries to recover, another huge blot of ink will drop from above like the unavoidable catastrophe of war.

With her feelings for Leslie an intensely private affair that she found difficult to explain to anyone who would understand, Mansfield was drawn to stories in which characters who have survived similar traumatic experiences compare their feelings. One of her most complex short stories, 'His Sister's Keeper' (1909), written while Leslie was still alive, describes a meeting between two women on the train from Dieppe to Paris, both of them devoted sisters to their brothers, both strongly maternal in their protection of them. '"I was his sister and his mother,"' claims the narrator's Fellow Passenger. '"On him I based all the hopes and aspirations of my life."' Envisaging him as the perfect man to whom she was prepared to sacrifice all her own needs, the sister intends living with him when they grow up: '"I did not wish to marry, he filled my life, and I was sound asleep, really, you know."' Her story ends with a nightmarish account of going to a house in London, where she is locked in her room, and sexually assaulted by '"the idol, my brother"'. According to Pamela Dunbar, who reprints the story as an appendix to her critique of Mansfield, it engages in 'strategies of evasion and displacement'.[52] It either implies that the sister's unselfish, if excessive devotion is interpreted as a literal kind of sexual feeling, and that she is horrified by the visual suggestion of what her feelings really mean, or that the brother is cynically taking advantage of her adulation. Either way, the brother is an ambiguous figure, who repays his sister's childhood devotion in a way that shocks her.

Brother figures, captured at all different stages of their lives, appear in many of her stories, not just the most autobiographical ones about the Sheridan and Burnell families. While brothers are seen as attractive as party escorts (for example in 'Her First Ball'), Mansfield more frequently portrays them as unpredictable, a source of anxiety to their families. In 'Sun and Moon' (1918) from the *Bliss* collection, another story dealing with a sense of the corruption underlying human pleasure and beauty, Sun is the child who is disturbed by the party preparations and their disastrous aftermath which his sister Moon experiences far more superficially. In the ironically-titled 'An Ideal Family', the son Harold (which was the name of Mansfield's father), though worshipped by his mother and sisters, is a mysterious scapegrace who charms women with his strange little half smile, but stole money from his mother's purse when he was thirteen. Again, the resentment against an unfairly privileged family member is given to a parent, rather than a sister, and it is 'the girls', rather than his insouciant son, who make Mr Neave's home lively and welcoming on his return from the office. 'Where was Harold?' Mr Neave wonders as he dresses for dinner. 'Ah, it was no good expecting anything from Harold.'[53] One of Mansfield's stories is even entitled 'Father and the Girls'. In several of her stories, 'the girls' are lumped together as less important than the son: more numerous, less necessary. Glimpses of the relationship with their brother Benny in one of Mansfield's best stories, 'The Daughters of the Late Colonel' (1921) inadvertently disclose a subtext of resentment going back to their childhood. There had been an occasion, the end of Section 6 reveals, when Constantia had pushed Benny into the round pond' (Boddy, p. 247). Now married and away in Ceylon, Benny features as a distant version of their menacing father: 'His right hand shook up and down, as father's did when he was impatient' (p. 248). While Benny's son, Cyril, on whom their affections now concentrate, lets them down by being too full to eat their splendid tea, Benny let them down by never introducing them to anyone they could marry: one of the most important functions a brother could perform for his sisters. 'How did one meet men?' Josephine wonders at the end of the story (p. 255).

Conclusion

Josephine's plight highlights the one-sidedness of the sibling relationship during the period leading up to and including the War: the period of imperial expansion and shorter-term wars before the outbreak of the one no one could ignore. Though brothers clearly valued news from home and relied on their sisters for an angle on home life different from their mothers', the novels and autobiographies of the period testify to the overwhelming emotional dependence of sisters on brothers, which inevitably intensified when the brothers were away fighting. Now their brothers had a real excuse for not writing to them, and parents had a real excuse for overlooking their daughters' needs. The attention of the whole family was focused on the brother; his leaves marked one season of the year from another. Even a daughter serving in a VAD detachment was only close to the battlefield, rather than in it, and unlikely to be killed. In *Honourable Estate*, Brittain's heroine Ruth Alleyndeyne hears that she has graduated in History at Oxford with a First – only to have her pleasure immediately dashed by the news of her brother Richard's death (p. 312). Her favourite brother has spoilt her one longed-for achievement by dying when she has won her First. Coming from Brittain, this can hardly be blatant cynicism. It is, perhaps, a poignant reminder that women were unable to enjoy their own special triumph

– of having breached the barriers of Oxford and succeeded even in a 'masculine' discipline – without being outstripped by their brothers in a way that was permanent, final, and overwhelming. This was simply a competition sisters were unable to win.

Though the First World War is usually seen as releasing women into active work, and earning them the right to vote as responsible citizens – making them, in effect, full participants in society, it can also be viewed as the worst blow yet in their bid to be regarded as men's equals. The War branded them unimportant as no previous event had done, and also restricted what they could write. Brothers must be seen as heroic, their sacrifices a gift to their country. Their bodies must be honoured and commemorated, though this was a new challenge, on this scale, for sisters. Yet Katherine Mansfield knew her brother had died in a foolish, unfortunate accident, and Vera Brittain suspected that hers had been deliberately careless with his life; in fiction, Rose Macaulay's Paul falls apart and shoots himself, while Irene Rathbone's Jimmy survives the War only to die of pneumonia. Rebecca West and Virginia Woolf had to invent hero brothers who never existed, also to be killed in futile accidents, minor outbursts of fighting. Though Brittain describes her relationship with her brother as 'perfect', involving 'no jealousy and no agitation, but only the profoundest confidence, the most devoted understanding on either side', there was something in this and all the other brother–sister relationships discussed in this chapter, that potentially crushed the sister's identity, and made her role in the family and society not so much essential, as second-best, a consolation prize to the sister herself and her grieving parents.

The War polarized sibling experiences in an unprecedented way, and left an aftermath of inequality that persisted emotionally, as well as socially and politically, for many decades afterwards. The men had been doomed youth in a way that was simply not true of the women. Especially among the educated middle classes – with whom this book has been primarily concerned – the wastage left few families unaffected. As John Stevenson has pointed out, the young (20–24) university-educated officer-class were seen as 'the flower of their generation'; those left behind had been too young, old or unfit to fight, or had come back shell-shocked or disabled. The reality was, in fact, that war deaths represented something like 'one in eight of the six million men from the British Isles who had served in the Great War': not quite as devastating a statistic as might be supposed.[54] Vera Brittain, who had lost her brother, her fiancé, and the two male friends she most cared about, may have been exaggerating when she referred to the 'wholesale annihilation of my masculine contemporaries', but this was what it felt like to her.[55] Women, in the meantime, were praised for their war work, and rewarded with the vote – if they were over thirty. This in itself implied that while men scarcely out of their school uniforms were considered fit to risk their lives in trench warfare, women were too immature politically to be trusted with an opinion on the government of the country until they were well beyond the first flush of youth. Moreover, their war work was meant at the time to be only an emergency measure, as government statements made clear. When conscription was introduced in 1916, the War Office stressed that 'No man who is eligible for Military Service should be retained in civil employment if his place can be temporarily filled by a woman or by a man who is ineligible for Military Service.'[56] The key word here was 'temporarily'; in effect, this statement also equated an able-bodied woman with an old or weak man. Both classes would normally be left at home, but in a national emergency their services were needed. After the War, went the assumption, everything would return to normal.

The War had been a temporary, abnormal situation, an indefinite call on the national sense of energy and patriotism, when 'normal' assumptions about the sexes, though by no means abandoned, were at least in abeyance. Women, who had been valued second-class citizens during the fighting, were expected to take off their uniforms and resume their domestic roles when the troops returned home. Mutilated ex-servicemen, with legs sawn off and eyes blown out, were constant reminders of what men had gone through in the War. Few women carried visible battle scars of a kind to arouse public sympathy.

While it would be unfair to suggest there was a kind of jealousy among sisters for what their brothers had experienced, there is no doubt that the sisters who had taken second place to their brothers in the Victorian schoolroom and round the family meal table, found themselves in 1918 newly pushed into the background in a way that must have seemed final and difficult to contest. For four years, parents had agonized over whether their sons would come home alive. In many homes, there were now only daughters, sisters without brothers, and it was unclear what they were expected to do next. Relief at the end of hostilities mingled with a sense of flatness and let-down. As Vera Brittain puts it, 'the intense emotional relationships of the War' left 'an emptiness which not even the most intimate friendships could fill'. She felt like 'a haphazard survivor from another life, with no place in society, and no foothold on any permanent ladder...' (*Testament of Youth*, p. 579). Irene Rathbone's character Joan Seddon in *We That Were Young* (1932), feels adrift in a 'ghost world', having accepted the abnormal war world as '"so ordinary – it was just our life. Yes, we hated it, and loved it, both."'[57]

With no brothers left to turn to, sisters had, to all intents and purposes, lost their connection with childhood. The War in itself had destroyed much of this connection, but a surviving brother would have restored some sense of the companionship sacrificed by the physical and psychological divide between men and women during the fighting. In *Testament of Youth*, when Brittain describes her feelings at the end of the War, with Edward gone, and only his portrait left to dominate the dining-room, she sounds drained of all purpose in life, her future curtailed in sympathy with Edward's loss. 'Yet here I was,' Brittain confesses, 'in a world emptied of that unfailing consolation, most persistently, most unwillingly alive.'[58] By a cruel twist of historical circumstances, thousands of privileged brothers had been removed from families and 'Arthur's Education Fund' left without an object. The sisters who remained, however, commemorated them in strange ways. Their images of brothers as 'eyeless', and yet all-seeing, like pagan gods; as Christlike and as 'dotted all over the field'; as kissing their sisters on the mouth and merging with them – suggest something other than the pious platitudes of the mourner, but rather an elegy for someone who was both a lover and a powerful compeer, unexpectedly disempowered.

Conclusion

What was the long-term effect of the First World War on brother–sister relationships? Were the old Victorian divisions finally eliminated? The dual image of the brother as a sympathetic companion or the forbidding patriarch; the favoured prodigal or the idealized man? If the War hastened other changes in the political and social structures of this country, did it also modernize the old family networks of dependency and vicarious living?

In the immediate aftermath of the War, emotional emptiness was the initial problem, closely followed by lack of occupation. Although the Sex Disqualification (Removal) Act of 1919 was supposed to remove the bar on women (even married ones) working in the professions, in Carol Dyhouse's words, 'it seems to have been wholly ineffectual'.[1] Women were still expected to give up work when they married – a view that persisted into the 1950s – and entry into the higher level of the professions remained a problem for the rest of the century. Brothers, meanwhile, were far from forgotten. Most of the War novels cited in the previous chapter that were tributes to lost brothers were actually written in the 1930s (*Honourable Estate*, 1936, *We That Were Young*, 1932); Rebecca West's *The Fountain Overflows* (1957) follows nearly 40 years after her first War novel, *The Return of the Soldier* (1918). Rosamond Lehmann's *Invitation to the Waltz* (1932) partly celebrates the promise of her younger brother John, who had, in fact, been too young to fight in the War, while the sibling pair of Vita Sackville-West's *The Edwardians* (1930), Viola and Sebastian, are fond of each other 'in the uncomfortably remote manner of affection between brothers and sisters': theirs is a relationship not yet fully explored by themselves.[2] Ivy Compton-Burnett, shattered by the deaths of her only two brothers (Guy died of influenza in 1905, but Noel was killed in 1916), wrote obsessively about brother–sister relationships throughout her long career as a novelist: '"Them both dying like that," she said many times, "quite smashed my life up, it quite smashed my life up."'[3] Her novel *Brothers and Sisters* (1929), set in a sibling society where almost everyone belongs to a brother–sister pair like a married couple, looks unashamedly at the implications of an incestuous marriage between half siblings. '"So I am Father's sister,"' says Sophia Stace, less shocked by the revelation than her children expect. '"Well, I am not troubled about that. It only seems to draw us closer."'[4]

Those novelists who write about sibling relationships after the War do largely invoke patterns of family intensity that if anything surpass the Victorian models discussed earlier. Evelyn Waugh's *Brideshead Revisited* (1945) shows how difficult it is for Sebastian and Julia Flyte to escape the morality of their Catholic nursery, shared with two other siblings who wholly accept it, while L. P. Hartley's nearly contemporary *Eustace and Hilda* (1944) charts its hero's lifelong effort to qualify for his older sister's approval, which eventually kills him. He recalls that Hilda was 'a task-mistress, leading the chorus, undefined, unrecognised, but clearly felt, of those who thought he ought to try more, do more, be more, than he had it in him to try, or do, or be' (p. 256). Also tormented by his sister in real life was J. R. Ackerley, literary editor of *The Listener* and friend of E. M. Forster. Observers at the time felt that they had each ruined the other's life: 'Together, they were more like a married couple than a brother and sister; but like a married couple who have decided that, on balance, they had better stick together, even though everyone else knows that a divorce would be best for them.'[5] Though Nancy herself had been married and had a son, her dependency on her brother drove her to suicide attempts and emotional blackmail. Joe Ackerley had to remind himself in his diary that he was only her brother, and not her husband or lover: the police expected him to accept personal responsibility for her in much the same way as Charles Lamb did for his sister Mary (p. 79). Where a sibling couple managed to split – as was the case with Gertrude and Leo Stein in 1914 – feelings could be so strong that a total break seemed a better option than partial reconciliation. Uncompromisingly, Gertrude summarized the situation as one of artistic rejection: 'Leo's response to her writing "destroyed him for me and it destroyed me for him"'.[6] Where each felt s/he was the genius of the family, and the other had achieved nothing of importance, there was little room for negotiation.

Sibling incest themes, largely in abeyance during the nineteenth century after a period of popularity in Jacobean drama and the Gothic/Romantic novel of the late eighteenth century, returned with gusto in the twentieth. While most of Ivy Compton-Burnett's siblings in *Brothers and Sisters* would ideally like to marry each other, in Iris Murdoch's *A Severed Head* (1961), Martin Lynch Gibbon, the adulterous hero, finds Palmer Anderson and Honor Klein, a half-brother and sister actually in bed together, and becomes fascinated by the notion of sibling incest. He even dreams of ice-skating with his own sister Rosemary, and wanting to embrace her, but as he does so, he is 'impeded by the sword which hung down stiffly between us, its hilt biting into me and causing a sharp pain'. For further good measure, their father's face comes towards them, clearly frowning on this breach of an ancient taboo by his children.[7] In Ian McEwan's *The Cement Garden* (1978), the two older siblings, Julie and Jack, undress, explore each other's bodies, and have sex together; while in Jay McInerney's *Model Behaviour* (1998), Connor McKnight shares an embrace with his sister Brooke and wishes he could marry her.[8] In Penelope Lively's *Moon Tiger* (1987), Claudia Hampton finds most men wanting in comparison with her brother Gordon: 'I tested myself for the *frisson* that Gordon induced, and it was not there.' Making the point that incest is close to narcissism, Claudia sees in Gordon's maleness 'an erotic flicker' of herself: 'Other people became, for a while, for a couple of contemptuous years, a proletariat. We were an aristocracy of two.'[9]

One could go on. Unwise though it is to summarize the development of a theme over a period of many years, it is hard to avoid the conclusion that in the twentieth century, the brother–sister plot – so far as it remained an interest – became more extreme, more violent. To a large extent this is attributable to the relaxation of censorship and the sensationalizing of many relationships in modern fiction. By the 1980s there was little left to say that was too shocking for publication. What is surprising, perhaps, is the continuing fascination with brother–sister relationships, given the wider dispersal of families, the richer opportunities for forming connections outside the home, and the apparent diversity of people's emotional experiences. These, on the other hand, may be good reasons for re-invoking the stable, lifelong relationships of the past as counterweights to the atomization of modern life. The appeal of a ready-made friendship with someone who has had the same upbringing and whom one is free to kiss and embrace, does, on the face of it, sound too good to be true – even if its underside is a lifelong association, however neglected or despised, with a rival for parental affection and most of the other prizes of life.

A less reassuring explanation for the upsurge of interest in writing about impassioned and twisted sibling relationships may be the rise of recorded instances of child abuse, including incest, from the 1960s onwards. Ian Hacking, in an extended survey of Western attitudes to child abuse, argues that 'sexual offences against children used to be kept completely distinct from cruelty to children'. The two – specifically incest as a form of child abuse – came together in the 1970s, since when the incidence of sibling incest has been increased by the need for single or working parents to leave older brothers and sisters in charge of younger ones. *The Cement Garden* in particular seems a natural product of this newly violent and sexualized awareness of sibling relations which Hacking sees as a kind of paradigm-shift. 'People do many of the same vile things to children, for sure, that they did a century ago. But we've been almost unwittingly changing the very definitions of abuse and revising our values and our moral codes accordingly,' Hacking suggests.[10]

The Janus-face of the brother–sister relationship has been the underpinning theme of this study, with all that this implies more widely for non-familial heterosexual relationships. Through the sibling bond, girls and boys, men and women, rehearse the complexities of the connections they will have with other men, other women, as adults. While the brother stands for a deeply rooted inequality in private life which is then transposed on to the public sphere, he also functions as a concerned guardian, a protector of his sister's chastity and safety – unless, of course, he takes advantage of his special intimacy with her to breach them. While the sister functions as a second mother devoted to him and not sharing him with his father, she may suddenly, unaccountably, demand a life of her own, compete with him in public, or leave him altogether. The relationship is more multi-faceted than that of husband–wife, despite the blood tie which forbids so much, because of the lack of any legal bond or specific duties. The range of permitted emotions and functions is wider and fuller; the opportunities for reconciliation after an argument more numerous; the stages of life passed through, from babyhood to old age, those of the whole human life-span and not just of the sexually mature years.

The contention of this book has been that by using the sibling bond as a model, nineteenth-century novelists and poets were better able to explore the full emotional range between men and women within the limits set by contemporary censorship. Having cleansed the relationship of the incestuous overtones popularized by the Gothic novel, the Victorians reconstructed the brother–sister relationship as uniquely demonstrative, the one chaste but warmly affectionate contract possible between young people of the opposite sex, outside marriage. In some ways, the Victorians were freer to express themselves than we are today. Through relationship to a brother or sister, they learnt how to articulate their feelings in a way that we now, in a post-Freudian, abuse-conscious culture, consider embarrassingly open. They practised a form of courtship in the home, and in some of the best models cited in earlier chapters, developed the capacity for intellectual and emotional companionship within safe parameters before they were of marriageable age. As a natural corollary of this, romantic friendships that were brother and sister-*like* – Edmund Bertram's feelings for Fanny Price, Emma Woodhouse's for Mr Knightley, Florence Dombey's for Walter Gay, Roger Hamley's for Molly Gibson, Helen Huntingdon's for Gilbert Markham, John Graham Bretton's for Lucy Snowe – became a new and regular feature of the nineteenth-century novel, and a further destabilizing influence on its heterosexual relationships. As the line between real and pseudo-siblings became less distinguishable, often as one partner came to want more than the steady support of a friend, the blurring of sexual and non-sexual feelings extended the emotional range of the novel, and permitted the exploration of subtler, more elusive shades of attraction and sympathy.

At the same time, the full gamut of competitive feelings, from intellectual rivalry to sexual jealousy, was also part of the experience of growing up with brothers and sisters. By displacing their sense of the irreconcilable differences between male and female on to sibling relationships, British writers from the Romantics to the First World War, gave themselves the opportunity to take their exploration of human psychology at a time of rapid change into new and unexplored territories. The War itself left sisters in a state of permanent moral defeat: unable to claim equality with brothers who had died for their country, they were emotionally immobilized, symbolically adrift. Jealous retaliation was no longer an option in a society where it would be unthinkable to complain of men as the favoured sex. The chance to answer back was finally cancelled.

Brothers' dependency on their sisters seems to have declined during the nineteenth century, but sisters' need of their brothers remained persistent. Before the War, brothers were still required as escorts and chaperones in the world of education, social life and business outside the home. After the War, sisters largely faced these challenges on their own: forbidden to take men's jobs, yet in many cases responsible for their parents' support; expected to marry, yet with their options severely reduced. If the Victorians charted the century-long rivalry and friendship between brothers and sisters, post-1918 Britain saw the sisters apparently triumphant – enfranchised and politically of age, survivors of the worst war in modern civilization – but in reality with their life choices and relationships to remake afresh. Henceforward, they could no longer count on their brothers as lifelong companions of their mental and material world, or as safe escorts through the increasingly intricate labyrinth of heterosexual relations.

Notes

Introduction

1. T. B. Macaulay to his sisters Margaret and Hannah, 6 July 1832, quoted by John Clive, *Thomas Babington Macaulay: The Shaping of the Historian* (London: Secker & Warburg, 1973), p. 273.
2. Juliet Mitchell, *Mad Men and Medusas: Reclaiming Hysteria and the Effect of Sibling Relationships on the Human Condition* (London: Allen Lane: Penguin Press, 2000), p. 23.
3. Victor G. Cicirelli, *Sibling Relationships Across the Life Span* (New York and London: Plenum Press, 1995), p. 222.
4. Stephen P. Bank and Michael D. Kahn, *The Sibling Bond* (New York: Basic Books, 1982), p. 11.
5. The most extensive study of sibling relationships in Jane Austen is Glenda A. Hudson's *Sibling Love and Incest in Jane Austen's Fiction* (London and Basingstoke: Macmillan – now Palgrave, 1992); work on Dickens includes Harry Stone's 'The Love Pattern in Dickens' Novels,' in *Dickens the Craftsman: Strategies of Presentation*, ed. Robert B. Partlow, Jr (Carbondale and Edwardsville: Southern Illinois University Press, and London and Amsterdam: Feffer & Simons, 1970), and Albert J. Guerard, *The Triumph of the Novel: Dickens, Dostoevsky, Faulkner* (New York: Oxford University Press, 1976). Jane Miller includes a chapter on brothers in her *Women Writing About Men* (London: Virago, 1986).
6. Most recently by Kathleen Jones in *A Passionate Sisterhood* (London: Virago, 1998), but most Wordsworth scholars mention it, one of the best-known being F. W. Bateson in *Wordsworth: A Reinterpretation* (London: Longman, 1954). There was a major debate in the *Times Literary Supplement* from August to November 1974 to which scholars such as Alethea Hayter, Mary Moorman and Molly Lefebure contributed.
7. Juliet Barker, *The Brontës* (London: Weidenfeld & Nicolson, 1994).
8. A classic case is Philip Larkin, whose older sister Catherine (Kitty) seems to have played only the smallest part in his life. Contrast Allon White, who in 'Too Close to the Bone', suggests that the 'most important single event' in his childhood was the death of his younger sister Carol (*Carnival, Hysteria and Writing: Collected Essays and Autobiography*, Oxford: Clarendon Press, 1993, p. 39).
9. For instance in the writing of Ivy Compton-Burnett, Evelyn Waugh, Rebecca West, the Sitwells, Vita Sackville-West, Virginia Woolf, L. P. Hartley, and later, Iris Murdoch (*A Severed Head*, 1961) and Ian McEwan (*The Cement Garden*, 1978).
10. Diana Gittins, *The Family in Question: Changing Households and Familiar Ideologies* (London and Basingstoke: Macmillan – now Palgrave 1985), p. 28.
11. Michel Foucault, *The History of Sexuality: An Introduction*, trans. Robert Hurley (1976; repr. Harmondsworth: Penguin, 1990), p. 46.

12 Leonore Davidoff, Megan Doolittle, Janet Fink and Katherine Holden, *The Family Story: Blood, Contract and Intimacy, 1830–1960* (Harlow, Essex: Longman, 1999), p. 20.
13 Barry Smart, *Postmodernity* (London and New York: Routledge, 1993), pp. 62–3. For a survey of attitudes to child abuse in Western culture, see Ian Hacking, 'The Making and Molding of Child Abuse', *Critical Inquiry* (Winter 1991), pp. 253–88.
14 Herodotus tells a story in which King Darius asks the wife of Intaphernes which of her kinsmen she should save, and she replies, 'If the King grants me the life of one alone, I make choice of my brother.' Asked why, she replies that she may replace her husband and children: 'But as my father and mother are no more, it is impossible that I should have another brother.' Darius is so impressed by this answer that he spares her eldest son as well as her brother. (*The History of Herodotus*, trans. George Rawlinson (London: J. M. Dent, 1910, Book III, p. 267).
15 Otto Rank, *The Incest Theme in Literature and Legend: Fundamentals of a Psychology of Literary Creation* (1912; repr. trans. Gregory C. Richter, Baltimore and London: Johns Hopkins University Press, 1992).
16 George Steiner, *Antigones: The Antigone Myth in Western Literature, Art and Thought* (1984; Oxford: Oxford University Press, 1986), p. 16.
17 In fact, this idea ultimately derives from a story told by Aristophanes in Plato's *Symposium*. At one time, he says, there were three types of human being: male, female, and an androgynous type, completely round, with two faces, exactly alike, on a rounded neck. When the androgynes attacked the gods, Zeus sliced them in two, and ever since, each of us is a ' "matching half" of a human whole, because each was sliced like a flatfish, two out of one, and each of us is always seeking the half that matches him' (Plato's *Symposium*, 190–1, in *Complete Works of Plato*, ed. John M. Cooper (Indianapolis and Cambridge: Hackett Publishing, 1997), p. 474.
18 G. W. F. Hegel, *The Phenomenology of Mind* (1807; trans. J. B. Baillie: London: George Allen & Unwin, 1971), pp. 475–6.
19 Christina Battersby, *Gender and Genius: Towards a Feminist Aesthetics* (London: Women's Press, 1989), p. 148. Elizabeth A. Fay, however, in *Becoming Wordsworthian: A Performative Aesthetics* (Amherst: University of Massachusetts Press, 1995) rejects the notion of 'male genius and his sister companion', and suggests that Romantic siblinghood should be seen as 'twinship, or twinned souls', p. 17.
20 John Herdman, *The Double in Nineteenth Century Fiction* (Basingstoke and London: Macmillan – now Palgrave, 1990), p. 2.
21 Mary Shelley, *Frankenstein* (1818; repr. Harmondsworth: Penguin, 1985), p. 102 (ch.5).
22 See, for example, J. M. S. Tompkins, *The Popular Novel in England, 1770–1800* (London, 1932; repr. 1969); Glenda A. Hudson, *Sibling Love and Incest in Jane Austen's Fiction*; and James B. Twitchell, *Forbidden Partners: The Incest Taboo in Modern Culture* (New York: Columbia University Press, 1987).
23 Frances Burney, *Evelina or the History of a Young Lady's Entrance into the World* (1778; repr. Oxford University Press, 1970), p. 184.
24 Steven Mintz, *A Prison of Expectations: The Family in Victorian Culture* (New York and London: New York University Press, 1983), pp. 147–8.

25 Bram Stoker, *Dracula* (1897; repr. Oxford: World's Classics, 1983), pp. 230–1.
26 *My Sister and Myself: The Diaries of J. R. Ackerley*, ed. Francis King (London: Hutchinson, 1982), p. 22.
27 *Manful Assertions: Masculinities in Britain since 1800*, ed. Michael Roper and John Tosh (London and New York: Routledge, 1991), p. 8.

Chapter 1   The Brother and Sister Culture

1 S. T. Coleridge on Charles and Mary Lamb, letter to Robert Southey, 29 December 1794, in *Collected Letters of Samuel Taylor Coleridge*, ed. Earl Leslie Griggs, vol I (Oxford: Clarendon Press, 1956), p. 147.
2 Christopher Hibbert, *Edward VII: A Portrait* (London: Allen Lane, 1976), p. 8.
3 Ibid, p. 12.
4 Karl Miller, *Doubles: Studies in Literary History* (Oxford: Oxford University Press, 1985), p. 24.
5 Lawrence Stone, *The Family, Sex and Marriage in England 1500–1800* (1977; abridged edition, Harmondsworth: Penguin, 1985), p. 423. Stone sees this phase as peaking from 1800 to 1860.
6 Foucault, *The History of Sexuality: An Introduction*, pp. 108–9.
7 *The Letters and Diaries of John Henry Newman*, ed. Ian Ker and Thomas Gornall, SJ Oxford: Clarendon Press, 1978), II, 1979.
8 David Newsome, *On the Edge of Paradise: A. C. Benson: The Diarist* (London: John Murray, 1980), p. 13.
9 Betty Askwith, *Two Victorian Families* (London: Chatto & Windus, 1971), p. 222. For an excellent study of the Bensons' marriage, see John Tosh's essay in *Manful Assertions: Masculinities in Britain since 1800*, ed. Michael Roper and John Tosh (London and New York: Routledge, 1991). David Williams's *Genesis and Exodus: A Portrait of the Benson Family* (London: Hamish Hamilton, 1979) provides a fascinating account of the whole family.
10 Eleanor Farjeon, *A Nursery in the Nineties* (Oxford: Oxford University Press, 1980), p. 324.
11 From several letters of 1874 in the Benson papers (3/47), New Bodleian Library, Oxford.
12 Virginia to Thoby Stephen, 6 March 1896 and 1 February 1897, in *The Flight of the Mind: The Letters of Virginia Woolf*, ed. Nigel Nicolson and Joanne Trautmann (London: Hogarth Press, 1975), pp. 2,4.
13 Sir George Otto Trevelyan, *The Life and Letters of Lord Macaulay* (1876; London: Longmans, Green, 1889), p. 209; Robert Blake, *Disraeli* (London: Eyre & Spottiswode, 1966), p. 69: this was on the death of Sarah's fiancé and Disraeli's friend, William Meredith.
14 Benjamin and Sarah Disraeli, *A Year at Hartlebury; or the Election* (1834; repr. London: John Murray, 1983), Preface. They took the pseudonymns 'Cherry and Fair Star'; Sarah wrote most of the first volume and Benjamin the second.
15 *The Letters of William and Dorothy Wordsworth: The Early Years 1787–1805*, ed. Ernest De Selincourt (Oxford: Clarendon Press, 1967), p. 102.
16 *Selected Letters of Edith Sitwell*, ed. Richard Greene (London: Virago, 1997), p. 7.
17 Jean Strouse, *Alice James: A Biography* (London: Jonathan Cape, 1981), pp. 52–3.

18 The letters of Vera and Edward Brittain, for example – perhaps the best-known sibling war correspondence – are less emotionally flamboyant than the examples cited. See *Letters from a Lost Generation: First World War Letters of Vera Brittain and Four Friends*, ed. Alan Bishop and Mark Bostridge (London: Abacus, 1999). The restrained language of these letters may of course be due to consciousness of censorship, and what Edward called their 'incomplete' (ie. polite, undemonstrative) upbringing (p. 316).
19 This (perhaps surprising) view is expressed by Ian Hacking in 'The Making and Molding of Child Abuse', *Critical Inquiry* (Winter 1991), p. 287. He argues that the Victorians 'never medicalized cruelty. Cruel parents were not deemed sick or even pathological' – and dates the start of 'child abuse' as such in 1962.
20 Park Honan, *Matthew Arnold: A Life* (London: Weidenfeld & Nicolson, 1981), p. 101.
21 Clinton Machann, *Matthew Arnold, A Literary Life* (Basingstoke and London: Macmillan – now Palgrave, 1998), p. 22.
22 Carol Dyhouse, *Girls Growing Up in Late Victorian and Edwardian England* (London: Routledge & Kegan Paul, 1981), p. 12.
23 *The Young Lady's Friend, by a Lady* [E. W. Farrar], (Boston: American Stationers' Company, 1836), pp. 221–2.
24 Charlotte M. Yonge, *The Girl's Little Book* (London: Skeffington, 1893), p. 12.
25 *The Hard Way Up: The Autobiography of Hannah Mitchell, Suffragette and Rebel*, ed. Geoffrey Mitchell (London: Faber & Faber, 1968), p. 43.
26 M. V. Hughes, *A London Child of the 1870s* (1934; repr. Oxford: Oxford University Press, 1980), pp. 7–8.
27 *Harriet Martineau's Autobiography* (1877) ed. Gaby Weiner (2 vols: London: Virago, 1983), I, 99.
28 *The Mothers of England: Their Influence and Responsibility, by the Author of the 'Women of England'* [Mrs Ellis], (London: Fisher, son, Co, 1843), pp. 329–30.
29 [Isaac Taylor], *Home Education* (London: Jackson & Walford, 1838), p. 25.
30 Maria Edgeworth, *Harry and Lucy Concluded* (1813; repr. 4th edn, 3 vols, London: Simpkin, Marshall, 1846), I, pp. 2–3.
31 Charles and Mary Lamb, *Poetry for Children* (1809).
32 George Eliot, *The Mill on the Floss* (1860; repr. Everyman: London: Dent, 1974), p. 140.
33 Charlotte M. Yonge, *The Daisy Chain, or Aspirations: A Family Chronicle* (1856; repr. London: Macmillan, 1890), pp. 162–3.
34 *Life of Mrs Sherwood*, pp. 40–1.
35 Elizabeth Barrett, 'Glimpses into My Own Life and Literary Character' (1820) in *Two Autobiographical Essays by Elizabeth Barrett*, ed. William S Peterson, *Browning Institute Studies* II (New York, 1974), p. 127.
36 *Personal Recollections, from Early Life to Old Age, of Mary Somerville*, ed. Martha Somerville (London: John Murray, 1873), pp. 36–7; p. 53.
37 Naomi Mitchison, *Small Talk: Memories of an Edwardian Childhood* (London: Bodley Head, 1973), p. 54.
38 Hilary Spurling, *Ivy When Young: The Early Life of I. Compton-Burnett 1884–1919* (London: Victor Gollancz, 1974), p. 66.
39 Penelope Lively, *Moon Tiger* (1987; Harmondsworth: Penguin, 1988), p. 25.

190 *Notes*

40 J. R. de S. Honey, *Tom Brown's Universe: The Development of the Victorian Public School* (London: Millington Books, 1977), pp. 209, 223.
41 Harriet Martineau to Fanny Wedgwood, 11 February 1843, in *Harriet Martineau's Letters to Fanny Wedgwood*, ed. Elisabeth Sanders Arbuckle (Stanford: Stanford University Press, 1983), pp. 47–8.
42 Thomas Hughes, *Tom Brown's Schooldays* (1857; Harmondsworth: Puffin Books, 1984), pp. 174, 185.
43 *The Letters and Diaries of John Henry Newman*, vol I, ed. Ian Ker and Thomas Gornall (Oxford: Clarendon Press, 1978), pp. 24–5, 69, 84.
44 Charles to Elizabeth Dodgson, 24 May [1849], *The Letters of Lewis Carroll*, ed. Morton N. Cohen, 2 vols (London: Macmillan – now Palgrave, 1979), I, 11–12.
45 Hughes, *A London Child*, p. 30.
46 Benson papers, New Bodleian Library, Oxford: correspondence of Eleanor Mary Benson with her brother Martin. Several letters have no date. Others cited here are from 12 July 1874, 19 December 1875, 24 June 1877, and 16 September 1877.
47 Hughes, *A London Child*, p. 57.
48 Vera Brittain, *Testament of Youth* (1933; repr. London: Virago, 1978), p. 89.
49 As Woolf explains, the phrase 'Arthur's Education Fund' comes from ch. 18 of Thackeray's novel *The History of Pendennis* (1848), and refers to the 'voracious receptacle' of money set aside by middle-class parents to pay for their sons' education: Virginia Woolf, *Three Guineas* (1938; repr. Harmondsworth: Penguin Books, 1978), pp. 7–8.
50 Virginia to Thoby Stephen, 15 June 1898, *The Flight of the Mind*, p. 17.
51 Peter M. Lewis, 'Mummy, Matron and the Maids: Feminine presence and absence in male institutions, 1934–63,' in John Tosh and Michael Roper, eds, *Manful Assertions*, pp. 168–9.
52 Lionel James, *A Forgotten Genius: Sewell of St Columba's and Radley* (London: Faber & Faber, 1945), pp. 141, 146.
53 Grevel Lindop, *The Opium-Eater: A Life of Thomas De Quincey* (London: Weidenfeld & Nicolson, 1981), p. 10.
54 E. F. Benson, *Our Family Affairs 1867–1896* (London: Cassell, 1920), p.50; A. C. Benson, *Life and Letters of Maggie Benson by her Brother Arthur Christopher Benson* (London: John Murray, 1917), p. 20.
55 Tosh, 'Domesticity and Manliness,' p. 57.
56 A. C. Benson, *Life and Letters of Maggie Benson*, p. 40; Virginia Woolf, 'A Sketch of the Past', in *Moments of Being*, ed. Jeanne Schulkind (London: Harcourt Brace, 1985), p. 129.
57 Thomas L. Hankins, *Sir William Rowan Hamilton* (Baltimore and London: Johns Hopkins University Press, 1980), p. 17.
58 Eleanor Farjeon, *A Nursery in the Nineties* (Oxford: Oxford University Press, 1980), pp. 205, 321.
59 In stories such as *Five Children and It* (1902) and *The Phoenix and the Carpet* (1904), the children's mother is often away visiting relatives and their father is absent on business, while the children have secret adventures with a sand-fairy, a phoenix and a magic carpet.
60 Stephen Gwynn, *The Life of Mary Kingsley* (London: Macmillan – now Palgrave, 1932), p. 27.

61 'Henry's approbation hitherto is even equal to my wishes,' she wrote of his response to *Mansfield Park* in 1814: *Jane Austen's Letters*, ed. Deirdre Le Faye (Oxford: Oxford University Press, 1995), p. 255. Hers and Henry's correspondence with John Murray, 20 October/3 November 1815, pp. 293–4.
62 Daphne Bennett, *Emily Davies and the Liberation of Women 1830–1921* (London: André Deutsch, 1990), pp. 104–5, 25–6.
63 Virginia to Thoby Stephen, July 1901 and May 1903, *The Flight of the Mind*, pp. 42, 76.
64 Elizabeth Tollett, 'To My Brother at St John's College in Cambridge,' in *Eighteenth Century Women Poets: An Oxford Anthology*, ed. Roger Lonsdale (Oxford: Oxford University Press, 1989), p. 97.
65 *A Memoir of Anne Jemima Clough By her Niece, Blanche Athena Clough* (London and New York: Edward Arnold, 1897), p. 16.
66 Deborah Gorham, *The Victorian Girl and the Feminine Ideal* (London and Canberra: Croom Helm, 1982), p. 141. This includes a particularly useful discussion of brother–sister relationships – mostly different examples from the ones I have chosen.
67 John Maynard, *Browning's Youth* (Cambridge, Mass. and London: Harvard University Press, 1977), p. 36.
68 Michael Polowetzsky, *Prominent Sisters: Mary Lamb, Dorothy Wordsworth, and Sarah Disraeli* (Westport, Conn. and London: Praeger, 1996), p. 105.
69 Disraeli dedicated *Tancred* to Sarah, and portrayed her as Eva, the Maiden of Bethany.
70 John Lehmann, *The Whispering Gallery* (London: Longmans, Green, 1955).
71 Victoria Glendinning, *Edith Sitwell: A Unicorn Among Lions* (1981; Oxford: Oxford University Press, 1983), pp. 54, 71.
72 *My Sister and Myself*, pp. 125, 14.
73 Theodore Zeldin, *An Intimate History of Humanity* (1994; London: Vintage, 1998), p. 387.

Chapter 2   Brother–Sister Collaborative Relationships

1 Charlotte Brontë, 'Captain Henry Hastings', *Five Novelettes*, ed. Winifred Gérin (London: Folio Press, 1971), p. 201.
2 He proposed in 1819 to the actress Fanny Kelly; she turned him down because she would have had to share their house with Mary Lamb.
3 Almost everyone who comments on the Wordsworths at length mentions this, but perhaps the most celebrated debate took place in the *Times Literary Supplement* from August to November 1974.
4 Molly Lefebure, *Samuel Taylor Coleridge: A Bondage of Opium* (London: Victor Gollancz: 1974), p. 343.
5 Charles Lamb to Dorothy Wordsworth, 14 June 1805, in *The Letters of Charles and Mary Anne Lamb*, ed. Edwin W. Marrs (Ithaca and London: Cornell University Press, 1978), II, 169.
6 *The Letters of Charles and Mary Anne Lamb*, vol II, 1801–1809, ed. Edwin W Marrs, Jr, (Ithaca and London: Cornell University Press, 1978), pp. 228–9.
7 Charles Lamb, 'Mrs Battle's Opinions on Whist', *The Essays of Elia* (1823) (London: J. M. Dent, 1962), p. 44.

8. *The Letters of William and Dorothy Wordsworth: The Early Years 1787–1805*, ed. Ernest De Selincourt (Oxford: Clarendon Press, 1967), p. 98; pp. 102–3.
9. *Collected Letters of Samuel Taylor Coleridge*, ed. E. L. Griggs (Oxford: Oxford University Press, 1956–72), no. 270.
10. De Quincey quoted in Kathleen Jones, *A Passionate Sisterhood: The sisters, wives and daughters of the Lake Poets* (London: Virago, 1998), p. 115.
11. Charles Lamb, 'A Bachelor's Complaint of the Behaviour of Married People', *The Essays of Elia*, p. 148.
12. Alan Grob, 'William and Dorothy: A Case Study in the Hermeneutics of Disparagement', *ELH* 65 (1998), 217.
13. Charles Lamb, 'Mackery End, in Hertfordshire', *The Essays of Elia*, p. 88.
14. Charles Lamb, letter of 3 October 1796.
15. Ibid, p. 89.
16. Hélène Cixous, 'The Laugh of the Medusa' (1975), in *Feminisms: an anthology of literary theory and criticism*, ed. Robyn R. Warhol and Diane Price Herndl, revised edition (Basingstoke: Macmillan – now Palgrave, 1997), p. 356.
17. Charles Lamb, 'Old China', *Last Essays of Elia* (1833) in Everyman edition above, pp. 287–92.
18. Alison Hickey, 'Double Bonds: Charles Lamb's Romantic Collaborations,' *ELH* 63 (1996), p. 761.
19. Jane Aaron, *A Double Singleness: Gender and the Writings of Charles and Mary Lamb* (Oxford: Clarendon Press, 1991), p. 180.
20. Charles and Mary Lamb, *Mrs Leicester's School* (1808 repr. London: J. M. Dent, 1899), p. 93; p.102.
21. Charles Lamb, 'Arabella Hardy; or, the Sea Voyage,' Ibid., p. 124.
22. Aaron, *A Double Singleness*, p. 32.
23. Thomas De Quincey, *Recollections of the English Lake Poets* (1834–9; repr. London: Dent, n.d.), p.153, p. 97.
24. James Soderholm, 'Dorothy Wordsworth's Return to Tintern Abbey', *New Literary History* 26 (1995), 309–22. John Barrell, whom Soderholm discusses, comments that Wordsworth needs to believe that 'Dorothy will grow up and sober up, for by doing so she will naturalise and legitimate his own loss of immediate pleasure in nature', John Barrell, *Poetry, Language and Politics* (Manchester: Manchester University Press, 1988), p. 162.
25. These cancelled lines of 'Nutting' are reproduced in *The Poetical Works of William Wordsworth*, ed. E. de Selincourt, 2nd edition (Oxford: Oxford University Press, 1952), vol. II, pp. 504–5. Astolpho was a well-mannered English knight and suitor of Angelica in Ariosto's *Orlando Furioso* (1532).
26. Gregory Jones, '"Rude Intercourse": Uncensoring Wordsworth's "Nutting"', *Studies in Romanticism* 35 (Summer 1996), pp. 238–9.
27. Dorothy Wordsworth, *Grasmere Journal*, 13 March 1802, *Journals of Dorothy Wordsworth*, ed. Ernest de Selincourt, 2 vols (London: Macmillan – now Palgrave, 1952), I, 123.
28. Douglass H. Thomson, 'Wordsworth's Lucy of "Nutting",' *Studies in Romanticism* 18 (Summer 1979), p. 287.
29. Kenneth R. Johnston, *The Hidden Wordsworth: Poet, Lover, Rebel, Spy* (New York and London: W. W. Norton, 1998), p. 652.
30. Compare Wordsworth's poem 'Resolution and Independence' with DW's description of the Leech Gatherer, 3 October 1800, *Grasmere Journals*, I, 63.

31 Her poem 'Thoughts on my sick-bed', incorporates allusions to 'Tintern Abbey' and 'A Slumber did my spirit seal', which Susan Levin sees as further undermining Dorothy's identity in that she accepts William's classification of her as passive and intellectually inferior.
32 Christine Alexander, *The Early Writings of Charlotte Brontë* (New York: Prometheus Books, 1983), p. 2.
33 *An Edition of The Early Writings of Charlotte Brontë*, ed. Christine Alexander (Shakespeare Head Press: Basil Blackwell, 1987), I, 25.
34 Ibid, p. 197.
35 *The Early Writings*, pp. 126–7.
36 *The Early Writings*, pp. 190–1; p. 195.
37 Winifred Gerin, *Branwell Brontë* (London: Thomas Nelson, 1961), p. 71.
38 Ibid, p. 132.
39 Charlotte Brontë, *Five Novelettes*, ed. Winifred Gerin (London: Folio Press, 1971), pp. 201, 242.
40 Tom Winnifrith, 'The Life of Patrick Branwell Brontë', *Brontë Society Transactions* 24 (April 1999), p. 2.
41 Jane Miller, *Women Writing About Men* (London: Virago, 1986), pp. 77, 82.
42 *The Early Writings*, p. 220.
43 Gérin, *Branwell Brontë*, p. 4.
44 *The Poems of Patrick Branwell Brontë*, ed. Tom Winnifrith (Oxford: Shakespeare Head Press/Basil Blackwell, 1983) pp. 30, 29; p. 115; U. C. Knoepflmacher, *Emily Brontë: Wuthering Heights* (Landmarks of World Literature series, Cambridge: Cambridge University Press, 1989), p. 102.
45 Gerin, *Branwell Brontë*, p, 71.
46 His best-known portraits of her are in 'The Girlhood of Mary Virgin' (1849) and 'Ecce Ancilla Domini' (1850); the caricature was drawn in response to a *Times* reviewer who commented of her *Goblin Market* volume (1862): 'Miss Rossetti can point to work which could not easily be mended.' See William Michael Rossetti's 'Memoir' of his sister, in *The Poetical Works of Christina Georgina Rossetti*, ed William Michael Rossetti (London: Macmillan – now Palgrave, 1928), p. lxiii.
47 Jan Marsh, *Christina Rossetti: A Literary Biography* (1994; London: Pimlico, 1995), p. 326.
48 *The Poetical Works of Dante Gabriel Rossetti*, ed. with Preface by William M. Rossetti (London: Ellis & Elvey, 1898), p. xxi; 'Memoir', *The Poetical Works of Christina Georgina Rossetti*, p. lxvii.
49 Angela Leighton, *Victorian Women Poets: Writing Against the Heart* (New York and London: Harvester Wheatsheaf, 1992), p. 120.
50 *The Family Letters of Christina Georgina Rossetti*, ed. W. M. Rossetti (1908; New York: Haskell House, 1968), p. 87.
51 Jan Marsh, p. 323.
52 Both poems, written in 1853, can be found in her *Poetical Works*.
53 Jan Marsh, p. 326.
54 Germaine Greer, *Slip-Shod Sibyls: Recognition, Rejection and the Woman Poet* (London: Viking, 1995), p. 379.
55 Dolores Rosenblum, *Christina Rossetti: The Poetry of Endurance* (Carbondale and Edwardsville: Southern Illinois University Press, 1986), pp. 146–7.

56 'Few things written by Christina contain more of her innermost self than this,' *Poetical Works*, p. 472.
57 *Family Letters*, p. 83.
58 Aldous Huxley to Julian Huxley, 3 August 1917, *Letters of Aldous Huxley* ed. Grover Smith (London: Chatto & Windus, 1969), p. 132.
59 Wyndham Lewis, *The Apes of God* (London: Grayson & Grayson, 1931), p. 488.
60 Virginia Woolf to Jacques Raverat, 30 July 1923, *A Change of Perspective: The Letters of Virginia Woolf 1923–1928*, ed. Nigel Nicolson and Joanne Trautmann (London: Hogarth Press, 1977), p. 60.
61 F. R. Leavis, *New Bearings in English Poetry* (London: Chatto & Windus, 1932), p. 73.
62 Edith Sitwell to Rache Lovat Dickson, 14 July 1949, *Edith Sitwell: Selected Letters*, ed. John Lehmann and Derek Parker (London and Basingstoke: Macmillan – now Palgrave, 1970), p. 168.
63 Edith to Sacheverell Sitwell, January 1932, *Sitwell Letters*, p. 124; November 1934, ibid. p. 157.
64 Victoria Glendinning, *Edith Sitwell: A Unicorn Among Lions* (Oxford University Press Paperback, 1983), p. 71.
65 Ibid, p. 36.
66 Osbert Sitwell, *Left Hand, Right Hand* (London: Macmillan – now Palgrave, 1945), p. 160.
67 *Selected Letters*, p. 125.
68 Edith Sitwell, *English Women* (London: William Collins, 1942).
69 *Sacheverell Sitwell: A Symposium*, ed. Derek Parker (London: Bertram Rota, 1975), p.5.
70 Edith Sitwell, *Taken Care Of: An Autobiography* (London: Hutchinson, 1965), p. 60.

Chapter 3 'One of the Highest Forms of Friendship'

1 George Eliot, 'Brother and Sister', Sonnet X, in George Eliot, *Selected Essays, Poems and Other Writings*, ed. A. S. Byatt and Nicholas Warren (Harmondsworth: Penguin, 1990).
2 Gertrude Stein, *Everybody's Autobiography* (1937; repr. London: Virago, 1985), p. 61.
3 *The Autobiography of Charles Darwin, 1809–1882*, ed. Nora Barlow (London: Collins, 1958), p. 22.
4 *Harriet Martineau's Autobiography* (1877, repr. ed. Gaby Weiner, 2 vols, London: Virago, 1983), I, 99–100.
5 James reviewed the book under the heading 'Mesmeric Atheism' in *The Prospective Review* 7 (April 1851), 224–61.
6 Juliet Barker, *The Brontës* (London: Weidenfeld & Nicolson, 1994), p. 568.
7 Charlotte Mary Yonge, 'Autobiography' (1877) in *Charlotte Mary Yonge: Her Life and Letters*, ed. Christabel Coleridge (London: Macmillan, 1903), p. 73.
8 *Harriet Martineau's Autobiography*, I, 13–14.
9 Mary Howitt, *An Autobiography*, ed. Margaret Howitt, 2 vols (London: William Isbister, 1889), I, 1889.

10 *The Autobiography of Margaret Oliphant: The Complete Text*, ed. Elisabeth Jay (Oxford: Oxford University Press, 1990), p. 19.
11 'Charlotte Elizabeth,' *Personal Recollections* (London: R. B. Seeley & W. Burnside, 1841), p. 67.
12 Stein, *Everybody's Autobiography*, p. 55.
13 Mary Martha Sherwood, *The Life of Mrs Sherwood*, p. 52.
14 *Harriet Martineau: Selected Letters*, ed. Valerie Sanders (Oxford: Clarendon Press, 1990), p. 16; Valerie Kossew Pichanick, *Harriet Martineau: The Woman and Her Work, 1802–76* (Ann Arbor: University of Michigan Press, 1980), p. 16.
15 Mrs Alex Tweedie, 'A Chat with Mrs. Lynn Linton', *Temple Bar* (July 1894), p. 355.
16 *The Autobiography of Elizabeth M. Sewell*, ed. Eleanor L. Sewell (London: Longmans, 1907), p. 42.
17 Oliphant, *Autobiography*, p. 26; p. 33.
18 '... in public she turned away from any allusion to the character of an authoress': Henry Austen, 'Biographical Notice of the Author' (1817), in *Northanger Abbey and Persuasion*, ed. John Davie (Oxford: Oxford University Press, 1971), p. 5.
19 Lionel James, *A Forgotten Genius: Sewell of St Columba's and Radley* (London: Faber & Faber, 1945), p. 123.
20 Juliet Barker, *The Brontës*, p. 568.
21 This was in March 1846 after Branwell had tricked their father into giving him a sovereign under pretence of paying a debt, and promptly spent it in a public house: *The Letters of Charlotte Bronte, Vol. I 1829–1847*, ed. Margaret Smith (Oxford: Clarendon Press, 1995), p. 455.
22 George Eliot, *Letters* II, 364; VII, 280.
23 *Some Last Words of the Rev. W. Sewell, D.D. ... with a Prefatory Notice by His Sister* (London: Rivingtons, 1876), pp. vii–viii.
24 James, *A Forgotten Genius*, p. 213.
25 James's manuscript of his *Biographical Memoranda*, p. 54, Harris Manchester College, Oxford. It was written at the request of his friend Charles Wicksteed for a biographical sketch in *The National Portrait Gallery* (1877).
26 James Martineau, *Biographical Memoranda*, p. 10; p. 38; see also James Drummond and C. B. Upton, *The Life and Letters of James Martineau*, 2 vols (London: James Nisbet, 1902), I, 222.
27 The story has to be gleaned from James's summaries of Harriet's letters for 1825–6 in the Library of Harris Manchester College, Oxford.
28 The letter is reproduced as an Appendix to Theodora Bosanquet's *Harriet Martineau: An Essay in Comprehension* (London: Haslewood Books, 1927), pp. 218–41.
29 Arbuckle *Letters*, p. 4.
30 *Selected Letters*, p. 47.
31 Ibid., p. 69.
32 Ibid., p. 100; p. 118.
33 Arbuckle, *Letters*, p. 140.
34 Harriet Martineau to Helen Martineau, 11 July [1851], Harriet Martineau Papers (HM631), University of Birmingham.

35 Harriet Martineau to Helen Martineau, 14 July [1851], Harriet Martineau Papers (HM631), University of Birmingham.
36 Ibid., p. 142.
37 [James Martineau], 'Comte's Life and Philosophy,' *National Review* XIII/7 (July 1858), 184–220, especially pp. 188–194. He was reviewing Richard Congreve's translation, *The Catechism of Positive Religion* (1858).
38 Drummond and Upton, I, 223; 'Mesmeric Atheism', *The Prospective Review* 17 (1851), p. 234.
39 *Daily News*, 30 December 1884, in Bosanquet, p. 239.
40 *The Prospective Review*, p. 227.
41 *Harriet Martineau's Autobiography* II, 330; 334 [James Martineau]. 'Science, Nescience, and Faith,' *National Review* 15 (October 1862), pp. 398, 418.
42 I am grateful to Carol Keller of San Antonio College, Texas, for drawing my attention to these two incidents. Harriet is here referring to a sermon James gave on 15 June 1851 at Hope Street Church, Liverpool, questioning Jesus's claim to be the Messiah. It was subsequently caricatured in the *British Quarterly Review* of September 1851. Harriet still remembered this sermon six years later in her correspondence of March 1857 with George Jacob Holyoake, arguing that as James's views were no longer representative of mainstream Unitarianism, he had no right to the Manchester College post (unpublished letter MS 42.726 no.21 in the British Library). The University College controversy of 1866–7 arose when James became a candidate for the Chair of Philosophy of Mind and Logic, but was opposed by George Grote who objected that he was, as a minister of religion, disqualified from holding office. Harriet followed the controversy through her correspondence (for example with Alexander Bain).
43 *The George Eliot Letters*, ed. Gordon S. Haight, 9 vols (New Haven: Yale University Press, 1954–78), VI, 353.
44 Constance W. Hassett, '"Siblings and Antislavery": The Literary and Political Relations of Harriet Martineau, James Martineau, and Maria Weston Chapman', *Signs* (Winter 1996), 21/2 (Winter 1996), p. 404.
45 'Maria grows more and more glorious', she told Fanny Wedgwood in November 1855, Arbuckle (ed.) *Letters*, p. 136.
46 Pichanick, p. 135; Hassett, p. 403.
47 Bosanquet, p. 240.
48 *The George Eliot Letters*, ed. Gordon S. Haight, VI, 371.
49 Recent studies of Martineau include Shelagh Hunter, *Harriet Martineau: The Politics of Moralism* (1995), and Susan Hoecker-Drysdale, *Harriet Martineau: First Woman Sociologist* (1992). A new biography is currently being written by Elisabeth Sanders Arbuckle.

Chapter 4 The Brother as Lover

1 Elizabeth M. Sewell, *Ursula: A Tale of Country Life* (1858; London: Longmans, 1886), p. 323.
2 Jay McInerney, *Model Behaviour* (London: Bloomsbury, 1998), p. 92.

3 Ovid, *Metamorphoses*, trans. Mary M. Innes (Harmondsworth: Penguin, 1955), pp. 234–5.
4 Sigmund Freud, 'General Theory of the Neuroses', in The Penguin Freud Library, vol. I, *Introductory Lectures on Psychoanalysis*, trans. James Strachey (Harmondsworth: Penguin, 1991), p. 377.
5 Jane Austen, *Mansfield Park* (1814; repr. Harmondsworth: Penguin, 1966), p. 243.
6 For example, Nicholas and Kate Nickleby in *Nicholas Nickleby*, Roderick and Madeline Usher in 'The Fall of the House of Usher', Helena and Neville Landless in *The Mystery of Edwin Drood*, Edgar and Isabella Linton in *Wuthering Heights*, George and Clara Talboys in *Lady Audley's Secret*, Angelica and Diavolo in Sarah Grand's *The Heavenly Twins* (discussed in chapter 6); but not, of course, Maggie and Tom Tulliver.
7 Charles Dickens, *David Copperfield* (1850; repr. Harmondsworth: Penguin, 1966), p. 436.
8 Adrienne Rich, 'Natural Resources' in *The Dream of a Common Language: Poems 1974–1977* (New York and London: W. W. Norton, 1978), p. 62.
9 Elizabeth Rose Gruner, 'Born and Made: Sisters, Brothers, and the Deceased Wife's Sister Bill,' *Signs* 24 (Winter 1999), p. 445.
10 E. Lynn Linton, *Lizzie Lorton of Greyrigg* (London: Tinsley Brothers, 1867), p. 329.
11 Jane Austen, *Northanger Abbey* (1818; repr. Harmondsworth: Penguin, 1972), p. 67.
12 While Julia Prewitt Brown thinks the ending of *Mansfield Park* is static and pessimistic (*Jane Austen's Novels*: Cambridge, Mass. and London: Harvard University Press, 1979), Glenda A. Hudson suggests 'the endogamous unions safeguard the family circle and its values', *Sibling Love and Incest in Jane Austen's Fiction* (Basingstoke: Macmillan – now Palgrave, 1992), p. 35.
13 Jane Austen, *Emma* (1816; repr. Harmondsworth: Penguin, 1966), p. 139.
14 Jane Austen, *Pride and Prejudice* (1813; repr. Oxford: Oxford University Press, World's Classics, 1970), p. 34.
15 Mary Shelley, *Frankenstein; or, the Modern Prometheus* (1818; Harmondsworth: Penguin, 1985), p. 80.
16 Emily Brontë, *Wuthering Heights* (1847; Harmondsworth: Penguin, 1965), pp. 79, 78.
17 G. W. F. Hegel, *The Phenomenology of Mind*, trans J. B. Baillie (London: George Allen & Unwin, 1971), p. 231.
18 Shadia B. Drury, *Alexandre Kojeve: The Roots of Postmodern Politics* (Basingstoke: Macmillan – now Palgrave, 1994), p. 17.
19 Anne Brontë, *The Tenant of Wildfell Hall* (1848; repr. Oxford and New York: Oxford University Press, World's Classics, 1993), p. 52.
20 Charlotte Brontë, *Jane Eyre* (1847; repr. Harmondsworth: Penguin 1966), p. 141.
21 Linda H. Peterson, *Traditions of Victorian Women's Autobiography: The Poetics and Politics of Life Writing* (Charlottesville and London: University of Virginia Press, 1999), p. 93.
22 C. S. Forester, *The African Queen* (1935; repr. London: Michael Joseph, 1946), pp. 6–7. I am grateful to Pamela Spence for drawing my attention to this novel.

23. Charlotte Brontë, *Villette* (1853; repr. Harmondsworth: Penguin, 1979), pp. 83, 81.
24. Mary Elizabeth Braddon, *Lady Audley's Secret* (1862; repr. London: Virago, 1984), p. 171.
25. Elizabeth M. Sewell, *Ursula: A Tale of Country Life* (1858; repr. London: Longmans, 1886), p. 26.
26. Charlotte M. Yonge, *The Pillars of the House*, 2 vols (London: Macmillan, 1873), I, 130; 133.
27. Charlotte M. Yonge, *The Trial* (1864; repr. Stroud: Alan Sutton, 1996), p. 2.
28. Charlotte M. Yonge, *Heartsease; or the Brother's Wife* (London: Macmillan, 1854), p. 123.
29. Charles Dickens, *Martin Chuzzlewit* (1843–4; repr. Harmondworth: Penguin, 1968), p. 661.
30. Charles Dickens, *Dombey and Son* (1848; repr. Harmondsworth: Penguin, 1970), p. 134.
31. *George Eliot Letters* V, 402–3.
32. George Eliot, *The Mill on the Floss* (1860; repr. London: Dent, 1974), p. 370.
33. Joseph A. Boone and Deborah E. Nord, 'Brother and Sister: The Seductions of Siblinghood in Dickens, Eliot, and Brontë,' *Western Humanities Review* 46 (1992), 176–7.
34. George Eliot, *Daniel Deronda* (1876; repr. Harmondsworth: Penguin, 1967), p. 707.
35. Elizabeth Gaskell, *Wives and Daughters* (1866; repr. Harmondsworth: Penguin, 1969), p. 399.
36. Iris Murdoch, *The Sea, The Sea* (1978; repr. London: Triad/Panther, 1980), p. 460.

Chapter 5   The Family Revenge Novel

1. *Harriet Martineau's Autobiography*, I, 99.
2. Charles Brockden Brown, *Wieland* (1798; repr. Oxford: World's Classics, 1994), p. 80.
3. Nathaniel Hawthorne, 'Alice Doane's Appeal', *The Centenary Edition of the Works of Nathaniel Hawthorne*, vol. XI (Ohio State University Press, 1974), p. 270–2.
4. Mark Poster, *Critical Theory of the Family* (London: Pluto Press, 1978), p. xvii; Steven Mintz, *A Prison of Expectations: The Family in Victorian Culture* (New York and London: New York University Press, 1983), pp. 4, 151.
5. Cited by Karen Gold in 'Brother Cain, Sister Jane', *Times Higher Educational Supplement*, 4 February 2000, p. 18, in a review of *Mad Men and Medusas*; further comments from 'Start the Week', with Jeremy Paxman, BBC Radio 4, 24 April 2000.
6. Sigmund Freud, *Case Histories I: 'Dora' and 'Little Hans'*, trans. Alix and James Strachey (Harmondsworth: Penguin, 1985), p. 229. Cf. P. 228 and 232.
7. Sigmund Freud, *Case Histories 9: The Pelican Freud Library* (Harmondsworth: Penguin, 1979), pp. 241–2. See also Karen Gold in 'Brother Cain, Sister Jane' (*Times Higher Education Supplement*, 4 February 2000) for a discussion of why psychoanalysts have overlooked the importance of sibling rivalry in family relationships (pp. 18–19).

8. Sigmund Freud, 'General Theory of the Neuroses' (1916–1917) in *The Standard Edition of the Complete Psychological Works of Sigmund Freud*, trans. James Strachey, vol. 15 (London: Hogarth Press and Institute of Psychonalaysis, 1963), p. 377; cf. 'Symbolism in Dreams' (1916), Ibid., p. 186, and 'A Child is Being Beaten' (1919).
9. In *The Interpretation of Dreams*, (1900; trans. James Strachey, *The Standard Edition of the Complete Psychological Works of Sigmund Freud*: London: Hogarth Press and Institute of Psychoanalysis, vol V, 1953), pp. 250–3.
10. Leila S. May, '"Sympathies of a Scarcely Intelligible Nature": The Brother-Sister Bond in Poe's "Fall of the House of Usher"', *Studies in Short Fiction* 30 (Summer 1993), 387–96.
11. Edgar Allan Poe, 'The Fall of the House of Usher' (1839) in *The Complete Tales and Poems of Edgar Allan Poe*, ed. Harvey Allen, New York: Modern Library, 1938, p. 245.
12. Sigmund Freud, 'A Child is Being Beaten' (1919) in *Freud on Women: A Reader*, ed. Elisabeth Young-Bruehl (London and New York: W. W. Norton, 1990), pp. 222–4.
13. Michael Slater, *Dickens and Women* (London: J. M. Dent, 1983), p. 38.
14. Allon White, *Carnival, Hysteria, and Writing: Collected Essays and Autobiography* (Oxford: Clarendon Press, 1993), p. 42.
15. Charles Dickens, *Great Expectations* (1860–1; repr. Harmondsworth: Penguin, 1965), p. 437.
16. L. P. Hartley, *Eustace and Hilda* (1944; repr. London: Faber & Faber, 1979), p. 256.
17. Sigmund Freud, 'Civilised Sexual Morality and Modern Nervous Illness', cited by Elaine Showalter, *Sexual Anarchy: Gender and Culture at the Fin de Siècle* (London: Virago, 1992), p.120).
18. Charles Dickens, *Hard Times* (1854; repr. Harmondsworth: Penguin, 1969), p. 131.
19. Anthony Trollope, *Can You Forgive Her?*(1864–5; repr. Harmondsworth: Penguin, 1972), p.95.
20. [Margaret Oliphant], *Harry Muir: A Story of Scottish Life*, 3 vols (London: Hurst & Blackett, 1853), I, 31.
21. Mrs Oliphant, *The Doctor's Family* (1863; repr. London: Virago, 1986), p. 69.
22. Mrs Oliphant, *Phoebe Junior* (1876; repr. London: Virago, 1989), p. 53.
23. Mrs Oliphant, *Hester* (1883; repr. London: Virago, 1984), p. 248; cf. p. 271.
24. Elaine Showalter, introduction to Mary Cholmondeley, *Red Pottage* (1899; repr. London; Virago, 1985), p. xiii.
25. Mary Cholmondeley to Rhoda Broughton, 24 November 1917, unpublished letter, Cheshire Record Office, Chester (Delves Broughton Collection).
26. Linda H. Peterson, *Traditions of Victorian Women's Autobiography: The Poetics and Politics of Life Writing* (Charlottesville and London: University of Virginia Press, 1999), ch. VI, especially pp. 192–6.
27. Mary Cholmondeley, *Under One Roof: A Family Record* (London: John Murray, 1918), p. xiii.
28. Mary Cholmondeley to Rhoda Broughton, 30 October 1899, unpublished letter, Cheshire Record Office, Chester.
29. Mary Cholmondeley to Rhoda Broughton, 18 November 1918, unpublished letter, Cheshire Record Office, Chester.

30 I am especially grateful to Virginia Blain of Macquarie University, Sydney, for telling me about the Hamiltons, and suggesting I find out more about them.
31 Robert Perceval Graves, *Life of Sir William Rowan Hamilton* (3 vols, 1882–9; repr. New York: Arno Press, 1975), III, 27.
32 Thomas L. Hankins, *Sir William Rowan Hamilton* (Baltimore and London: Johns Hopkins University Press, 1980), p. 29.
33 See for example Hamilton's letter of 23 September 1829, giving Wordsworth's verdict on her poems: 'He thinks that they evince sensibility, feeling, and genius, but that they want much of perfection with respect to the art of composition,' *Life*, I, 342.

Chapter 6   Changing Places: Siblings and Cross-Gendering

1 Ian McEwan, *The Cement Garden* (1978; repr. London: Vintage, 1997), p. 46.
2 Elizabeth Gaskell, *Cranford* (1853; repr. Oxford: World's Classics, 1998), p. 51.
3 Vern L. Bullough and Bonnie Bullough, *Cross-Dressing, Sex, and Gender* (Philadelphia: University of Philadelphia Press, 1993), pp. 194, 160 and chapter 7 *passim* for extensive historical evidence of cross-dressed women functioning as men undetected for many years..
4 Judith Halberstam, *Female Masculinities* (Durham, NC and London: Duke University Press, 1998), p. xi.
5 Cited by Christina Battersby in *Gender and Genius: Towards a Feminist Aesthetics* (London: Women's Press, 1989), p. 129.
6 For example in early October 1871: *The Letters of Emily Dickinson*, ed. Thomas H. Johnson and Theodora Ward, 3 vols (Cambridge, Mass.,: Belknap Press, 1958), II, 491.
7 Judith Butler, *Gender Trouble: Feminism and the Subversion of Identity* (London: Routledge, 1990), pp. ix, 137.
8 Marjorie Garber, *Vested Interests: Cross-Dressing and Cultural Anxiety* (Harmondsworth: Penguin, 1993), p. 1.
9 Sigmund Freud, 'Femininity' (1932) in *Freud on Women: A Reader*, ed. Elisabeth Young-Bruehel (London and New York: W. W. Norton, 1990), p. 347.
10 Juliet Mitchell, *Mad Men and Medusas*, p. 103.
11 Juliet Mitchell, *Psychoanalysis and Feminism* (Harmondsworth: Penguin, 1974), p. 50.
12 Dinah M. Craik, *The Head of the Family*, 3 vols (London: Chapman & Hall, 1852), III, 5.
13 Joseph A. Boone and Deborah E. Nord, 'The Seductions of Siblinghood in Dickens, Eliot, and Brontë,' *Western Humanities Review* 46 (1992), p. 166.
14 Evelyn Waugh, *Brideshead Revisited* (1945; repr. Harmondsworth: Penguin, 1980), p. 172.
15 Eve Kosofsky Sedgwick, *Between Men: English Literature and Male Homosocial Desire* (New York: Columbia University Press, 1985), chapters 1 and 2, *passim*.
16 Elizabeth Gaskell, *North and South* (1855; repr. Harmondsworth: Penguin, 1970), pp. 262, 313.
17 Charles Dickens, *Nicholas Nickleby* (1839; repr. Harmondsworth: Penguin, 1978), p. 448.

18 *The Routledge Anthology of Cross-Gendered Verse*, ed. Alan Michael Parker and Mark Willhardt (London and New York: Routledge, 1996), p. 2.
19 Charlotte Brontë, *The Professor* (1857; repr. Oxford: Clarendon, 1987) p.16.
20 Victor A. Neufeldt (ed.), *The Poems of Patrick Branwell Brontë: A New Text and Commentary* (New York and London: Garland, 1990), p. 270.
21 *The Brontës: The Critical Heritage*, ed. Miriam Allott (London and Boston: Routledge & Kegan Paul, 1974), p. 98.
22 Walter Pater, *Imaginary Portraits* (1887; repr. *The Works of Walter Pater*, 8 vols, London: Macmillan, 1900) IV, p. 12.
23 David Dolan, 'Pater's Portrait of the Author as a Young Girl', *Australasian Victorian Studies Journal* 6 (2000), 122–7.
24 Michael Levey, *The Case of Walter Pater* (London: Thames & Hudson, 1978), pp. 44, 146.
25 William E. Buckler, *Walter Pater: The Critic as Artist of Ideas* (New York and London: New York University Press, 1987), p. 203.
26 Gerald Monsman, *Walter Pater's Art of Autobiography* (New Haven and London: Yale University Press, 1980), p. 70.
27 Walter Pater, *'Measure for Measure,'* repr. *Appreciations* (1889), p. 178.
28 Walter Pater, *Appreciations* (London: Macmillan, 1901), p. 119.
29 Walter Pater, *The Renaissance* (1873; repr. London: Macmillan, 1910), p. 115.
30 Jennifer Uglow (ed.), *Walter Pater: Essays on Literature and Art* (London: J. M. Dent, 1973), p. xxiii.
31 Sarah Grand, *The Heavenly Twins* (1893, repr. ed. Carol A. Senf, Ann Arbor: University of Michigan Press, 1992), p. 7.
32 George Somes Layard, *Mrs Lynn Linton: Her Life, Letters and Opinions* (London: Methuen, 1901), p. 21.
33 'A Chat with Mrs Lynn Linton' by Mrs Alec Tweedie, *Temple Bar* 102 (July 1894), p. 355.
34 Cited by Nancy Fix Anderson in her biography of Linton, *Woman against Women in Victorian England: A Life of Eliza Lynn Linton* (Bloomington and Indianapolis: Indiana University Press, 1987), p. 12.
35 Eliza Lynn Linton, *The Autobiography of Christopher Kirkland*, 3 vols (London: Richard Bentley and Son, 1885), I, 58.
36 As for instance in Moira West, heroine of *The One Too Many* (1894), whose feminine feebleness prevents her from resisting, and then surviving, an unsuitable arranged marriage; or Dora Drummond, the manipulative, ultra-feminine counter-heroine of *Patricia Kemball* (1875).
37 Tweedie, 'A Chat with Mrs Lynn Linton,' p. 355.
38 Sandra M. Gilbert and Susan Gubar, *No Man's Land: The Place of the Woman Writer in the Twentieth Century*, vol. 2, *Sexchanges* (New Haven and London: Yale University Press, 1989), p. 326.
39 Elaine Showalter, *Sexual Anarchy*, p. 120.
40 E. Lynn Linton, 'The Future Supremacy of Women,' *The National Review* (September 1886), p. 3.

Chapter 7 'Most Unwillingly Alive'

1 Lady Cynthia Asquith, *Diaries 1915–1918* (London: Hutchinson, 1968), p. 90.

2. The best known of these articles was Harriet Martineau's 'Female Industry', in the *Edinburgh Review* 109 (April 1859), 293–336.
3. *Vera Brittain: Chronicle of Youth: War Diary 1913–1917*, ed. Alan Bishop with Tony Smart (Leicester: Charnwood, 1982), pp. 505–6.
4. Virginia Woolf, *Three Guineas* (1938; repr. Harmondsworth: Penguin, 1978), pp. 99, 19. See note 49 in chapter 1 for the origins of 'Arthur's Education Fund'.
5. Virginia Woolf, *The Pargiters*, ed. Mitchell A. Leaska (London: Hogarth Press, 1978) p. 30.
6. Barbara Caine, *Destined to be Wives: The Sisters of Beatrice Webb* (Oxford: Clarendon Press, 1986), pp. 142, 144.
7. Gwen Raverat, *Period Piece: A Cambridge Childhood* (London: Faber & Faber, 1952), pp. 61–74, *passim*.
8. D. H. Lawrence, *Lady Chatterley's Lover* (1928; repr. Harmondsworth: Penguin, 1960) p. 18.
9. May Sinclair, *Mary Olivier: A Life* (1919; repr. London: Virago, 1980), p. 117.
10. H. G. Wells, *Ann Veronica* (1909; repr. London: Virago, 1984), pp. 100–1.
11. H. G. Wells, *Joan and Peter* (1918; repr. London 1933), p. 232.
12. E. M. Forster, *Howards End* (1910; repr.Harmondsworth: Penguin, 1976), p. 251.
13. Virginia Woolf, *The Years* (1937; repr. London: Triad/Panther, 1977), p. 28.
14. *Vera Brittain: Chronicle of Youth: War Diary 1913–1917*, p. 222.
15. Her biographers, Paul Berry and Mark Bostridge, note her wish for children expressed in these terms: 'I should like to recreate my brother as far as such a thing is possible': *Vera Brittain: A Life* (London: Chatto & Windus, 1995), p. 193.
16. *Autobiography of Storm Jameson: Journey from the North Vol. I* (1969; repr. London: Virago, 1984), p. 102.
17. From Clare Leighton's Preface to *Vera Brittain, Chronicle of Youth* (p. 5); Lady Cynthia Asquith, *Diaries 1915–1918* (London: Hutchinson, 1968), p. 90; p. 182; p. 217.
18. Vera Brittain, *Honourable Estate* (1936; repr. London: Virago, 2000), p. 315.
19. *Letters from a Lost Generation: First World War Letters of Vera Brittain and Four Friends*, ed. Alan Bishop and Mark Bostridge (London: Abacus, 1999), p. 84.
20. Irene Rathbone, *We That Were Young* (1932; repr. London: Virago, 1988), pp. 26–7.
21. N. A. Taylor papers (90/28/1), Imperial War Museum, London.
22. Rose Macaulay, *Non-Combatants and Others* (London: Methuen, 1916), p. 10.
23. Francesca M. Wilson, *Rebel Daughter of a Country House: The Life of Eglantyne Jebb* (London: George Allen & Unwin, 1967), p. 74.
24. Hilary Spurling, *Ivy When Young 1884–1919* (London: Victor Gollancz, 1975), p. 142.
25. Cited by Mitchell Leaska in *Granite and Rainbow*, p. 127.
26. *A Passionate Apprentice: The Early Journals 1897–1909: Virginia Woolf*, ed. Mitchell A. Leaska (London: Hogarth Press, 1990), p. 7.
27. For example on p. 125 of *Moments of Being*, 2nd edn ed. Jeanne Schulkind (Harvest Book, New York: Harcourt, Brace, 1985). 'A Sketch of the Past', written in 1939–40, is one of Woolf's autobiographical pieces included in this collection.
28. This is the point where Mr Ramsay says: '"Well done!" James had steered them like a born sailor': Virginia Woolf, *To the Lighthouse* (1927; repr. 1976: Harmondsworth: Penguin), p. 234.

29 *The Flight of the Mind: The Letters of Virginia Woolf, Vol I: 1888–1912 (Virginia Stephen)*, ed. Nigel Nicolson and Joanne Trautmann (London: Hogarth Press, 1975), pp. 250, 266.
30 Virginia Woolf, *Jacob's Room* (1922; repr. London: Triad/Panther, 1976), p. 98.
31 Sara Ruddick, 'Private Brother, Public World', in *New Feminist Essays on Virginia Woolf*, ed. Jane Marcus (Basingstoke: Macmillan – now Palgrave, 1981), p. 204. Woolf herself undoubtedly saw Percival as a version of Thoby. She asked Vanessa: 'You didn't think it sentimental, did you, about Thoby? I had him so much in my mind –' (*Letters 1929–1931*, pp. 390–1). In her diary, she wondered whether she could write 'Julian Thoby Stephen 1881 [*sic*]–1906' on the novel's first page: 'I suppose not' (*The Diary of Virginia Woolf, Vol. IV 1931–1935*, ed. Anne Olivier Bell and Andrew McNeillie, London: Hogarth Press, 1982, p. 10).
32 Hermione Lee, *Virginia Woolf* (London: Chatto & Windus, 1996), p. 341.
33 Vera Brittain, *Chronicle of Youth:*, p. 231. Mrs Leighton also thought his 'unctuous seriousness' equipped him for being either 'a clergyman or a clerk', *Ibid*, p. 126.
34 Berry and Bostridge, *Vera Brittain: A Life*, p. 42.
35 *Letters from a Lost Generation: First World War Letters of Vera Brittain and Four Friends*, ed. Alan Bishop and Mark Bostridge (London: Abacus, 1999), pp. 316, 320.
36 *Ibid.*, p. 6.
37 Vera Brittain, *Honourable Estate* (1936, repr. London: Virago, 2000), pp. 336–7.
38 Rebecca West, *The Fountain Overflows* (1957; repr. London: Virago, 1984), p. 72.
39 Rebecca West, *This Real Night* (1984; repr. London: Virago, 1987), pp. 17, 152.
40 *The Fountain Overflows*, p. 8.
41 *The Collected Letters of Katherine Mansfield*, ed. Vincent O'Sullivan and Margaret Scott, vol. 1 1903–1917 (Oxford: Clarendon Press, 1984), p. 41.
42 *The Katherine Mansfield Notebooks*, vol. 2, ed. Margaret Scott (New Zealand: Lincoln University Press, 1997), p. 16.
43 John Middleton Murry, *Between Two Worlds: An Autobiography* (London: Jonathan Cape, 1935), pp. 373–4.
44 *The Collected Letters of Katherine Mansfield*, ed. Vincent O'Sullivan with Margaret Scott, vol. 2 1918–1919 (Oxford: Clarendon Press, 1987), p. 54.
45 *Journals of Katherine Mansfield*, ed. John Middleton Murry (New York: Alfred A Knopf, 1927), p. 47.
46 Katherine Mansfield, 'Awake, awake! My little boy', *Unbound Papers*, p. 15.
47 'To L. H. B. (1894–1915)' in *Poems of Katherine Mansfield*, ed. Vincent O'Sullivan (Oxford, Auckland and Melbourne: Oxford University Press, 1988), p. 54.
48 Katherine Mansfield, *The Doves' Nest and Other Stories*, Centenary Edition, ed. C.A. Hankin (New Zealand: Century Hutchinson, 1988), p. 94.
49 *The Collected Stories of Katherine Mansfield* (Harmondsworth: Penguin, 1981), p. 223.
50 Gillian Boddy, *Katherine Mansfield: The Woman and the Writer* (Harmondsworth: Penguin Books, 1988), p. 304.
51 *Ibid*, p. 302.
52 Pamela Dunbar, *Radical Mansfield: Double Discourse in Katherine Mansfield's Short Stories* (Basingstoke: Macmillan – now Palgrave, 1997), p. 100. The story covers pp. 180–3.

53 *Collected Stories*, p.374.
54 John Stevenson, *British Society 1914–45* (Harmondsworth: Penguin, 1984), p. 94. Stevenson suggests that about 30 per cent of all men aged 20–24 in 1914 were killed.
55 Vera Brittain, *Testament of Youth*, p. 579.
56 Quoted by Midge Mackenzie in *Shoulder to Shoulder: A Documentary* (New York: Vintage Books, 1988), p. 306.
57 Irene Rathbone, *We That Were Young*, pp. 463, 465.
58 Vera Brittain, *Testament of Youth*, p. 444.

Conclusion

1 Carol Dyhouse, *Feminism and the Family in England 1880–1939* (Oxford: Basil Blackwell, 1989), p. 79.
2 Vita Sackville-West, *The Edwardians* (1930; repr. London: Virago, 1983), pp. 240–1.
3 Hilary Spurling, *Ivy When Young: The Early Life of I. Compton-Burnett, 1884–1919* (London: Victor Gollancz, 1974), p. 256.
4 Ivy Compton-Burnett, *Brothers and Sisters* (London: Allison Busby, 1929), p. 178.
5 *My Sister & Myself: The Diaries of J R Ackerley*, ed. Francis King (London: Hutchinson, 1982), p. 13.
6 Brenda Wineapple, *Sister Brother: Gertrude and Leo Stein* (London: Bloomsbury, 1996), p. 355.
7 Iris Murdoch, *A Severed Head* (Harmondsworth: Penguin, 1961), p. 135.
8 Jay McInerney, *Model Behaviour* (Lodnon: Bloomsbury, 1998), p. 100.
9 Penelope Lively, *Moon Tiger* (1987; repr. Harmondsworth: Penguin, 1988), pp. 136–7.
10 Ian Hacking, 'The Making and Molding of Child Abuse,' *Critical Inquiry* (Winter 1991), 253–88, especially pp. 274–7.

Bibliography

Unpublished materials

Harriet Martineau's letters to her sister-in-law, Helen Martineau: Harriet Martineau Papers, University of Birmingham Library.
The Benson Family Papers, Bodleian Library, Oxford.
Harriet Martineau's letters to George Jacob Holyoake: British Library.
Mary Cholmondeley's letters to Rhoda Broughton: Cheshire Record Office.
James Martineau's *Biographical Memoranda* and transcripts of letters: Harris Manchester College, Oxford.
Brother–sister wartime correspondence: Imperial War Museum, London.

Primary sources

Ackerley, J. R. *My Sister and Myself: The Diaries of J. R. Ackerley*, ed. Francis King (London: Hutchinson, 1982).
Alexander, Christine (ed.). *An Edition of the Early Writings of Charlotte Brontë* vol. I (Oxford: Basil Blackwell/Shakespeare Head Press, 1987).
Asquith, Lady Cynthia. *Diaries 1915–1918* (London: Hutchinson, 1968).
Austen, Jane. *Emma* (1816; repr. Harmondsworth: Penguin, 1966).
——. *Mansfield Park* (1814; repr. Harmondsworth: Penguin, 1966).
——. *Northanger Abbey* (1818; repr. Harmondsworth: Penguin, 1972).
——. *Pride and Prejudice* (1813; repr. Oxford: World's Classics, 1998).
Bagnold, Enid. *Enid Bagnold's Autobiography* (London: Heinemann, 1969).
Benson, E. F. *Our Family Affairs 1867–1896* (London: Cassell, 1920).
Bishop, Alan and Mark Bostridge (ed.). *Letters from a Lost Generation: First World War Letters of Vera Brittain and Four Friends* (London: Abacus, 1999).
Bishop, Alan and Tony Smart (eds). *Vera Brittain, Chronicle of Youth: War Diary 1913–1917* (Leicester: Charnwood, 1982).
Braddon, Mary Elizabeth. *Lady Audley's Secret* (1862; repr. London: Virago, 1985).
Brittain, Vera. *Honourable Estate*. (1936; repr. London: Virago, 2000).
——. *Testament of Youth: An Autobiography of the Years 1900–1925* (1933; repr. London Virago, 1978).
——. *Verses of a V. A. D.* (1918; repr. London: Imperial War Museum of Printed Books, 1995).
Brontë, Anne. *The Tenant of Wildfell Hall* (1848; repr. Oxford and New York: World's Classics, 1993).
Brontë, Charlotte. *Five Novelettes*, ed. Winifred Gérin (London: Folio Press, 1971).
——. *Jane Eyre* (1847; repr. Harmondsworth: Penguin, 1966).
——. *The Professor* (1857, repr. Oxford: Clarendon Press, 1987).
——. *Villette* (1853; repr. Harmondsworth: Penguin, 1979).
Brontë, Emily. *Wuthering Heights* (1847; repr. Harmondsworth: Penguin, 1965).
Brown, Charles Brockden. *Wieland* (1798; repr. Oxford: World's Classics, 1994).

Burnett, Frances Hodgson. *The One I Knew Best of All* (1893; repr. London: Frederick Warne, 1974).
Burney, Frances. *Evelina* (1778; repr. Oxford: Oxford University Press, 1970).
Cholmondeley, Mary. *Red Pottage* (1899; repr. London: Virago, 1985).
———. *Under One Roof: A Family Record* (London: John Murray, 1918).
Compton-Burnett, Ivy. *Brothers and Sisters* (London: Allison & Busby, 1929).
Conrad, Joseph. *The Secret Agent* (1907; repr. Harmondsworth: Penguin, 1986).
———. *Under Western Eyes* (1911; repr. Harmondsworth: Penguin, 1996).
Craik, Dinah M. *The Head of the Family*, 3 vols: (London: Chapman & Hall, 1852).
Croft, Sir Herbert. *A Brother's Advice to His Sisters* (London:: J. Wilkie, 1775).
Darwin, Charles. *The Autobiography of Charles Darwin 1809–1882*, ed. Nora Barlow (London: Collins, 1958).
De Quincey, Thomas. *Recollections of the English Lake Poets* (1834–9; repr. London: Dent, n.d.).
Dickens, Charles. *David Copperfield* (1850; repr. Harmondsworth: Penguin, 1966).
———. *Dombey and Son* (1848; repr. Harmondsworth: Penguin 1970).
———. *Great Expectations* (1860; repr. Harmondsworth: Penguin, 1965).
———. *Hard Times* (1854; repr. Harmondsworth: Penguin, 1969).
———. *The Haunted Man* (1848; repr. London: Chapman & Hall, 1906).
———. *Martin Chuzzlewit* (1843–4; repr. Harmondsworth: Penguin, 1968).
———. *The Mystery of Edwin Drood* (1870; repr. Harmondsworth: Penguin, 1974).
———. *Nicholas Nickleby* (1839; repr. Harmondsworth: Penguin, 1978).
———. *Our Mutual Friend* (1864–5; repr. Harmondsworth: Penguin, 1971).
Disraeli, Benjamin and Sarah. *A Year at Hartlebury; or, the Election* (1834; repr. London: John Murray, 1983).
Edgeworth, Maria. *Harry and Lucy Concluded* (1825; repr. 4th edn 3 vols: London: Simpkin, Marshall, 1846).
Eliot, George. *Daniel Deronda* (1876; repr, Harmondsworth, Penguin, 1967).
———. *The Mill on the Floss* (1860; repr. London: Dent Everyman's Library, 1974).
———. *Selected Essays, Poems and Other Writings*, ed. A. S. Byatt and Nicholas Warren. (Harmondsworth: Penguin, 1990).
Ellis, Sarah. *The Mothers of England: Their Influence and Responsibility* (London: Fisher, 1843).
Farjeon, Eleanor. *A Nursery in the Nineties* (Oxford: Oxford University Press, 1980).
Farningham, Marianne. *Brothers and Sisters* (London: J. Clarke, 1873).
Farrar, E. W. *The Young Lady's Friend, by a Lady* (Boston: American Stationers' Company, 1836).
Ford, John. *'Tis Pity She's a Whore* (1633; repr. London: New Mermaids, 1993).
Forester, C. S. *The African Queen* (1935; repr. London: Michael Joseph, 1946).
Forster, E. M. *Howards End* (1910: repr. Harmondsworth: Penguin, 1976).
Gaskell, Elizabeth. *Cranford* (1853; repr. Oxford: World's Classics, 1998).
———. *The Moorland Cottage* (1850; repr. Oxford: World's Classics, 1995).
———. *North and South* (1855; repr. Harmondsworth: Penguin, 1970).
———. *Wives and Daughters* (1866; repr. Harmondsworth: Penguin, 1969).
Grand, Sarah. *The Heavenly Twins* (1893; repr. Ann Arbor Paperbacks: University of Michigan Press, 1992).
Grimm Brothers. *Fairy Tales* (London: Wordsworth Classics, 1993).
Hamilton, Cicely, *Life Errant* (London: J. M. Dent, 1935).
Hartley, L. P. *Eustace and Hilda* (1944; repr. London: Faber & Faber, 1979).

Hawthorne, Nathaniel. 'Alice Doane's Appeal' (1835) in *The Century Edition of the Works of Nathaniel Hawthorne* XI (Ohio: Ohio State University Press, 1974).

Herodotus. *History* 2 vols (trans. George Rawlinson: London: J. M. Dent, 1910).

Hobhouse, Stephen. *Forty Years and An Epilogue: An Autobiography (1881–1951)* (London: James Clarke, 1951).

Howitt, Mary. *My Own Story; or, The Autobiography of a Child* (London: Thomas Tegg, 1845).

Hughes, M. V. *A London Child of the 1870s* (1934; repr. Oxford: Oxford University Press, 1980).

Ibsen, Henrik. *Little Eyolf* (1894; repr. in *The Master Builder and Other Plays* Harmondsworth: Penguin 1958).

Jameson, Storm, *Journey from the North I* (1969; repr. London: Virago, 1984).

———. *No Time Like the Present* (London: Cassell, 1933).

Keppel, Sonia. *Edwardian Daughter* (London: Hamish Hamilton, 1958).

Kipling, Rudyard. 'Baa Baa, Black Sheep' in *Wee Willie Winkie and Other Stories* (London: Macmillan – now Palgrave 1896).

Lamb, Charles. *Essays of Elia and Last Essays of Elia* (London and New York: Dent Everyman's Library, 1962).

——— and Mary Lamb. *Mrs Leicester's School* (1808, repr. London: J. M. Dent, 1899).

Lawrence, D. H. *Lady Chatterley's Lover* (1928; repr. Harmondsworth: Penguin, 1960).

Lehmann, John. *The Whispering Gallery* (London: Longmans, Green, 1955).

Lehmann, Rosamond. *Invitation to the Waltz* (1932; repr. London: Virago, 1999).

Lewis, Wyndham. *The Apes of God* (London: Grayson & Grayson, 1931).

Linton, Eliza Lynn. *The Autobiography of Christopher Kirkland*, 3 vols (London: Richard Bentley, 1885).

———. *Lizzie Lorton of Greyrigg* (London: Tinsley Brothers, 1866).

Lively, Penelope. *Moon Tiger* (Harmondsworth: Penguin, 1988).

Macaulay, Rose. *Non-Combatants and Others* (London: Methuen, 1916).

Mansfield, Katherine. *The Collected Stories of Katherine Mansfield* (Harmondsworth: Penguin, 1981).

———. *Journal* (New York: Alfred A. Knopf, 1927).

Martineau, Harriet. *Harriet Martineau's Autobiography* (3 vols, 1877; repr. 2 vols, London: Virago, 1983).

Maurice, F. D. *Eustace Conway: or, The Brother and Sister: A Novel*, 3 vols (London: Richard Bentley, 1834).

McEwan, Ian. *The Cement Garden* (1978; repr. London: Vintage, 1997).

McInerney, Jay. *Model Behaviour* (London: Bloomsbury, 1998).

Mitchell, Hannah. *The Hard Way Up: The Autobiography of Hannah Mitchell, Suffragette and Rebel* (London: Faber & Faber, 1968).

Mitchison, Naomi. *All Change Here* (London: Bodley Head, 1975).

———. *Small Talk: Memories of an Edwardian Childhood* (London: Bodley Head, 1973).

Murdoch, Iris. *A Severed Head* (1961; repr. Harmondsworth: Penguin 1963).

———. *The Sea, The Sea* (1978; repr. London: Triad/Panther, 1980).

Murry, John Middleton. *Between Two Worlds: An Autobiography* (London: Jonathan Cape, 1935).

Neufeldt, Victor A. (ed.). *The Poems of Patrick Branwell Brontë: A New Text and Commentary* (New York and London: Garland, 1990).

Oliphant, Margaret. *Harry Muir: A Story of Scottish Life*, 3 vols (London: Hurst & Blackett, 1853).
——. *Hester* (1883; repr. London: Virago, 1984).
——. *Janet*, 3 vols (London: Hurst & Blackett, 1891).
——. *Phoebe Junior* (1876; repr. London: Virago, 1989).
——. *The Rector and the Doctor's Family* (1863; repr. London: Virago, 1986).
Ovid. *Metamorphoses*, trans. Mary M. Innes (Harmondsworth: Penguin, 1955).
Pankhurst, Emmeline. *My Own Story* (London: Eveleigh Nash, 1914).
Pater, Walter. *Appreciations* (1878; repr. London: Macmillan – now Palgrave, 1901).
——. *Essays on Literature and Art* (ed. Jennifer Uglow: London: J. M. Dent, 1973).
——. *Imaginary Portraits* (1887; repr. *The Works of Walter Pater*, 8 vols: vol. IV: London: Macmillan – now Palgrave, 1900).
——. *The Renaissance: Studies in Art and Poetry* (1873; repr. London: Macmillan – now Palgrave, 1910).
Plato. *Symposium* in *Complete Works*, ed. John M. Cooper (Indianapolis and Cambridge: Hackett, 1997).
Poe, Edgar Allan. 'The Fall of the House of Usher' (1839) in *The Complete Tales and Poems of Edgar Allan Poe*, ed. Henry Allen (New York: Modern Library, 1938).
Rathbone, Irene. *We That Were Young* (1932; repr. London: Virago, 1988).
Raverat, Gwen. *Period Piece: A Cambridge Childhood* (London: Faber & Faber, 1952).
Rich, Adrienne. *The Dream of a Common Language: Poems 1974–1977* (New York and London: W. W. Norton, 1978).
Rossetti, William Michael (ed.). *The Poetical Works of Christina Georgina Rossetti* (London: Macmillan – now Palgrave, 1928).
—— (ed.). *The Poetical Works of Dante Gabriel Rossetti* (London: Ellis & Elvey, 1898).
Sackville-West, Vita. *The Edwardians* (1930; repr. London: Virago, 1983).
Sewell, Elizabeth M. *Ursula: A Tale of Country Life* (1858; repr. London: Longmans, 1886).
——. *The Autobiography of Elizabeth M. Sewell*, edited by her niece, Eleanor M. Sewell (London: Longmans, 1907).
Sewell, William. *Some Last Words of the Rev. W. Sewell* (London: Longmans, 1876).
Shelley Mary. *Frankenstein* (1818; repr. Harmondsworth: Penguin, 1985).
Sinclair, May. *Mary Olivier: A Life* (1919; repr. London: Virago, 1980).
Sitwell, Edith. *The Sleeping Beauty* (London: Duckworth, 1924).
——. *Taken Care Of: An Autobiography* (London: Hutchinson, 1965).
Sitwell, Osbert. *Left Hand, Right Hand: An Autobiography* (London: Macmillan – now Palgrave, 1945).
Sitwell, Sacheverell. *An Indian Summer* (London: Macmillan – now Palgrave, 1964).
Stein, Gertrude. *Everybody's Autobiography* (1937; repr. London: Virago, 1985).
Stoker, Bram. *Dracula* (1897; repr. Oxford: World's Classics, 1983).
Thackeray, William M. *The History of Pendennis* (1848–50; repr. Harmondsworth: Penguin, 1972).
Trollope, Anthony. *Can You Forgive Her?* (1864–5; repr. Harmondsworth: Penguin, 1972).
Waugh, Evelyn. *Brideshead Revisited* (1945; repr. Harmondsworth: Penguin, 1980).

Wells, H. G. *Ann Veronica* (1909; repr. London: Virago, 1984).
——. *Joan and Peter* (1918, repr. London: no publisher's name on title page, 1933).
West, Rebecca.. *The Fountain Overflows* (1957; repr. London: Virago, 1984).
——. *This Real Night* (1984; repr. London: Virago, 1987).
Winnifrith, Tom (ed.). *The Poems of Patrick Branwell Brontë* (Oxford: Basil Blackwell/Shakespeare Head Press, 1983).
Woolf, Virginia. *Jacob's Room* (1922; repr. London: Triad/Panther, 1976).
——. *Moments of Being*, ed. Jeanne Schulkind, 2nd edn (London and New York: Harcourt Brace, 1985).
——. *The Pargiters* (1932; repr. ed. Mitchell A. Leaska: London: Hogarth Press, 1978).
——. *Three Guineas* (1938; repr. Harmondsworth: Penguin, 1977).
——. *To the Lighthouse* (1927; repr. Harmondsworth: Penguin, 1976).
——. *The Waves* (1931; repr. Harmondsworth: Penguin, 1974).
——. *The Years* (1937; repr. London: Triad/Panther, 1971).
Wordsworth, Dorothy. *Grasmere Journals* (ed. Mary Moorman: Oxford: Oxford University Press, 1971).
Wordsworth, William. *The Poetical Works of William Wordsworth*, ed. Ernest De Selincourt, 5 vols (Oxford: Clarendon Press, 1940).
Yonge, Charlotte M. *The Daisy Chain* (1856; repr. London: Macmillan – now Palgrave, 1901).
——. *Heartsease* (1854. repr. London: Macmillan – now Palgrave, 1901).
——. *The Pillars of the House*, 2 vols (1873; repr. London: Macmillan – now Palgrave, 1901).
——. *The Trial* (1864; repr. Stroud: Alan Sutton, 1996).

Secondary sources

Aaron, Jane. *A Double Singleness: Gender and the Writings of Charles and Mary Lamb* (Oxford: Clarendon Press, 1991).
Ackroyd, Peter. *Dickens* (London: Minerva, 1991).
Alexander, Christine. *The Early Writings of Charlotte Brontë* (New York: Prometheus Books, 1983).
Allott, Miriam (ed.). *The Brontës: The Critical Heritage* (London and Boston: Routledge & Kegan Paul, 1974).
Alpers, Antony. *The Life of Katherine Mansfield* (New York: Viking Press, 1980).
Anderson, Nancy Fix. *Woman against Women in Victorian England: A Life of Eliza Lynn Linton* (Bloomington and Indianapolis: Indiana University Press, 1987).
Arbuckle, Elisabeth Sanders. *Harriet Martineau's Letters to Fanny Wedgwood* (Stanford: Stanford University Press, 1983).
Armstrong, Isobel. *Victorian Poetry: Poetry, Poetics and Politics* (London and New York: Routledge, 1993).
Askwith, Betty. *Two Victorian Families* (London: Chatto & Windus, 1971).
Bank, Stephen P. and Michael D. Kahn. *The Sibling Bond* (New York: Basic Books, 1982).
Barker, Juliet. *The Brontës* (London: Weidenfeld and Nicolson, 1994).
Bateson, F. W. *Wordsworth: A Reinterpretation* (London: Longman, 1954).

Battersby, Christina. *Gender and Genius: Towards a Feminist Aesthetics* (London: Women's Press, 1989).
Battestin, Martin C. and Clive T. Probyn (eds). *The Correspondence of Henry and Sarah Fielding* (Oxford: Clarendon Press, 1993).
Bauman, Zygmunt. *Modernity and Ambivalence* (Cambridge: Polity Press, 1991).
Bell, Susan Groag and Marilyn Yalom (eds). *Revealing Lives: Autobiography, Biography, and Gender* (Albany: State University of New York Press, 1990).
Bennett, Daphne. *Emily Davies and the Liberation of Women 1830–1921* (London: André Deutsch, 1990).
Benson, A. C. *Life and Letters of Maggie Benson by her Brother, Arthur Christopher Benson* (London: John Murray, 1917).
Benson, E. F. *As We Were: A Victorian Peep-Show* (London: Longmans, Green, 1930).
Berry, Paul and Mark Bostridge. *Vera Brittain: A Life* (London: Chatto & Windus, 1995).
Black, Helen C. *Notable Women Authors of the Day* (Glasgow: David Bryce, 1893).
Blake, Robert. *Disraeli* (London: Eyre & Spottiswode, 1966).
Boddy, Gillian. *Katherine Mansfield: The Woman and the Writer* (Harmondsworth: Penguin, 1988).
Boone, Joseph A. and Deborah E. Nord. 'Brother and Sister: The Seductions of Siblinghood in Dickens, Eliot, and Brontë,' *Western Humanities Review*, 46 (2) (1992) 164–88.
Bosanquet, Theodora. *Harriet Martineau: An Essay in Comprehension* (London: Frederick Etchells and Hugh Macdonald, Haslewood Books, 1927).
Bowie, Fiona, Deborah Kirkwood and Shirley Ardener (eds). *Women and Missions: Past and Present: Anthropological and Historical Perceptions* (Providence and Oxford: Berg, 1993).
Brissenden, R. F. '*Mansfield Park*: Freedom and the Family', in *Jane Austen: Bicentenary Essays*, ed. J. Halperin (Cambridge: Cambridge University Press, 1975).
Brown, Julia Prewitt. *Jane Austen's Novels* (Cambridge, Mass. and London: Harvard University Press, 1979).
Buckler, William E. *Walter Pater: The Critic as Artist of Ideas* (New York and London: New York University Press, 1987).
Bullough, Vern L. and Bonnie Bullough. *Cross-Dressing, Sex, and Gender* (Philadelphia: University of Pennsylvania Press, 1993).
Butler, Judith. *Gender Trouble: Feminism and the Subversion of Identity* (London: Routledge, 1990).
Cadogan, Mary and Patricia Craig. *Women and Children First: The Fiction of Two World Wars* (London: Victor Gollancz, 1978).
Caine, Barbara. *Destined to be Wives: The Sisters of Beatrice Webb* (Oxford: Clarendon Press, 1986).
Carpenter, J. Estlin. *James Martineau: Theologian and Teacher: A Study of His Life and Thought* (London: Philip Green, 1905).
Chitham, Edward. *A Life of Anne Brontë* (Oxford: Blackwell, 1991).
——. *A Life of Emily Brontë* (Oxford: Basil Blackwell, 1987).
Cicirelli, Victor G. *Sibling Relationships Across the Life Span* (New York and London: Plenum Press, 1995).
Citron, Marcia J. (ed.). *The Letters of Fanny Hensel to Felix Mendelssohn* (London: Pendragon Press, 1987).

Clive, John. *Thomas Babington Macaulay: The Shaping of the Historian* (London: Secker & Warburg, 1973).
Clough, Blanche Athena (ed.). *A Memoir of Anne Jemima Clough* (London and New York: Edward Arnold, 1897).
Coburn, Kathleen (ed.). *The Notebooks of Samuel Taylor Coleridge*, Vol I 1794–1804 (London: Routledge & Kegan Paul, 1957).
Cockshut, A. O. J. *Truth to Life: The Art of Biography in the Nineteenth Century* (London: Collins, 1974).
Cohen, Morton N. (ed.). *The Letters of Lewis Carroll* 2 vols (London and Basingstoke: Macmillan – now Palgrave, 1979).
Conover, Robin St. John. 'Creating Angria: Charlotte and Branwell Brontë's Consciousness', *Brontë Society Transactions* 24 (1: April 1999) 16–32.
Cooke, Miriam and Angela Woollacott (eds). *Gendering War Talk* (Princeton: Princeton University Press, 1993).
Copeland, Edward and Juliet McMaster (eds). *The Cambridge Companion to Jane Austen* (Cambridge: Cambridge University Press, 1997).
Davidoff, Leonore, Megan Doolittle, Janet Fink and Katherine Holden. *The Family Story: Blood, Contract and Intimacy 1830–1960* (Harlow: Longman, 1999).
Davidoff, Leonore. *Worlds Between: Historical Perspectives on Gender and Class* (Cambridge: Polity Press, 1995).
Davies, Stevie. *Emily Brontë* (Brighton: Harvester Wheatsheaf, 1988).
Delamont, Sara. *The Nineteenth-Century Woman: Her Cultural and Physical World* (London: Croom Helm /New York: Barnes & Noble, 1978).
Dellamora, Richard. *Masculine Desire: The Sexual Politics of Victorian Aestheticism* (Chapel Hill and London: University of North Carolina Press, 1990).
De Selincourt, Ernest (ed.). *The Letters of William and Dorothy Wordsworth: The Early Years, 1787–1805* (Oxford: Clarendon Press, 1967).
——. *The Letters of William and Dorothy Wordsworth: The Later Years: Vol. II 1831–40* (Oxford: Clarendon Press, 1939).
Dinesen, Thomas. *My Sister, Isak Dinesen* (London: Michael Joseph, 1975).
Dolan, David. 'Pater's Portrait of the Author as a Young Girl', *Australasian Victorian Studies Journal* 6 (December 2000) 122–7.
Drummond, James and C. B. Upton (eds). *The Life and Letters of James Martineau*, 2 vols (London: James Nisbet, 1902).
Drury, Shadia B. *Alexandre Kojeve: The Roots of Postmodern Politics* (Basingstoke and London: Macmillan – now Palgrave, 1994).
Dunbar, Pamela, *Radical Mansfield: Double Discourse in Katherine Mansfield's Short Stories* (London and Basingstoke: Macmillan – now Palgrave, 1997).
Dunn, Judy and Carol Kendrick. *Siblings: Love, Envy and Understanding* (London: Grant McIntyre, 1982).
Durbach, Errol. '"The Geschwister-Komplex": Romantic Attitudes to Brother-Sister Incest in Ibsen, Byron, and Emily Brontë', *Mosaic* 12/14 (Summer 1979) 61–73.
Dyhouse, Carol. *Feminism and the Family in England 1880–1939* (Oxford: Basil Blackwell, 1989).
——. *Girls Growing Up in Late Victorian and Edwardian England* (London: Routledge & Kegan Paul, 1981).
Evans, Lawrence (ed.). *Letters of Walter Pater* (Oxford: Clarendon Press, 1970).

Fay, Elizabeth A. *Becoming Wordsworthian: A Perfomative Aesthetics* (Amherst: University of Massachusetts Press, 1995).
Foucault, Michel. *The History of Sexuality: An Introduction* (1976; repr. Harmondsworth: Penguin, 1990).
Freud, Sigmund. *Case Histories I: 'Dora' and 'Little Hans'* (Harmondsworth: Penguin, Pelican Freud Library 1985).
——. 'A Child is Being Beaten' (1919) in *The Standard Edition of the Complete Psychological Works of Sigmund Freud*, trans. James Strachey, vol. XVII (London: Hogarth Press and Institute of Psychoanalysis, 1955).
——. 'Femininity' (1932): see Young-Bruehl.
——. 'From the History of an Infantile Neurosis' (1918; repr. Harmondsworth: Penguin, Pelican Freud Library, 1987).
——. 'General Theory of the Neuroses' (1916–17), *Complete Psychological Works*, trans. James Strachey, vol. 15 (London: Hogarth Press and Institute of Psychoanalysis, 1963).
——. *The Interpretation of Dreams* (1900) in *The Standard Edition of the Complete Psychological Works of Sigmund Freud*, trans James Strachey, vol. V (London: Hogarth Press and Institute of Psychoanalysis, 1953).
——. *Introductory Lectures on Psychoanalysis*, trans. Joan Riviere (London: George Allen & Unwin, 1922).
Garber, Marjorie. *Vested Interests: Cross-Dressing and Cultural Anxiety* (Harmondsworth: Penguin, 1993).
Gérin, Winifred. *Branwell Brontë* (London: Thomas Nelson, 1961).
Gibbs, F. W. 'The Education of a Prince', *Cornhill Magazine* (Spring 1951) 109–19.
Gilbert, Sandra M. and Susan Gubar. *No Man's Land: The Place of the Woman Writer in the Twentieth Century: Vol. 2: Sexchanges* (New Haven and London: Yale University Press, 1989).
Gill, Stephen. *William Wordsworth: A Life* (Oxford: Clarendon Press, 1989).
Gittins, Diana. *The Family in Question: Changing Households and Familiar Ideologies* (London and Basingstoke: Macmillan – now Palgrave, 1985).
Glendinning, Victoria. *Edith Sitwell: A Unicorn Among Lions* (Oxford: Oxford University Press, 1981).
——. *Rebecca West: A Life* (London: Weidenfeld & Nicolson, 1987).
Gold, Karen. 'Brother Cain, Sister Jane', *Times Higher Education Supplement*, 4 February 2000, 18–19.
Gorham, Deborah. *Vera Brittain: A Feminist Life* (Oxford: Blackwell, 1996).
——.*The Victorian Girl and the Feminine Ideal* (London and Canberra: Croom Helm, 1982).
Greene, Richard (ed.). *Selected Letters of Edith Sitwell* (London: Virago, 1997).
Greer, Germaine. *Slip-Shod Sibyls: Recognition, Rejection and the Woman Poet* (London: Viking, 1995).
Griggs, Earl Leslie. *Collected Letters of Samuel Taylor Coleridge Vol. I 1785–1800* (Oxford: Clarendon Press, 1956).
Grob, Alan. 'William and Dorothy: A Case Study in the Hermeneutics of Disparagement', *English Literary History* 65 (1998) 187–221.
Gruner, Elisabeth Rose. 'Born and Made: Sisters, Brothers, and the Deceased Wife's Sister Bill', *Signs* 24 (Winter 1999) 423–47.
Guerard, Albert J. *The Triumph of the Novel: Dickens, Dostoevsky, Faulkner* (New York: Oxford University Press, 1976).

Gwynn, Stephen. *The Life of Mary Kingsley* (London: Macmillan – now Palgrave, 1932).

Hacking, Ian. 'The Making and Molding of Child Abuse', *Critical Inquiry* (Winter 1991) 253–88.

Haight, Gordon S. (ed.). *The George Eliot Letters*, 9 vols (New Haven and London: Yale University Press, 1954–1975).

Halberstam, Judith. *Female Masculinity* (Durham, NC and London: Duke University Press, 1998).

Hankin, C. A. *Katherine Mansfield and her Confessional Stories* (London and Basingstoke: Macmillan – now Palgrave, 1983).

Hankins, Thomas L. *Sir William Rowan Hamilton* (London and Baltimore: Johns Hopkins University Press, 1980).

Hassett, Constance W. '"Siblings and Antislavery": The Literary and Political Relations of Harriet Martineau, James Martineau, and Maria Weston Chapman', *Signs* (Winter 1996) 374–409.

Hayter, Alethea. 'Victorian Brothers and Sisters', *Times Literary Supplement* (9 August 1974) 859.

Hegel, G. W. F. *The Phenomenology of Mind* (1807; repr. trans. J. B. Baillie, London: George Allen and Unwin, 1964).

Herdman, John. *The Double in Nineteenth-Century Fiction* (Basingstoke and London: Macmillan – now Palgrave, 1990).

Hewlett, Dorothy. *Elizabeth Barrett Browning: A Life* (1952; repr. New York: Octagon Books, 1972).

Hibbert, Christopher. *Edward VII: A Portrait* (London: Allen Lane, 1976).

Hickey, Alison. '"Double Bonds": Charles Lamb's Romantic Collaborations', *English Literary History* 63 (1996) 735–71.

Hill, Alan G. (ed.). *The Letters of Dorothy Wordsworth* (Oxford: Oxford University Press, 1981).

Homans, Margaret. *Women Writers and Poetic Identity: Dorothy Wordsworth, Emily Brontë and Emily Dickinson* (Princeton: Princeton University Press, 1980).

Honan, Park. *Matthew Arnold: A Life* (London: Weidenfeld & Nicolson, 1981).

Honey, J. R. de S. *Tom Brown's Universe: The Development of the Victorian Public School* (London: Millington Books, 1977).

Hudson, Glenda A. *Sibling Love and Incest in Jane Austen's Fiction* (Basingstoke: Macmillan – now Palgrave, 1992).

Jalland, Pat. *Women, Marriage and Politics 1860–1914* (Oxford: Clarendon Press, 1986).

James, Lionel. *A Forgotten Genius: Sewell of St Columba's and Radley* (London: Faber & Faber, 1945).

Jenkins, Roy. *Gladstone* (London: Macmillan – now Palgrave, 1995).

Johnston, Kenneth R. *The Hidden Wordsworth: Poet, Lover, Rebel, Spy* (London and New York: W. W. Norton, 1998).

Jones, Frederick L.(ed.). *The Letters of Percy Bysshe Shelley, Vol. II* (Oxford: Clarendon Press, 1964).

Jones, Gregory. '"Rude Intercourse": Uncensoring Wordsworth's *Nutting*', *Studies in Romanticism* 35 (Summer 1996) 213–43.

Jones, Kathleen. *A Passionate Sisterhood* (London: Virago, 1998).

Karl, Frederick R. *George Eliot: Voice of a Century* (London and New York: W. W. Norton, 1995).

214 Bibliography

Kelley, Mary (ed.). *The Power of Her Sympathy: The Autobiography and Journal of Catharine Maria Sedgwick* (Boston: Massachusetts Historical Society, 1993).

Kent, David A. (ed.). *The Achievement of Christina Rossetti* (Ithaca and London: Cornell University Press, 1987).

—— and P. G. Stanwood (ed.). *Selected Prose of Christina Rossetti* (Basingstoke and London: Macmillan – now Palgrave, 1998).

Ker, Ian and Thomas Gornall, SJ (eds). *The Letters and Diaries of John Henry Newman*, vols 1–2 (Oxford: Clarendon Press, 1978, 1979).

Keynes, Geoffrey and Brian Hill (eds). *Letters Between Samuel Butler and Miss G. M. A. Savage 1871–1885* (London: Jonathan Cape 1935).

Kidd, Alan, and David Nicholls (eds). *The Making of the British Middle Class? Studies of Regional and Cultural Diversity since the Eighteenth Century* (Stroud, Gloucestershire: Sutton Publishing, 1998).

Klein, Melanie. *Love, Guilt and Reparation and Other Works 1921–1945* (London: Virago, 1988).

Knoepflmacher, U. C. *Wuthering Heights* (Cambridge: Cambridge University Press, 1989).

Leaska, Mitchell. *Granite and Rainbow: The Hidden Life of Virginia Woolf* (London: Picador 1998).

Lee, Hermione. *Virginia Woolf* (London: Chatto & Windus, 1996).

Lefebure, Molly. *Samuel Taylor Coleridge: A Bondage of Opium* (London: Victor Gollancz, 1974).

Lehmann, John and Derek Parker (ed.). *Edith Sitwell: Selected Letters* (Basingstoke and London: Macmillan – now Palgrave, 1970).

Leighton, Angela. *Victorian Women Poets: Writing Against the Heart* (New York and London: Harvester Wheatsheaf, 1992).

Levey, Michael. *The Case of Walter Pater* (London: Thames & Hudson, 1978).

Lewis, Jane. *Women in England 1870–1950: Sexual Divisions and Social Change* (Brighton: Wheatsheaf Books, 1984).

Lindop, Grevel. *The Opium-Eater: A Life of Thomas De Quincey* (London: Weidenfeld & Nicolson, 1981).

MacConnell, Juliet Flower. *The Regime of the Brother: After the Patriarchy.* (London and New York: Routledge, 1991).

Machann, Clinton. *Matthew Arnold: A Literary Life* (Basingstoke and London: Macmillan – now Palgrave, 1998).

Mackenzie, Midge. *Shoulder to Shoulder: A Documentary* (New York: Vintage Books, 1988).

Mahoney, John L. *William Wordsworth: A Poetic Life* (New York: Fordham University Press, 1997).

Marchand, Leslie A. *Byron: A Bibliography*, 3 vols (London: John Murray, 1957).

Marcus, Jane. *New Feminist Essays on Virginia Woolf* (Basingstoke and London: Macmillan – now Palgrave, 1981).

Marples, Morris. *Six Royal Sisters: Daughters of George III* (London: Michael Joseph, 1969).

Marrs, Edwin W. Jr. (ed.). *The Letters of Charles and Mary Anne Lamb, Vol. II 1801–1809* (Ithaca and London: Cornell University Press, 1976).

Marsh, Jan. *Christina Rossetti: A Literary Biography* (London: Pimlico, 1995).

Martineau, James. 'Comte's Life and Philosophy', *National Review* XIII/ 7 (July 1858) 184–220.

——. *Essays, Reviews and Addresses*, 3 vols (London: Longman, Green, 1890).

——. 'Mesmeric Atheism,' *Prospective Review* 7 (April 1851) 224–62.

May, Leila S. ' "Sympathies of a Scarcely Intelligible Nature": The Brother-Sister Bond in Poe's "Fall of the House of Usher" ', *Studies in Short Fiction* 30 (Summer 1993) 387–96.

Maynard, John. *Browning's Youth* (Cambridge, Mass. and London: Harvard University Press, 1977).

McNeillie, Andrew (ed.). *The Essays of Virginia Woolf, vol. II, 1912–1918* (London: Hogarth Press, 1987).

Megroz, R. L. *The Three Sitwells: A Biographical and Critical Study* (London: Richards Press, 1927).

Miller, Jane. *Women Writing About Men* (London: Virago, 1986).

Miller, Karl. *Doubles: Studies in Literary History* (Oxford: Oxford University Press, 1985).

Minow-Pinkney, Makiko. *Virginia Woolf and the Problem of the Subject: Feminine Writing in the Major Novels* (Brighton: Harvester, 1987).

Mintz, Steven. *A Prison of Expectations: The Family in Victorian Culture* (New York and London: New York University Press, 1983).

Mitchell, Juliet. *Mad Men and Medusas: Reclaiming Hysteria and the Effect of Sibling Relationships on the Human Condition* (London: Allen Lane: Penguin Press, 2000).

——. *Psychoanalysis and Feminism* (Harmondsworth: Penguin: 1975).

Moers, Ellen. *Literary Women* (London: Women's Press, 1978).

Moglen, Helene. *Charlotte Brontë: The Self Conceived* (New York: W. W. Norton, 1976).

Monsman, Gerald. *Walter Pater's Art of Autobiography* (New Haven and London: Yale University Press, 1980).

Moorman, Mary. *William Wordsworth: A Biography: The Early Years, 1770–1803* (Oxford: Clarendon Press, 1957).

Murry, John Middleton (ed.). *The Scrapbook of Katherine Mansfield* (New York: Alfred A. Knopf, 1940).

New Society. 'The Family Circle: Brothers and Sisters, 15 June 1967.

Newsome, David. *On the Edge of Paradise: A. C. Benson: The Diarist* (London: John Murray, 1980).

Nicolson, Nigel and Joanne Trautmann (eds). *The Flight of the Mind: The Letters of Virginia Woolf Vol. I 1888–1912 (Virginia Stephen)* (London: Hogarth Press, 1975).

——. *The Reflection of the Other Person: The Letters of Virginia Woolf 1929–1931* (London: Hogarth Press, 1978).

O'Sullivan, Vincent and Margaret Scott (eds). *The Collected Letters of Katherine Mansfield Vol. I 1903–1917* (Oxford: Clarendon Press, 1984).

——. *The Collected Letters of Katherine Mansfield Vol. II 1918–1919* (Oxford: Clarendon Press, 1987).

Ouditt, Sharon. *Fighting Forces: Writing Women: Identity and Ideology in the First World War* (London and New York: Routledge, 1994).

Ovid, *Metamorphoses* (Harmondsworth: Penguin 1955).

Parker, Alan Michael and Mark Willhardt (eds). *The Routledge Anthology of Cross-Gendered Verse* (London and New York: Routledge, 1996).

Parker, Derek (ed.). *Sacheverell Sitwell: A Symposium* (London: Bertram Rota, 1975).

Partlow, Robert B. Jr. (ed.). *Dickens the Craftsman: Strategies of Presentation* (Carbondale and Edwardsville: Southern Illinois University Press/London & Amsterdam: Feffer & Simons, 1970).

Pearson, John. *Facades: Edith, Osbert and Sacheverell Sitwell* (London: Macmillan – now Palgrave, 1978).
Peterson, M. Jeanne. *Family, Love, and Work in the Lives of Victorian Gentlewomen* (Bloomington and Indianapolis: Indiana University Press, 1989).
Pichanick, Valerie Kossew. *Harriet Martineau: The Woman and Her Work, 1802–76* (Ann Arbor: University of Michigan Press, 1980).
Polowetzsky, Michael. *Prominent Sisters: Mary Lamb, Dorothy Wordsworth, and Sarah Disraeli* (Westport, Connecticut and London: Praeger, 1996).
Poole, Roger. *The Unknown Virginia Woolf* (Cambridge: Cambridge University Press, 1975).
Poster, Mark. *Critical Theory of the Family* (London: Pluto Press, 1978).
Raikes, Elizabeth. *Dorothea Beale of Cheltenham* (London: Archibald Constable, 1908).
Rank, Otto. *The Incest Theme in Literature and Legend: Fundamentals of a Psychology of Literary Creation* (1912; repr. trans. Gregory C. Richter: Baltimore and London: Johns Hopkins University Press, 1992).
Reiman, Donald H. 'Brothers and Sisters', *Times Literary Supplement* (13 September 1974) 979–80; (27 December 1974) 1464.
Richardson, Alan. 'The Dangers of Sympathy: Sibling Incest in English Romantic Poetry', *Studies in English Literature 1500–1900* 25 (1985) 737–54.
Roper, Michael and John Tosh. *Manful Assertions: Masculinities in Britain since 1800* (London and New York: Routledge, 1991).
Rosenblum, Dolores. *Christina Rossetti: The Poetry of Endurance* (Carbondale and Edwardsville: Southern Illinois University Press, 1986).
Rossetti, William Michael (ed.). *The Family Letters of Christina Georgina Rossetti* (1908; repr. New York: Haskell House, 1968).
Sabean, David Warren. 'Fanny and Felix Mendelssohn-Bartholdy and the Question of Incest', *The Musical Quarterly* 77 (no. 4) (Winter 1993) 709–17.
Sanders, Valerie (ed.). *Harriet Martineau: Selected Letters* (Oxford: Clarendon Press, 1990).
Showalter, Elaine. *Sexual Anarchy: Gender and Culture at the Fin-de-Siècle* (London: Virago, 1992).
Silver, Arnold (ed.) *The Family Letters of Samuel Butler 1841–1886* (London: Jonathan Cape, 1962).
Sitwell, Edith. *Aspects of Modern Poetry* (London: Duckworth, 1934).
——. *The English Eccentrics* (London: Faber & Faber 1933).
Slater, Michael. *Dickens and Women* (London: J. M. Dent, 1983).
Smart, Barry. *Postmodernity* (London and New York: Routledge, 1993).
Smith, Margaret (ed.). *The Letters of Charlotte Brontë Vol. I 1829–1847* (Oxford: Clarendon Press, 1995).
Soderholm, James. 'Dorothy Wordsworth's Return to Tintern Abbey', *New Literary History* 26 (1995) 309–22.
Solomon, Eric. 'The Incest Theme in *Wuthering Heights*', *Nineteenth Century Fiction* 14 (June 1959) 80–3.
Spurling, Hilary. *Ivy When Young: The Early Life of I. Compton-Burnett 1884–1919* (London: Victor Gollancz, 1974).
Steiner, George. *Antigones: The Antigone Myth in Western Literature, Art and Thought* (Oxford: Oxford University Press 1986).
Stevenson, John. *British Society 1914–45* (Harmondsworth: Penguin, 1984).

Stone, Lawrence. *The Family, Sex and Marriage in England 1500–1800* (1977; repr. abridged: Harmondsworth: Penguin, 1985).
Strouse, Jean M. *Alice James: A Biography* (London: Jonathan Cape, 1981).
Sussman, Herbert. *Victorian Masculinities: Manhood and Masculine Poetics in Early Victorian Literature and Art* (Cambridge: Cambridge University Press, 1995).
[Taylor, Isaac]. *Home Education* (London: Jackson & Walford, 1838).
Thomson, Douglass H. 'Wordsworth's Lucy of "Nutting" ', *Studies in Romanticism* 18 (Summer 1979) 287–98.
Todd, Janet. *Women's Friendship in Literature* (New York: Columbia University Press, 1980).
Tomalin, Claire. *Jane Austen: A Life* (London: Viking, 1997).
Tompkins, J. M. S. *The Popular Novel in England 1770–1800* (London: Constable, 1932).
Trevelyan, Sir George Otto (ed.). *The Life and Letters of Lord Macaulay* (London: Longmans, Green, 1889).
Twain, Mark. *The Adventures of Huckleberry Finn* (1884; repr. Harmondsworth: Penguin, 1966).
Twitchell, James B. *Forbidden Partners: The Incest Taboo in Modern Culture* (New York: Columbia University Press, 1987).
Tylee, Claire M. *The Great War and Women's Consciousness* (Basingstoke and London: Macmillan – now Palgrave, 1990).
Van Ghent, Dorothy. *The English Novel, Form and Function* (1953; repr. New York: Harper & Row, Harper Torchbooks, 1961).
——. 'The Window Figure and the Two-Children Figure in *Wuthering Heights,*' *Nineteenth-Century Fiction* (7) (September 1952) 189–97.
Webb, R. K. *Harriet Martineau: A Radical Victorian* (London: William Heinemann, 1960).
White, Allon. *Carnival, Hysteria, and Writing: Collected Essays and Autobiography* (Oxford: Clarendon Press, 1993).
Whitelaw, Lis. *The Life and Rebellious Times of Cicely Hamilton* (London: Women's Press, 1990).
Williams, David. *Genesis and Exodus: A Portrait of the Benson Family* (London: Hamish Hamilton, 1979).
Wilson, Francesca M. *Rebel Daughter of a Country House: The Life of Eglantyne Jebb* (London: George Allen & Unwin, 1967).
Wilson, Romer. *All Alone: The Life and Private History of Emily Jane Brontë* (London: Chatto & Windus, 1928).
Wineapple, Brenda. *Sister Brother: Gertrude and Leo Stein* (London: Bloomsbury, 1996).
Winnifrith, Tom. 'The Life of Patrick Branwell Brontë', *Brontë Society Transactions* 24 Part I (April 1999) 1–10.
Wolfram, Sybil. *In-Laws and Outlaws* (London: Croom Helm, 1987).
Yonge, Charlotte M. *The Girl's Little Book* (London: Skeffington, 1893).
Young-Bruehl, Elisabeth (ed.). *Freud on Women: A Reader* (London and New York: W. W. Norton, 1990).
Zeldin, Theodore. *An Intimate History of Humanity* (London: Vintage 1998).
Ziegler, Philip. *Osbert Sitwell* (London: Chatto & Windus 1998).

Index

Note: entries in bold indicate main areas of discussion.
Book titles are listed under authors' names.

Aaron, Jane, 37–8, 192
Ackerley, J. R., 9, 30–1, 181, 188, 204
Ackerley, Nancy, 9, 30–1, 181
Alexander, Christine, 44, 193
Anderson, Nancy Fix, 152, 201
Arbuckle, Elisabeth Sanders, 190, 195, 196
Arnold, Matthew, 2, 16, 189
Askwith, Betty, 13, 188
Asquith, Lady Cynthia, 155, 160, 161, 201, 202
Atkinson, Henry G., 58, 72, 74
Austen, Henry, 28, 64, 83, 126, 191, 195
Austen, Jane, 1–2, 8, 28, **83–7**, 126, 184, 186, 191, 195
   Emma, 28, 83–4, 86–7, 184, 197
   Mansfield Park, 8, 27, 28, 81, 82, 84–6, 87, 184, 191, 197
   Northanger Abbey, 83–87 p*assim*, 197
   Pride and Prejudice, 27, 83, 87, 197
   Sense and Sensibility, 28, 84, 87

Bank, Stephen P. and Michael D. Kahn, 186
Barker, Juliet, 2, 58, 186, 194, 195
Barrell, John, 192
Barrett, Elizabeth, 21, 131, 189
Bateson, F. W., 186
Battersby, Christina, 6, 187, 200
Bauman, Zygmunt, 4
Beauchamp, Leslie, 170–6
Bennett, Daphne, 28, 191
Benson, A. C., 13, 25, 26, 188, 190
Benson, E. F., 13, 25–6, 190
Benson, Edward White, 13
Benson, Eleanor, 13, 14–15, 22, 23, 26, 190
Benson family, 12, 23, 25, 26
Benson, Maggie, 13, 23, 25, 26
Benson, Martin, 13, 14–15, 23, 25, 190
Benson, Mary, 13, 25
Berry, Paul and Mark Bostridge, 202, 203
Bishop, Alan, and Mark Bostridge, 168, 202, 203
Bishop, Alan, and Terry Smart, 189
Boddy, Gillian, 174, 203
Boone, Joseph A., and Deborah E. Nord, 102, 133, 197, 200
Bosanquet, Theodora, 195, 196
Braddon, Mary Elizabeth, 91, 96, 133–4, 197, 198
Brittain, Edward, 23, 155–6, 160, 161, 163, 168, 189, 202, 203
Brittain, Vera, 23, 155–6, 160–1, 163, 167, 168–9, 177–9, 189, 202, 203, 204
   Honourable Estate, 161, 168–9, 176–7, 180, 202, 203
   Testament of Youth, 157, 159, 178–9, 204
Brontë, Anne, 46, 47, 95, 142, 150
   The Tenant of Wildfell Hall, 82, 90–1, 139–40, 141–2, 150, 184, 197
Brontë, Branwell, 50, 52, 54, 56, 58, 59, 65, 67, 94, 133, 140–2, 144, 153, 193
   'Caroline' poems, 140–1
   juvenilia, 43–7
Brontë, Charlotte, 33, 50, 54, 58, 59, 67, 117, 140, 150, 191, 193, 201
   Jane Eyre, 46, 59, **91–3**, 94, 110, 113, 115, 123, 139, 142, 197
   juvenilia, 43–7
   The Professor, 46, 47, 96, 139–40, 150, 201
   Shirley, 46, 93
   Villette, 46, **93–6**, 102, 184, 198

Brontë, Emily, 46, 47, 56, 67, 93, 95, 140, 193
  Wuthering Heights, 8, 88–90, 110, 128, 132, 136, 139, 141–2, 197
Brontë family, 2, 14, 25, 32, 43–7, 125, 139–42, 201
Brontë, Maria, 25, 46–7, 140, 153
brother–sister relationship
  bad brothers, 116–28
  bad sisters, 112–15, 116
  educational differences, 17–25, 108, 155–7, 158
  fairy tales, 106–7
  historical background, 2–10
  households, adult sibling, 27–8, 33–6, 42–3, 52, 63, 96–7, 104, 106, 143, 157, 181
  games, 25–6
  Gothic representations, 2, 7–8, 110–13, 181, 183
  incest, 5, 7, 12, 14, 21, 33, 40, 42, 46, 81, 88, 93, 99, 106, 181–3, 186, 191
  language of, 14–15
  murder, 8, 108, 110, 118, 124
  psychoanalysis, 1, 10, 108–10, 132
  psychologists, recent interest of, 1
  resemblance of siblings.81, 133–5, 197
  rivalry, 1, 78–9, 107–10, 112, 128–9, 124, 130, 198
  Romanticism, 5–7, **34–43**, 57, 106
  War, effect of, 2, 9, 15, 154–81
Brown, Charles Brockden, 106, 108, 110–11, 198
Brown, Julia Prewitt, 197
Browning, Elizabeth
  see under Barrett, Elizabeth
Browning, Robert, 30, 37
Browning, Sarianna, 30
Buckler, William E., 143–4, 201
Bullough, Vern L. and Bonnie, 131, 200
Burney, Fanny, 7, 187
Butler, Judith, 131–2, 133, 200
Byron, Lord, 5, 6

Caine, Barbara, 156, 202
Carroll, Lewis, 22–3, 26, 190

Cholmondeley, Hester, 125–6, 128
Cholmondeley, Mary, 27, **123–6**, 127, 128, 199
  Red Pottage, 27, 123–6, 127
  Under One Roof, 124–6, 199
Cicirelli, Victor G., 1, 186
Cixous, Hélène, 37, 192
Clive, John, 186
Clough, A. H., 2, 29
Clough, Anne Jemima, 29
Coleridge, S. T., 35, 44, 188
Compton-Burnett, Guy, 164, 180–1
Compton-Burnett, Ivy, 21, 164, 180–1, 182, 186
  Brothers and Sisters, 164, 181, 204
Compton-Burnett, Noel, 164, 180–1
Conrad, Joseph, 133, 136, 157
Coward, Noel, 52
Craik, Dinah M., 133, 200

Darwin, Caroline, 57
Darwin, Catherine, 57
Darwin, Charles, 57, 194
Davidoff, Leonore, 3, 4, 187
Davies, Emily, 28
Davies, Llewelyn, 28
Defoe, Daniel, 7, 138
De Quincey, Elizabeth, 25
De Quincey, Thomas, 25, 35, 38, 57, 192
Dickens, Charles, 2, 7, 28, 99–100, 112, 186
  Bleak House, 138
  David Copperfield, 81, 99, 112, 197
  Dombey and Son, 100, 102, 136, 184, 198
  Edwin Drood, The Mystery of, 132–3, 197
  Great Expectations, 99, 113–15, 199
  Hard Times, 116, 117, 136, 199
  Little Dorrit, 112
  Martin Chuzzlewit, 99–100, 112, 122, 198
  Nicholas Nickleby, 136, 137, 138, 197, 200
  Our Mutual Friend, 116
Dickinson, Emily, 131, 140, 200
Disraeli, Benjamin, 15, 32, 33, 188, 191
Disraeli, Sarah, 15, 30, 32, 188, 191

Dolan, David, 143, 201
Drury, Shadia B., 89, 197
Duckworth, George, 14, 165
Duckworth, Gerald, 14, 165
Duckworth, Stella, 14, 156, 164
Dunbar, Pamela, 175, 203
Dyhouse, Carol, 16, 180, 189, 204

Edgeworth, Maria, 189
  Harry and Lucy Concluded, 18–19, 20
Edward VII, 11, 109, 188
Eliot, George, 2, 59, 60, 62, 65, 67, 73, 76, 77, 101–3, 124
  'Brother and Sister' sonnets, 57, 60–1, 194
  Daniel Deronda, 103–4, 198
  Middlemarch, 103
  The Mill on the Floss, 8, 11, 19, 24, 26, 53, 60, **101–3**, 113–14, 116, 117, 168, 198
  relationship with brother, 60, 65, 67
Ellis, Sarah, 17, 189

Farjeon, Eleanor, 14, 26, 188, 190
Farjeon, family, 12, 14, 26
Farrar, E. W., 16
Fay, Elizabeth A., 187
First World War, 2, 9, 15, **154–81**
Forester, C. S., 93, 197
Forster, E. M., 158, 202
Foucault, Michel, 3, 12, 186, 188
Freud, Sigmund, 80–1, 108–12, 116, 131–2, 153, 197, 198–9, 200
  bisexuality, theory of, 131–2, 153
  'A Child is Being Beaten', 112, 199
  'Dora', 108, 132
  'Femininity', 132, 200
  'Little Hans', 108
  siblings as vermin, 110
  'Wolf Man', 109–10

Garber, Marjorie, 132, 200
Gaskell, Elizabeth
  Cranford, 130–1, 135, 200
  The Moorland Cottage, 116–17
  North and South, 117, 136–8, 200
  Ruth, 27
  Wives and Daughters, 104–5, 184, 198
Gérin, Winifred, 46, 193

Gilbert, Sandra, and Susan Gubar, 153, 201
Gittins, Diana, 3, 186
Gladstone, W. E., 30
Glendinning, Victoria, 191, 194
Goethe, 5
Gold, Karen, 108, 198
Gorham, Deborah, 29, 191
Gothic
  see under brother–sister relationship
Grand, Sarah, 133, **145–7**, 153–4, 197
Greer, Germaine, 50, 193
Grimm brothers, 107
Grob, Alan, 36, 192
Gruner, Elisabeth Rose, 82, 197

Hacking, Ian, 183, 189, 204
Halberstam, Judith, 131, 200
Hamilton, Cicely, 187
Hamilton, Eliza, 126–9, 200
Hamilton, Sir William Rowan, 2, 16, 26, 126–9, 190, 200
Hankins, Thomas L., 127, 128, 190, 200
Hartley, L. P.,
  Eustace and Hilda, 9, **113–15**, 116, 181, 186, 199
Hassett, Constance W., 76, 196
Hawthorne, Nathaniel
  'Alice Doane's Appeal', 106, 198
Hayter, Alethea, 186
Hegel, G. W. F., 5–6, 89, 187, 197
Herodotus, 187
Herdman, John, 6, 187
Herschel, William and Caroline, 16, 128
Hickey, Alison, 37, 192
Hobhouse, Stephen, 156
Honan, Park, 15–16, 189
Honey, J. R. de S., 21, 190
Howitt, Mary, 59, 194
Hudson, Glenda A., 186, 187, 197
Hughes, M. V., 16, 23, 189
Hughes, Thomas, 22, 190
Hunt, Leigh, 57
Huxley, Aldous, 52, 194

Ibsen, Henrik
  Hedda Gabler, 124, 135
  Little Eyolf, 135

James, Alice, 15, 32, 188
James, Henry, 27, 32, 164
James, Lionel, 190, 195
James, William, 15, 32, 33
Jameson, Storm, 160, 202
Jebb, Eglantyne, 26, 163, 202
Jewsbury, Geraldine, 148
Johnston, Kenneth R., 40, 192
Jones, Gregory, 39, 192
Jones, Kathleen, 186

Kant, Immanuel, 5
Kingsley, Charles, 27, 190
Knoepflmacher, U. C., 47, 193

Lamb, Charles, 33, 34–8, 40, 43, 56
   Essays of Elia, 34–5, 36–8, 192
Lamb, Mary, 34–8, 40–1, 43, 56
Lamb, Charles and Mary, 11, 19, 27, 31, 32, 33, 34–8, 40, 42–3, 144, 181, 188, 189, 191, 192
   Mrs Leicester's School, 37–8, 40–1, 133, 192
Latin, learning of, 19–21, 23
Lawrence, D. H., 3–4, 157, 202
Layard, George Somes, 147, 201
Lee, Hermione, 167, 203
Lefebure, Molly, 33, 186, 191
Lehmann, John, 9, 30, 180, 191
Lehmann, Rosamond, 9, 30, 180
Leighton, Angela, 49, 193
Leighton, Clare, 160
Leighton, Roland, 160, 163, 168
Levey, Michael, 143, 201
Levin, Susan, 193
Lewes, G. H., 67
Lewis, M. G., 7–8
Lewis, Peter M., 24, 190
Lewis, Wyndham, 52–3, 194
Linton, Eliza Lynn, 62, 133, 201
   Autobiography of Christopher Kirkland, **147–54**
   Lizzie Lorton of Greyrigg, 82–3, 197
Linton, W. J., 149, 151
Lively, Penelope,
   Moon Tiger, 21, 182, 189, 204

Macaulay, Hannah and Margaret, 15
Macaulay, Rose, 163, 177, 202

Macaulay, T. B., 1, 2, 14, 15, 16, 27, 186, 188
Mansfield, Katherine, **170–6**, 177, 203
   'An Ideal Family', 175–6
   'At the Bay', 174
   'The Daughters of the Late Colonel', 176
   'The Fly', 174–5
   'His Sister's Keeper', 175
   'Sun and Moon', 175
Marsh, Jan, 50, 193
Martineau, Harriet, 14, 17, 21–2, 57–8, 59, 62, 63, 65, **69–78**, 106, 189, 190, 194, 195–6, 202
   breakdown of relationship with James, 69–78, 196
   on brother-sister relationship, 17, 21–2, 57–8, 106
   Harriet Martineau's Autobiography, 59, 62, 63, 70–3, 75–8, 189, 194
Martineau, James, 14, 21, 58, 59, 62, 63, **69–78**
   Prospective Review article on sister, 72–5
Martineau, Thomas, 63, 70
Maurice, F. D., 136
May, Leila S., 111, 199
McEwan, Ian,
   The Cement Garden, 130, 182–3, 186, 200
McInerney, Jay,
   Model Behaviour, 80, 182, 196, 204
Miller, Jane, 46, 186, 193
Miller, Karl, 12, 188
Mintz, Steven, 8, 108, 187, 197
Mitchell, Hannah, 16, 189
Mitchell, Juliet, 1, 10, 108, 128, 132, 186, 198, 200
Mitchison, Naomi, 21, 189
Monsman, Gerald, 144, 201
Mozley, Harriett, 12–13, 22, 57, 65
Mozley, Jemima, 12, 22, 24, 57
Mozley, Thomas, 12, 65
Murdoch, Iris,
   A Severed Head, 182, 186, 204
   The Sea, The Sea, 105, 198
Murry, John Middleton, 171–2, 203

Index

Nesbit, E., 27, 190
Newman family, 12
Newman, Harriett and Jemima
  see under Mozley
Newman, John Henry, 12–13, 22, 24, 57, 188, 190
Newman, Mary, 13, 22, 57
Norton, Caroline, 4

Oliphant, Margaret, 60, 64–6, 79, 118–22, 199
  Autobiography, 65–6
  The Doctor's Family, 121, 199
  Harry Muir, 119–20, 199
  Hester, 122, 199
  Phoebe Junior, 121–2, 199
  relationship with brothers, 60, 64–6, 119, 121
Ovid, 80, 197

Pater, Clara and Hester, 126, 143
Pater, Walter, 27, 126, 142–5, 153–4
  on Charles and Mary Lamb, 144
  'A Prince of Court Painters', **142–4**, 201
  'Measure for Measure', 144–5
  on Mona Lisa, 145
Peterson, Linda, 93, 125, 197, 199
Pichanick, Valerie Kossew, 77, 196
Plato, 187
Poe, Edgar Allan,
  'The Fall of the House of Usher', 111, 113, 115, 133, 197, 199
Poster, Mark, 109–10, 198

Rank, Otto, 5, 187
Rathbone, Irene,
  We That Were Young, 161–2, 177, 178–9, 180, 202, 204
Raverat, Gwen, 157, 202
Rich, Adrienne, 81–2, 197
Romanticism, 5–7, 34–43, 57, 106
Roper, Michael, and John Tosh, 9, 188, 190
Rosenblum, Dolores, 50, 193
Rossetti, Christina, 32, 33, **48–52**, 56, 193–4

Rossetti, Dante Gabriel, 32, 43, **48–52**, 56, 193
Rossetti family, 2, 14, 32, 43, 48, 52, 126
Rossetti, William Michael, 33, 43, 48, 51, 52, 126, 193
Ruddick, Sara, 165, 203
Ruskin, John, 59

Sackville-West, Vita, 180, 186
Sedgwick, Eve Kosofsky, 134, 200
Sewell, Elizabeth Missing, 62–3, 64–5, 67–9, 79, 96–7, 195
  Autobiography, 64–5, 67–9
  and brother William, 62–3, 79
  Ursula, 80, 96–7, 196, 198
Sewell, William, 24, 62–3, 64–5, 67–9, 79, 97, 195
Shelley, Mary, 7, 87–8, 187, 197
  Frankenstein, 7, 87–8
Shelley, Percy Bysshe, 5, 6–7
Sherwood, Mary Martha, 20, 61–2, 195
Showalter, Elaine, 123, 153, 199, 201
Sinclair, May, 156, 157–8, 202
Sitwell, Edith, 15, 30, **52–6**, 157, 188, 194
Sitwell family, 9, 32, 33, 52–6, 186
Sitwell, Osbert, 30, 52–6, 157, 194
Sitwell, Sacheverell, 15, 30, 33, 52–6, 194
Slater, Michael, 112, 199
Soderholm, James, 38, 40, 192
Somerville, Mary, 21, 189
Sophocles, 29
  Antigone, 5, 160
Spurling, Hilary, 164, 189, 202, 204
Stein, Gertrude, 32, 52, 57, 60, 157, 181, 194
Stein, Leo, 32, 33, 52, 60, 157, 181
Steiner, George, 5, 187
Stephen, Adrian, 14, 27, 52, 165
Stephen family, 12, 13, 25, 52, 156
Stephen, Sir Leslie, 13, 156, 164, 165
Stephen, Thoby, 13–14, 15, 24, 28–9, 52, 164–8, 169, 188, 190, 191, 203
  and *Jacob's Room*, 165–6
  and *To the Lighthouse*, 164, 202
  and *The Waves*, 166–8, 203
Stephen, Vanessa, 13, 28, 156, 164

Stephen, Virginia
  see under Woolf, Virginia
Stevenson, John, 177, 204
Stoker, Bram
  Dracula, 8–9, 188
Stone, Lawrence, 12, 188

Taylor, Isaac, 17–18, 189
Taylor, Norman Austin, 162–3, 202
Thackeray, W. M., 156, 190
Thomson, Douglass H., 40, 192
Tollet, Elizabeth, 29, 191
Tonna, Charlotte Elizabeth, 60, 195
Tosh, John, 25, 188
  see also under Roper, Michael
Trollope, Anthony, 57, 108, 122
  Can You Forgive Her? **117–19**, 136, 199
Twitchell, James B., 187

Uglow, Jennifer, 145, 201

Victoria, Queen, 11, 53, 109
Victoria, Princess Royal, 11, 53, 109

Waugh, Evelyn, 9, 134, 181
  Brideshead Revisited, 134, 181, 200
Wells, H. G.,
  Ann Veronica, 158, 202
  Joan and Peter, 158, 202
West, Rebecca, 169–70, 177, 186, 203
  The Fountain Overflows, 169–70, 180, 203
  This Real Night, 169–70, 203
White, Allon, 112, 128–9, 186, 199
Winnifrith, Tom, 46, 193

Wollstonecraft, Mary, 4
Woolf, Virginia, 2, 13, 15, 22, 24, 25, 26, 27, 28–9, 52, 53, 156, **164–8**, 177, 186, 188, 191, 194, 203
  relationship with brother Thoby, 13–14, 15, 28–9, **164–8**, 203
  Jacob's Room, 165–6, 203
  Moments of Being, 164, 202
  Mrs Dalloway, 167
  The Pargiters, 156, 159, 202
  Three Guineas, 24, 190, 202
  To the Lighthouse, 164, 165, 167, 202
  The Waves, **165–8**, 203
Wordsworth, Dorothy, 2, 15, 27, 32, 33, 34–6, **38–43**, 56, 171, 188, 191, 192–3
  incest rumours, 2, 33, 35, 42, 191
  wildness, 38–40
Wordsworth, William, 2, 15, 27, 32, 33, 34–6, **38–43**, 56, 126, 127, 171, 186, 188, 191, 192–3, 200
  incest rumours, *see under* Wordsworth, Dorothy
  'Nutting', 39, 40, 42
  'Tintern Abbey', 38, 39–40

Yonge, Charlotte M., 16, 59, 65, 96, 97–9, 134–5, 189, 194, 198
  The Daisy Chain, 19–20, 98, 99, 100, 134–5
  The Girl's Little Book, 16
  Heartsease, 98–9
  The Pillars of the House, 97–8, 99, 133, 135
Yonge, Julian, 59, 65

Zeldin, Theodore, 31, 191